TIMOTHY EGAN

AUTHOR OF THE NATIONAL BOOK AWARD–WINNING
The Worst Hard Time

The

BIG
BURN

"In prose so sizzling it crackles,
The Big Burn keeps alive the
conservation dreams of Teddy
Roosevelt by allowing this story
to rise from the ashes, once
again." — DENVER POST

TEDDY ROOSEVELT
& THE FIRE THAT SAVED AMERICA

TIMOTHY EGAN

The
BIG BURN

Teddy Roosevelt *and the*
Fire That Saved America

Mariner Books · *Houghton Mifflin Harcourt*
BOSTON   NEW YORK

First Mariner Books edition 2010

www.hmhbooks.com

Library of Congress Cataloging-in-Publication Data
Egan, Timothy.
  The big burn : Teddy Roosevelt and the fire that saved America /
Timothy Egan.
     p. cm.
  Includes bibliographical references and index.
  ISBN 978-0-618-96841-1
  1. Roosevelt, Theodore, 1858–1919. 2. Presidents — United States — Bi-
ography. 3. Conservationists — United States — Biography. 4. Pinchot,
Gifford, 1865–1946. 5. Forest conservation — United States — History.
6. Nature conservation — United States — History. 7. National parks
and reserves — United States — History. 8. United States. National
Park Service — History. 9. Forest fires — Montana — History. 10. Forest
fires — Idaho — History. I. Title.
  E757.E325 2009
  973.911 — dc22   2009021881
  ISBN 978-0-547-39460-2 (pbk.)

Book design by Melissa Lotfy
Map by Jaques Chazaud

Printed in the United States of America

DOC 10 9 8 7 6 5 4 3 2 1

To Sam Howe Verhovek

*Friend, editor, writer, and adopted son of
the Pacific Northwest, no bow-tied bum-kisser he*

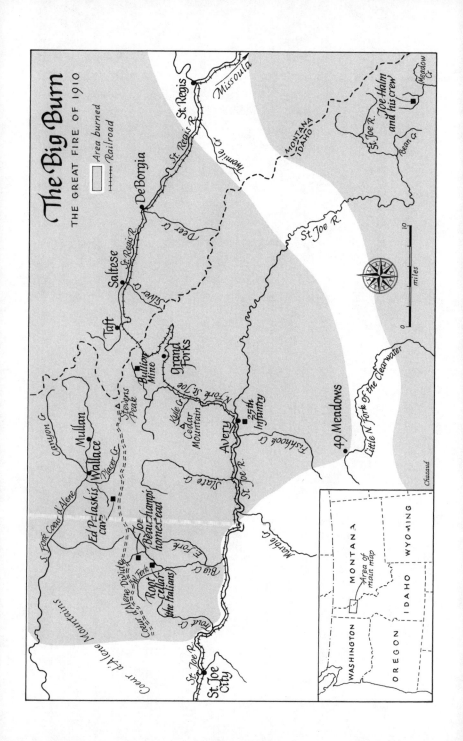

CONTENTS

If now the dead of this fire should awaken and I should be stopped beside a cross, I would no longer be nervous if asked the first and last question of life, How did it happen?

— NORMAN MACLEAN, *Young Men and Fire*

PROLOGUE

A Fire at the End of the World

H ERE NOW CAME the fire down from the Bitterroot Mountains and showered embers and forest shrapnel onto the town that was supposed to be protected by all those men with faraway accents and empty stomachs. For days, people had watched it from their gabled houses, from front porches and ash-covered streets, and there was some safety in the distance, some fascination even — *see there, way up on the ridgeline, just candles flickering in the trees.* But now it was on them, an element transformed from Out There to Here, and just as suddenly on their front lawns, in their hair, snuffing out the life of a drunk on a hotel mattress, torching a veranda. The sky had been dark for some time on this Saturday in August 1910, the town covered in a warm fog so opaque that the lights were turned on at three o'clock in the afternoon. People took stock of what to take, what to leave behind. A woman buried her sewing machine out back in a shallow grave. A pressman dug a hole for his trunk of family possessions, but before he could finish, the fire caught him on the face, the arms, the neck.

How much time did they have until Wallace burned to the ground? An hour or two? Perhaps not even that? When the town had been consumed by flame twenty years earlier, it fell in a deep exhale — painted clapboards, plank sidewalks, varnished storefronts.

Whoooommmppffffff! Then they did what all western boomers did after a combustible punch: got up from the floor and rebuilt, with brick, stone, and steel, shaking a fist again at nature. And since there was so much treasure being stripped from the veins of these mountains on the high divide between Montana and Idaho, they rebuilt in a style befitting their status as the source of many a bauble in the late Gilded Age. Italian marble sinks went into barber shops. Cornices were crafted of cast iron. Terracotta trim decorated bank windows. The saloons, the bordellos, the rooming houses, the men's clubs, the hotels — *fireproof,* it said on their stationery. Most impressive of all was the new train depot of the Northern Pacific Railroad. Designed in the Chateau style, the depot's buff-colored bricks formed a Roman arch over the main window. Three stories, counting the magnificent turret, and shingled in green. The depot was an apt hub for a region that promised to produce more silver, lead, and white pine than any other on the planet.

"It seemed like a toy city," a novice forest ranger said after he had crested the mountains by train and caught his first sight of Wallace, Idaho, "clean and spotless, and very much up to date, with fine homes and fine people."

In the early evening, the young mayor, Walter Hanson, checked with his fire chief, and he summoned his assistant, and they said, yes, it was time — *sound the alarm!* That was it; everyone knew they had to make a dash for the getaway trains. Women and children only, the mayor said, with a Victorian gentleman's reflex common even in the Far West. He deputized an instant force of local men to back him up. Troops were available as well, the "negro soldiers" of the 25th Infantry, I Company, who had just pitched a hurried camp on the Wallace baseball field after withdrawing from the aggressive front line of the fire. Over the years, they had chased Indians in the Dakotas, put down insurrections in the Philippines, and helped to establish civil order during western labor wars, but never in the history of the 25th Infantry had these Buffalo Soldiers been asked to tame a mountain range on fire. In a state with fewer than seven hundred blacks, the troops were greeted with curiosity and skepticism by polite citizens, scorn and open hostility by others. On Saturday, after they pulled back from the flames up high and regrouped on the baseball field, the retreat fed the scolds who said a black battalion could never save a town, much less fight a wildfire nearly as large as the state of Connecticut.

Even as the bell rang, the special trains were being fitted, with not enough space for half the town of 3,500 people. Rail workers stripped away cargo and some seats to make room for the exodus. The men could not leave, the mayor insisted; they must stay behind and fight. The elderly, the infirm, and little boys, of course, even those who looked like men, could go. Everyone else was told to get a garden hose and go up on their roofs, or jump aboard one of the horse-drawn fire carriages, or grab a shovel and get on a bicycle. Or pray. The mayor was asked about the jail — *do we let the prisoners burn?* Needing the manpower, he ordered the cells opened and the inmates sent to Bank Street, right in front of the courthouse, to form a human fire line. Only two would remain handcuffed, a murderer and a bank robber.

The evacuation was not orderly, not at all as the mayor had imagined days earlier when he first drew up plans with the United States Forest Service to save Wallace. People dashed through the streets, stumbling, bumping into each other, shouting rumors, crying, unsure exactly where to go. Some carried babies under wet towels. Some insisted on carting away large objects. It felt as if the town was under artillery fire, the mile-high walls of the Bitterroots shooting flaming branches onto the squat of houses in the narrow valley below. Between flareups and blowups, the hot wind delivered a continuous stream of sparks and detritus.

Earlier in the day, ashes had fallen like soft snow through the haze. At the edge of town, where visibility was better, people looked up and saw thunderheads of smoke, flat-bottomed and ragged-topped, reaching far into the sky. Then the wind had calmed to a whisper for the better part of an hour, a truce of sorts, and it seemed

that the town might be spared. But at 5 P.M., leaves on trees rustled
and flags unfurled in slow flaps as winds picked up to twenty miles
an hour. By 6 P.M., telephone lines and utility wires whistled with
another kick in velocity. And before the hour passed, big evergreens
groaned at the waist and twigs snapped off—the air galloping to
gale force, forty-five to sixty miles an hour, a wildfire's best stimu-
lant. So by nightfall, when the evacuation began, the blows were
approaching hurricane force, extended gusts of seventy-four miles
an hour or more. Everyone knew about Palousers, the warm winds
from the southwest; they could pack a punch, though they were rare
in the Bitterroots. But a Palouser hissing flames at high speed—this
was a peek beyond the gates of Hell.

In the pandemonium, to be heard on the streets required a shout.
Strong men knocked down women, ignoring the mayor's order
and betting that the newly constituted fire militia—their neighbors—would never shoot them for fleeing. "I have been in panics,"
said Carl Getz, visiting from Seattle, "but the one at Wallace was
the worst I have ever seen."

John Boyd, father of a town fire captain, was worried about his
bird, the parrot that kept him company in his old age. He covered
the cage with a sheet, but the bird squawked something terrible
when menaced by the smoke and wind. *Forget it*, his son told him.
Get out! Don't take the bird. The orders stipulated that no pets would
be evacuated, and no baggage allowed beyond what a person could
carry and fit in her lap. It was the only way to ensure enough room
to get all the women and children out of town. Boyd left his house
and started for the exit trains, aided by his son, who was quickly
called away to his fire duties. But Boyd couldn't stop thinking about
his parrot, and when his son was out of sight, the old man doubled
back toward his house.

Just after 9 P.M., an ember the size of a horse's thigh fell from
the sky and landed next to buckets of press grease and rags that had
been soaked in solvent at the *Wallace Times.* The wooden rear side
of the newspaper building went up in a flash; inside, reporters, ed-

itors, and pressmen fled with barely enough time to find the exits. From there, flames jumped to a mill, a rooming house, two hotels, and the depot of the Oregon Railway & Navigation Company, the town's second line, designated for the main evacuation service. The roof of the four-story Sunset Brewery collapsed in flames. Beer spilled out the side of the building and ran down the streets. The defense line had been drawn a few blocks west, where a buttress of solid stone buildings stood. But soon came a *pop, pop, pop* of glass as some windows of the courthouse broke in the heat or cracked as the wood trim curled, the fire now challenging the boundary of resistance. From the streets, it looked as if all of Wallace was burning, the storm setting off near-constant explosions of its own—gas tanks, oil vats, and other containers of liquid combustibles blowing up.

The mass of exiles clustered along the tracks, unsure where to meet the train, waiting, stomping feet, shuffling, surrounded on all sides by what looked like an amphitheater of flame. The mayor tried to assure the crowd: the train was coming—*don't panic!* The plan was to make a run west for Spokane, 103 miles away. People were drenched in sweat; all their worldly possessions—that is, the clothes on their backs—picked up ash from above. Wrapped in a swirl of hot air and gas, some fainted or buckled over from dehydration. When the train whistle screeched the crowd moved closer to the tracks, more pushing, more jostling, more screaming. The mayor hurried to address the mob, leading a handful of troops and his fire chief, Fred Kelly. Their job, he had told the troops, was simply to keep people from turning on each other, to maintain order. Again he issued the command: no able-bodied man was allowed on the train, no baggage but what you could hold in your lap. The train whistle blared constantly in the dark, but it was almost drowned out as tanks continued to blow up, scattering flammables to other parts of town.

The train came into view, moving very slowly, an eternity to those in the exodus scrum. It lumbered to a stop, engines still fired, wheezing smoke and steam. Doors opened, and with a heave people poured into the cars, all seats and standing room filled as if by water gushing into a ship's cargo hold. A woman separated from her child cried out, "My baby! My baby!" One man yanked a woman from her seat and took it as his own. He was pulled from the train and kicked to the ground by those who were overseeing the evacuation. Within minutes, all space was taken, even on the flatbeds, and yet men of strong build in fine clothes spurned the mayor's orders and bullied their way onto the train.

"Men fought with women for precedence, well-dressed men eager to get into the coaches and save themselves," the *Idaho Press* reported in its eyewitness dispatch. The men were cowards, the railroad's freight agent said. "The women were the heroines." To the mayor's dismay, among the weak men were prominent citizens who had talked earlier of holding the line, of fighting for the town and setting an example for the children, for the community. In truth, they came to this mountain town to get rich, and damned if they were going to die trying to save the place. The mayor consulted with his fire chief about ejecting all the men by force. Before he could issue an order, a soldier removed a well-known roustabout from the train, "a fat gambler," as the papers called him; he was forced off at the end of a fixed bayonet. Still, men dodged, slipped, and pressed to get on; they were in life-flight, bloated with adrenaline.

"Let the bastards go," Chief Kelly said to Mayor Hanson.

Missing from the rescue train was John Boyd. He had ignored his son's pleading, returning to the house to rescue his parrot. He found the bird in a frenzy. Boyd took the cage outside, then paused and set it on the ground. Perhaps the house could be saved. He turned on the garden hose and sprayed the outside walls, the roof, the porch — just enough water for good measure, and surely his son would thank him for thinking like a fireman and not like a coward in abject confusion. Then he picked up the bird cage and hustled for the rail tracks. His gait was unsteady. Snagged by smoke and heat, he gasped and trembled. He had trouble getting a deep breath in the heated air that smothered the town, and it hurt his chest to cough. He sat and rested on the street, taking slow, deliberate breaths, mumbling promises to his parrot. Now when he stood it was difficult to take more than a step or two. After walking a few hesitant paces, he fell to the ground, his grip tight on the birdcage no more. John Boyd and his parrot died on the streets of Wallace, of smoke inhalation.

Also missing from the train was Emma Pulaski. Her husband was a ranger with the Forest Service who had spent the month of August trying to knock down small blazes in the mountains. He had nearly three hundred men under his command at one point, working a few miles from Wallace. If anyone could keep the fire from jumping into town, it was thought to be Ed Pulaski, one of the few rangers in the fledgling Forest Service who knew the region — its trails, creekbeds, and ridgelines. He knew the winds, the mining holes, the path of afternoon thunderstorms. He knew how to calm a horse when lightning struck, and could craft a tool from a plank of rough cedar, and could pitch a lean-to in less time than it took other rangers to finish a sentence. Chronically short of supplies while commanding a brigade of confused men, Pulaski had fought a rear-guard, defensive action, trying to hold flames in check by digging lines that would deprive the fire of fresh fuel. The strategy was simply to keep the fire a safe distance from Wallace, the biggest town in the valley. On Friday, the day before the evacuation, Pulaski had returned to Wallace for food, blankets, shovels — anything to restock his bedraggled crew. He stopped by his house to see Emma and their ten-year-old daughter, Elsie. He had a bad feeling about the next twenty-four hours, he told them.

"Wallace will surely burn," Pulaski said to his wife. "Be prepared to save yourselves." His was a voice of doom, not a hint of optimism. Wallace had never looked so vulnerable: all this fuel, in this narrow slot of humanity, at the base of a dense forest that had not seen noticeable rain for months. Pulaski and Emma discussed the town evacuation plan first, then another idea of staying behind and hunkering down near the mine tailings by the river, a berm of graveled waste. He was not long into his visit when another ranger rushed up to the house—a fresh fire, much bigger than anything to date, was moving close to town. Pulaski had to go back into the mountains and tend to his firefighters; his orders were to corral this thing before it advanced any farther down the valley. Emma and Elsie went with him to the trailhead, an eight-mile ride from town.

At road's end, Pulaski faced his wife and daughter. In his fashion, he was blunt, devoid of sentiment, telling them this might be the final goodbye. He turned and started up the steep, faint trail, a corkscrew that had been hacked along a creek by miners. Emma and Elsie rode back to town through a thicket of smoke and blowing embers, Emma's eyes red from the sting of the air.

When Emma and Elsie reached home, the front yard was littered with burning bark and the porch was covered in ash. They spent a sleepless night. The next day, Saturday, as the winds picked up in the early evening, the house shook so violently Emma thought it might be pushed off its foundation. Those who did not head for the train streamed out of town, their furniture, pots, pans, blankets, and linens piled onto horse-drawn jalopies. Emma still thought she could ride it out. She put her child to bed at 8:30 P.M., closed the doors and windows. In the dark of Saturday night, a neighbor banged on the door.

"Mrs. Pulaski," she said, "leave the house!"

Emma glanced outside and saw flames far down the flanks of the mountains, lapping at homes in the foothills. She woke Elsie, grabbed a few blankets, and made a run for the mine tailings. She would try to survive the night in a bed of crushed mineral waste—one thing that would not ignite. Her thoughts were up higher, with her husband in the chop of flame.

No living person in the United States had seen anything like the flames that roared through the Bitterroots in the summer of 1910:

at its peak, the storm would consume three million acres in barely two days. In the weeks leading up to the blowup, before Wallace was evacuated, nearly ten thousand men had been thrown together in three states, Montana, Idaho, and Washington. The woods were a snarl of smoke, thousands of small blazes consuming a prime piece of the Rockies, and it looked as if many lives were at risk. After sending out a rescue call to save the national forests, the government enlisted college boys from California; day workers from Denver, Salt Lake City, Butte, Missoula, Spokane, Seattle, and Portland; and immigrants, thousands of foreigners—from mining camps in Arizona and Colorado, from irrigation ditches in California, from timber towns in the coastal Pacific Northwest, people working at jobs that American citizens would not take. It was the greatest force yet assembled to fight a wildfire in the country.

President William H. Taft had also sent Army troops to the region. Taft was 335 pounds of insecurity, growing politically weaker and physically bigger by the day. A year and a half into his first term, he was never out of the strong wake of his predecessor, the peripatetic Theodore Roosevelt. At the same time that Taft monitored the fires from his summer home in Beverly, Massachusetts, Roosevelt was beginning a nationwide speaking tour—a firestorm of his own, heading west, arena by arena, his spectacles steamed as he barked on behalf of ideals he had promoted in the new century. The road show of high-minded rhetoric would further highlight the inadequacies of the man Roosevelt had handpicked to follow him in office, a man he would soon abandon.

The Republican Party that Teddy Roosevelt had built—the uneasy meld of progressives, Main Street capitalists, and the founding voices of American conservation—was falling apart. One big reason: the establishment of national forests in an expanse of wild country that Roosevelt and his chief forester, Gifford Pinchot, had kept from the control of men they castigated as robber barons and plunderers of the public domain. The land that had not been settled, not been promised to vanquished Indian tribes, not been given over to railroads, not been cleared for cities, factories, and farms—this big, rumpled, roadless quilt of original America belonged to everyone, Roosevelt said; it belonged to the ages. It was sweeping and simple as a philosophy, and maybe even obvious in retrospect. But this was a radical idea then, one formed over brisk, heart-pumping walks with the *über*-passionate Pinchot. It did not go over well in places where a fortune could still be made from the remains of Manifest Destiny. After cutting the great forests of Maine and Michigan, after leveling much of the Appalachian hardwoods and southern piney woods, the leading timber industrialists coveted Idaho and western Montana, the native nursery for the largest body of standing white pine on the planet, with trees 250 feet tall or more. The land was little changed since Lewis and Clark stumbled through it a century earlier.

The president's enemies in Congress had tried at every turn to blunt his biggest domestic policy dream. "Many rich men were stirred to hostility, and they used the Congressmen they controlled to assault us," T.R. wrote in his autobiography. Roosevelt and Pinchot reveled in the fight. They saw politics in stark terms: good versus evil, the people versus the powerful, the virtuous against the corrupt. They had the momentum of an idea in ascendancy, they felt, and it helped that Roosevelt had invented the bully pulpit—named for his favorite exclamation. He appealed to the expanding middle class in a century dawning with technological marvels, to new citizens from the Old World, to those without a trace of sentiment for something so foreign as preservation of wild land. Every American had this birthright: holding a citizen's share in an area nearly as large as France. Even if they never set foot on it, never saw it, never knew where it was, it was there, and it was *theirs*. Throughout his presidency, his grand plan grew ever more audacious: Why not quadruple the national forests? And the Grand Canyon, as American an icon as the Coliseum is to Rome—why not leave it as it is? Why not set aside marshes and rivers, high plains and low valleys, for the creatures that lived there—wildlife refuges all over the country? Of course, one reason to preserve those creatures was to have the opportunity to kill them later, as Roosevelt was not a passive observer of the food chain. But his love of nature was deep and consistent. "When I hear of the destruction of a species," he wrote as a young man, "I feel just as if all of the works of some great writer had perished."

After Roosevelt left office in 1909 and went off to Africa and Europe for more than a year, his enemies had an easy time with the befuddled Taft. He did not really want to be president, he said later, and certainly did not enjoy the job. He wanted to be a judge, and he wanted to be liked, and he wanted to eat his dinner in peace, without all the sniping and second-guessing about his weight. The papers said he looked like a walrus in a postprandial snooze.

With Taft's indifference, it fell to the Forest Service, an agency just five years old in 1910, to protect the new reserves of public land. The rangers were despised in much of the West, scorned as Teddy's boy scouts, or worse—hapless elites from the Yale School of Forestry. Around mining camps and logging towns, the places where agents for timber trusts set up shop to foil the new national forests, rangers were sometimes threatened at gunpoint or chased from the woods. In Congress, opponents tried to starve the Forest Service to death. Low salaries forced good people out, and the budget was squeezed so tight that by the time the fire tore through the Rockies a single ranger was responsible for more than 300,000 acres on average. With such a large beat, it was impossible to thwart timber thieves and assorted opportunists who were prowling public land like burglars in an unlocked house, let alone keep a fire from getting away from them. When the hot summer of 1910 got under way, some rangers had to pay firefighters out of their own pockets, from their meager salaries. To the enemies of the Forest Service, the fire was a chance to kill the crusade of conservation.

So on the afternoon of August 20, 1910, it appeared as if the land at the heart of Roosevelt's big idea would be lost or saved on the backs of ten thousand firefighters guided by a handful of young forest rangers. They had few tools, few pack animals, and only flimsy bedrolls to keep them warm on cold Rocky Mountain nights, when temperatures would dip into the thirties even in August. Some of them knew how to milk a cow or plow a field in a country where, for the last time, a majority of citizens still lived in rural areas. Some knew how to weld a broken axle together or frame a house. Some knew how to extract silver or copper from deep underground. Some could speak three languages, though many of them spoke no English at all. They came from the mountains of Serbia, or the Danish coast, or the stony hills of Sicily to the last place in the contiguous United States to be fully mapped and charted. As *Collier's* magazine put it: "There were Scotsmen and Negroes, Italians and Danes, Micks, Macks and Scandihoovians." With flames closing in on Wallace and four other towns, the fate of this land was in the hands of people often derided as bohunks, dagos, or "dusky dough boys." They came because it was a job, paying twenty-five cents an hour — though many were paid only with promises. Ranger and immigrant alike, they shared but a single thing: not one of them knew how to engage a wildfire of this magnitude.

In the East, the monied interests were well aware of what was at stake on the afternoon of August 20. On a map, the location of this fire looked far removed from anything, but it was known in many a mahogany-paneled boardroom. The resource kingdom of the northern Rockies was one of the last arenas for the clash of Gilded Age plutocrats, from E. H. Harriman and James J. Hill to the Rockefellers, Morgans, Guggenheims, and Weyerhaeusers. Fire could prove to be the mortal blow to the Forest Service, clearing the obstacle to further big-business control of the land. But it could also destroy the very thing the titans wanted to get their hands on. For the first time, the major newspapers covered the burning West, giving it as much attention as they gave to military battles in a foreign conflict. The enemy was on the rampage. Troops were assembled. Let the war begin.

"It was the first organized and large-scale battle against forest fires in the United States," wrote Stewart Holbrook, the western historian.

By 10 P.M., the streets of Wallace, Idaho—where President Roosevelt had walked seven years earlier—were overwhelmed by flames, and the forest he had set aside for future generations was in ruin. Hundreds of firefighters were lost and thought to be dead. Looking for guidance in a town where nearly half the buildings were on fire, people tried to find William Weigle, the commanding ranger, in charge of the Coeur d'Alene National Forest that surrounded the town. Weigle was missing, just like his brother rangers, wandering somewhere on the burning slopes of the Bitterroots. What about Ed Pulaski, then? People called his name. The most experienced ranger in the district was racing through another part of the mountains, chased by a crown fire, flames leaping from treetop to treetop, pushed by gusts approaching eighty miles an hour. His horses stumbled, whinnied in agony, panic evident in their movement; they might roast before his eyes. His men had nowhere to go. They sobbed and moaned about loved ones, wives and mothers, children, or in acute self-pity. They were going to die on this smoke-choked mountainside so far removed from their homes, going to die in the most painful, horrid way. To be buried alive was one thing. But to be burned while still breathing, every nerve ending screaming, the skin boiling, dragon breath inside the lungs, that was the worst.

Back in town, near midnight, a telegraph operator at the Northern Pacific office sent a message:

"Every hill around town is a mass of flames and the whole place looks like a death trap. No connections can be had with outside towns. Men, women and children are hysterical in streets and leave by every possible conveyance and route."

PART I

In On the Creation

1

"A Peculiar Intimacy"

FOR TWO DAYS snow had been falling in upstate New York, so it came as a surprise to Gifford Pinchot when he showed up at the executive mansion in Albany and found the second-story windows wide open and a barrel-chested man, the governor of New York, cajoling children down a rope to the ground. The cold air rushed in, the children slid out—a robust family brought to life inside a snow globe.

Teddy Roosevelt loved to play. On this winter day in February 1899, the governor imagined that the mansion was under attack by Indians and it was his job to help the kids escape through the window and down the rope. One by one, Roosevelt lowered the children onto the snow, whooping and hollering to highlight the drama. There went Teddy Jr., and Kermit, Edith, and Archie. (Quentin, not yet two, was too small to join them, and Alice, the eldest daughter, was away at school.) Pinchot was amused, though he seemed at first blush to be the kind of man who kept his distance from a good joke.

Gifford Pinchot was attractive in the old-school way, with a sizable enough family fortune to qualify as an English lord, and was still unmarried at age thirty-three. But at times he also brought to mind a character from Washington Irving's *Legend of Sleepy Hol-*

low, with his elongated, skeletal frame, huge feet, stilts for legs, brushy mustache draped over his upper lip, comb-resistant hair, high forehead, and wild, faraway gaze. "His eyes do not look as if they read books," said the writer Owen Wister, a Roosevelt intimate, "but as if they gazed upon a cause." Pinchot could be kinetic, especially when unbound by an idea, his long arms fluttering in conversation. Or he could appear formal and upper class — stiff with the inherited burden of accent and manners that came from prep school at Exeter; college at Yale, including membership in the most secret of clubs, Skull and Bones; and summers in a family castle in Pennsylvania, with sixty-three turrets and twenty-three fireplaces, the chateau known as Grey Towers. On occasion, he slept on a wooden pillow; most mornings he was awakened by a valet who threw cold water in his face. A good man, *a bit odd*, as friends said behind his back. But Pinchot was self-aware enough to know that he was considered strange, and though he was in on the joke, it fed his insecurity.

"Made an ass out of myself," he wrote in his diary after many a party.

Pinchot, who knew Roosevelt from sportsmen circles in the Empire State, came to the governor's mansion with Christopher Grant La Farge, son of the painter John La Farge, a close friend of Teddy's. They were in Albany on business of sorts. Pinchot was the national forester, a meaningless federal job. He wanted to get a good look at a large tract of trees in the nearby Adirondacks — something he and La Farge thought might make a book subject. Roosevelt knew a thing or two about the written word: just forty years old, he was about to publish his fourteenth book.

Teddy invited the two men in for a hot drink and to stay the night. In the evening, they talked of forest protection and the fear of a coming timber famine caused by industrial-age logging. On this they agreed: Americans had become much too shortsighted with the continent they now straddled. In an eyeblink, the great bounty had been exhausted; more than a billion acres had been given away to corporations, states, or private landowners to do with as they pleased. There was deep concern in many circles that the nation might well run short of natural resources in the process of remaking the land. An America stitched together by railroads and telephone lines suddenly seemed not just finite but small. They also traded gossip about the political cesspool in Albany. Learning his craft in New York at a time when public office was bought and sold by machine bosses, Roosevelt had developed a remarkably hard view of politics. "On one side there were corrupt and unscrupulous demagogues," he wrote of the New York State Assembly, "and on the other side corrupt and unscrupulous reactionaries."

Teddy's face lit up when Pinchot and La Farge told him about their real reason for traveling upstate in the midst of one of the coldest seasons on record: a winter ascent of Mount Marcy, at 5,344 feet the highest point in New York. Marcy in February was like upper Denali in Alaska: a haunt of killing cold with wind chills of thirty below zero and rocks coated in polished ice. The plan was to snowshoe to a cabin and spend the night, then start out for Lake Tear of the Clouds, the source of the Hudson River. The snow was twenty feet deep in parts, but in other places the wind had blown it down to hard ice. Roosevelt thought the plan was *bully;* he had some experience in mountaineering, and regularly inhaled risk as some men gulped vitamin supplements. Danger was stimulating to mind and body. Roosevelt had scrambled up Vesuvius in Italy and the Jungfrau in Switzerland. After climbing the Matterhorn, he shrugged off the feat in a letter to his sister: "A fairly hardy man, cautious but not cowardly, with good guides, has little to fear. Still, there is enough peril to make it exciting."

It was the prospect of peril that first united Pinchot and Roosevelt. Both were adrenaline addicts and thrill seekers, the longer the odds, the better. Roosevelt's idea of "great sport" was to go after a grizzly bear armed only with a knife, while Pinchot had once killed a fast-moving deer with a pistol. Teddy had sponsored Pinchot's membership in the Boone and Crockett Club, a group devoted to hunting and fishing by educated men who never wanted to stop being boys. Pinchot could coax a fish from the deepest hole and outshoot anyone in his class. And now this talk of climbing Mount Marcy got the pulse of both men going. Instead of more tea, Roosevelt wondered, would Pinchot be ready for a physical challenge of some sort? Would Pinchot like to fight Roosevelt? How about wrestling, stripped to the skivvies, on the governor's mat? Roosevelt had installed the big wrestling mat and tried to get the state to pay for it. When the comptroller questioned the bill, he explained that while most governors entertained with billiards, Teddy preferred to attack — for sport — his official visitors.

As governor of New York, pinned to the executive mansion by the daily intrigues of Tammany Hall legislators, Roosevelt had little time for extended expeditions. Boxing was his main outlet, though he liked to wrestle too. "Violent amusement," Roosevelt called both sports. The problem was finding a regular sparring partner. For several weeks, a smalltime prizefighter served as one of his regular pugilistic opponents. Then he disappeared, and Roosevelt did not hear from the man until he received a letter from jail — as it turned out, his boxing mate was a fugitive, wanted for burglary.

Pinchot and Roosevelt agreed to a fight in two parts: a wrestling match, followed by a break, then a round of boxing. At Yale, Pinchot was a backup quarterback on the football team coached by Walter Camp; he was quick on his feet for a big man. He expressed some concern about his six-inch height advantage over T.R., who stood five feet eight inches. Nonsense, Roosevelt told him: he'd exchanged blows with men taller than Pinchot. Plus, Roosevelt had nearly thirty-five pounds on the cadaverous forester.

A sickly child, asthmatic, frail and nearsighted, Teddy had willed his way to strength, defying the doctors who said he might not live long unless he cultivated the indoor life. "I will make my body" was his vow, spoken in a voice yet to crack into young manhood. As a boy, he was afraid of horses, afraid of wild animals, afraid of what lurked behind a tree in the dark. But he taught himself to *pretend* that he was brave, and in this way became fearless. "By acting as if I was not afraid I gradually ceased to be afraid," he said. He not only could climb mountains but also could walk cross-country at a fifteen-minute-mile pace and ride a horse for half a day without a break. He loved to snowshoe in winter and canoe in summer. He swam outdoors in all seasons, in any temperature. He could rope, ride, and shoot like an action figure in a Remington painting, and yet he had a delicate side, with a poet's appreciation for the wondrous symmetry of a flower or the hush of a still morning. "There are no words that can tell the hidden spirit of the wilderness, that can reveal its mysteries, its melancholy and its charms," he said. The outdoors may have shaped the body, but it clearly got into his soul.

Young Teddy had been a collector of insects and frogs, happiest when he fled the clutter of Manhattan for summers of scrubbed air in the country. When he enrolled at Harvard, a teenager of just 125 pounds, he intended to become a zoologist; his father, a wealthy businessman and philanthropist, cautioned him that as a man of science he would never make much money. Roosevelt wanted to be like John James Audubon, who had done for American bird life what Leonardo da Vinci did for the human form, or Dr. William Hornaday, who founded the National Zoo in Washington and tried to save a few American bison before the last ones disappeared. Audubon and Hornaday were Teddy's heroes, unusual choices for a city boy.

During Teddy's sophomore year, his father died of stomach cancer, at the age of forty-six; he said he lost "the best man I ever knew." To sideline the sorrow, Roosevelt kept busy at all hours, studying the orderly web of the natural world and working his fists and feet in the gym. As a fighter, he made it once to the semifinals in his weight category, but realized he would never be an extraordinary athlete. As a student of science, he was dismayed that virtually all the work took place indoors, in the concentrated claustrophobia of the laboratory. He wanted to crash and thump and charge and breathe in all the dimensions beyond the walls. He gave up the zo-ology dream — though not his passion for insects, animals, and their habitats — to study politics and history, followed by law school. He wasn't fit to be a lawyer either; he dropped out of Columbia without a law degree.

Delayed adolescence, full of earnest indecision and freeform travel, was not for Teddy Roosevelt. In little more than a year's time, he married the stunning Alice Hathaway Lee — "so radiantly pure and good and beautiful that I almost feel like worshipping her" — and was elected to the New York Assembly, from Manhat-tan. At age twenty-three, he was the state's youngest legislator; at twenty-five, he was Republican minority leader, though he showed little of a young man's naiveté. He knew whom the party bosses owned and could always tell when they left their fingerprints on a bill. With his father's inheritance, he could afford virtue, which was in short supply in Albany. Not all of his fellow assemblymen were one hundred percent crooked, Roosevelt said, but "there were a great many thoroughly corrupt men in the Legislature, perhaps a third of the whole number."

The blow of a lifetime came early, on Valentine's Day 1884, per-haps the best-known single day of trauma in the formative period of a future president. In the morning, Teddy's mother died of ty-phoid fever at the family house on Fifty-seventh Street; she was forty-six. A few hours later, the suddenly orphaned Roosevelt lost his bride in the same house, to Bright's disease, a kidney ailment, which had been masked by her pregnancy. He scrawled a big, shaky X on a diary page and wrote a single sentence: "The light has gone out of my life." He never said or wrote his wife's name again.

Roosevelt went west to the Badlands, west to a place far removed from Manhattan and Albany and friends from college and the fam-ily circle, west to a place where the markings on the map showed no major roads or cities of any size — only ranges and rivers, the West of anonymity, where he could be swallowed by the landscape. In the Dakotas, he would try to heal himself. When he arrived at the train depot on the Little Missouri and looked around at the vast brown emptiness, the prairie wind in his face, he felt born to this land.

In time, he built a small cabin of rough-hewn logs, with a sitting room in front of a big fireplace. There he put a rocking chair, hung buffalo robes and bear hides from animals he had killed, and spent the evenings with his books. He became another man, with cattle to run and horses to keep, with water to haul and fences to mend, a bespectacled cowboy from Harvard who punched a drunk in a bar who'd taunted him as "four-eyes," chased an outlaw through the canyons, suffered frostbite on a winter outing. He was no faux ranch hand: Teddy rode long days in the saddle, once breaking a shoulder and ribs while taming wild horses. "I have three weeks on the roundup and have worked as hard as any of the cowboys," he wrote in one letter. "Yesterday, I was 18 hours in the saddle, from 4 A.M., to 10 P.M."

The West of unlimited promise was in its last days. The tribes had been rounded up and shuttled off to little remnants of their native land. The indigenous bison herd, sixty million or more strong at one time, was down to a few hundred stragglers. The ecosystem of the high plains, which had been compared to Eden by Lewis and Clark, was being torn to pieces. Where birds had once blotted the skies of migratory flyways, it was hard at times to find a single duck on a fall afternoon. But even with the smell of death on it, the land made Roosevelt whole again. He found renewal in wilderness—the geography of hope, as it was called by westerners who followed him.

Back in Manhattan after two years, Roosevelt resumed his political career. He ran for mayor of New York City in 1886, and lost, but considered the whole venture a lark — "anyway, I had a bully time!" A month after the election, he married Edith Kermit Carow, whom he'd known since he was a kid on East Twentieth Street; while very young, they had watched Lincoln's funeral procession from an upstairs window of a house. In just over ten years, they had five children. During the same span, Roosevelt wrote nine books—histories of the West and New York, biographies, memoirs, war stories. In two years as the city's police commissioner, he saw New York's underside—ragged orphans working in overheated tenements, opium dens filled with frightened immigrants, illegal boxing matches in sweaty basements. The job both hardened him against crime and softened him about the woes of the underclass at a time of great wealth held by a few. The muckraking book by Jacob Riis, *How the Other Half Lives,* was an enormous influence. "I was still ignorant of the extent to which big men of great wealth played a mischievous part in our industrial and social life," Roosevelt said. Early on, he developed a disdain for the more gaudy members of the gilded class, the celebrity millionaires who took up column space in the penny papers and held parties where showy excess was the goal, a dinner with a Versailles theme being the peak of ostentation. The rich bored him.

Adventure called during the Spanish-American War. Again he became another man, someone who would charge into a hail of bullets because he had willed himself not to fear death. He despised politicians who talked of war and sent others off to fight. Colonel Roosevelt, with his sun-hardened troop of ranchers, broncobusters, drifters, and hunters—the Rough Riders, 1st Volunteer Cavalry Regiment—became the best-known man in America. The luster was enough to carry him into the governor's office in 1898. Yet even with a decade of New York reform politics and a season at war under his belt, what had saved the broken young man was his time in the open land of the Dakotas. He never forgot.

"I owe more than I can ever express to the West," Roosevelt said.

Stripped to gym shorts and tank tops, the governor and the forester faced each other. In a crouch, Gifford Pinchot was still taller than Roosevelt standing. Pinchot had a rangy athleticism, sinewy and hard, weighing barely 175 pounds. The two men circled each other, arms extended, hands at the ready, looking for advantage. They made thrusts and parries, grunting with every advance. Roosevelt liked to taunt an opponent, and it threw people off—that high, jabbing voice, a barking bulldog. He reached for Pinchot's neck, trying to corral him. He grabbed his shoulders, trying to throw him. He planted his foot on the mat and moved to trip him. Because Roosevelt's center of gravity was lower, it gave him an advantage for dropping a taller man. But Pinchot was not easy to bring down. The big man could squirm and dodge, and when dropped to the mat he could bounce to his feet with great speed. Roosevelt's best weapon was his chest—it was huge for a man his size, armored in muscle. At last, he flipped Pinchot to the floor, using his upper body and weight advantage to hold him. Roosevelt got his count—and victory. Pinchot stood, red-faced and defeated.

The second fight was with fists only, and here Roosevelt also seemed to have the advantage because of his regular sparring. But Pinchot had a much longer wingspan; he could simply slow-box around Roosevelt, keeping his distance, using his superior height and arm length. He laced his gloves, mulling his strategy. Go for the quick knockdown with a hook to the face? Or circle and exhaust the older, smaller Roosevelt?

Pinchot was a man of many moods, many calculations. He could be gothic with his dreadful long-distance stares. He could certainly be mystical, making some cryptic reference to the spirit world and often disappearing for no reason. "You see more and learn more when no one else is there," Pinchot said. He could be suddenly forceful and personable, enlivened by a cause. He could be impulsive and would not back down, even when facing certain defeat. And he was in perpetual motion.

"Action is what I craved," he said.

Pinchot had much in common with Roosevelt. Both were born to wealth, but disdained the rich. "Gilded idlers are just plain fools," Pinchot said. Both grew up in the cultured comfort of Manhattan and learned about the outdoors over long summers in the country.

Both were educated at the nation's premier colleges, but were bored by academic life. Both had lost a woman to early death, after falling deeply in love. Both were passionate about nature. Both were hyper-competitive. Both had a similar epiphany about their own country while wandering around Europe: the United States would never match the Old World for cathedrals and castles, but should glory in its endowment from the natural world. Both were reformists with acute self-righteous streaks. Both drank very little and were regular churchgoers. Both found the West restorative. Both men thought they could change the world, and would soon get a chance at it.

While Roosevelt came from Dutch Knickerbocker stock, Pinchot traced his lineage to Napoleonic France. His grandfather, a supporter of the emperor, fled to the United States after Napoleon was forced into his second exile. In America he became a timber baron of his own rank, establishing the family wealth by relieving entire sections of the New World of its tree cover. What Pinchot the forester played down for most of his life was how much his family had to do with *deforesting*. He seldom mentioned that the immigrant Pinchot became one of the wealthiest men in northeastern Pennsylvania by stripping trees in his adopted state. The founder of the American family line, Cyrille Constantine Désiré Pinchot was a speculator and a clear-cutter. Gifford's grandfather mowed down big swaths of native hemlock, white pine, oak, and other species. His wealth grew as the young nation fed the furnaces and the spoils of the industrial revolution, in time becoming the richest landowner in his county. His son certified their baronial status when he built Grey Towers, the massive family castle overlooking the Delaware — not too far from, but out of sight of, the hills denuded by his father's clear-cuts.

Gifford was raised in New York, Connecticut, and the blue-stone manse in Pennsylvania, in even greater wealth than his father had known. His mother, Mary, his closest confidant — Mamee, he called her — came from a big merchant and real estate family, one of the richest in New York. The merger through marriage with James Pinchot, who had parlayed his inherited money into a fortune in the restless ferment of New York, ensured that the children would always have the finest things in life. The family collected art and friends from among the best-connected people. But their main project was Gifford. He was bound for greatness, they told him early—he must choose his life's task with utmost care. Gifford learned his tennis and his table manners, his French and his music, what to wear and when to swear, but he never took to the smart set.

In Gifford Pinchot's version of the family narrative, he was born to service in the tradition of noblesse oblige. Perhaps. His parents were more refined than the earlier generation—the moneymakers. They were interested in philanthropy and the outdoors, in religion and music, and seldom got their hands dirty. Still, on Pinchot's side, wealth had come from the brute economics of felling trees fast. So Gifford's life could be seen as a corrective for what his grandfather had done. Pinchot recalled how his father approached him just before the young man went off to Yale. "How would you like to be a forester?" It was a strange question, Pinchot wrote, because there was no such concept then in the United States—no profession, school, job title, not so much as an aspiration. "The fact that Forestry was new and strange and promised action probably had as much to do with it as my love for the woods," he wrote.

Like Roosevelt, he wanted to roam on his own; he wanted to prove himself. After Yale, with no job prospects in a profession still unborn in the states, Pinchot went to France, where forestry was a fussy thing practiced by a mildewed gentry. He studied at l'École Nationale Forestière, a cluster of dark buildings in Nancy. The ascetic Pinchot noted that "the town was full of wicked students," and the neighboring hardwood forests were just as alien—trees grown like a crop, with nary a twig on the ground, the peasants banned even from making a campfire, subservient to the lords of the grounds. Everything was orderly, not at all like home. "I feel like being in real woods again," Pinchot wrote his parents from Europe. "I shall be glad to leave—all drink and no forestry is not my meat." To his surprise, everyone in European forestry circles wanted to talk about the American West, the big wild of the Rocky Mountains and beyond, which Pinchot had not yet seen. What a tabula rasa! What a place to practice *la foresterie!* Open country, ripe for grand themes!

When Pinchot returned home in 1890, he was dismayed at how Americans viewed their public domain. What was hailed in Europe as a glorious swath of unspoiled creation was viewed in his native land as a plunderer's buffet. "To waste timber was a virtue, not a crime," he wrote. While others saw a young country in full flex, stapling railroads along every river byway, leveling and burning the woods to make way for progress, overturning the prairie grass for farms, Pinchot saw chaos, death, soiling the garden—"a gigantic and lamentable massacre." The cut-and-run philosophy appalled him. Worse, most public land was being sold at a pittance or handed off to people (not unlike his grandfather) who could not see beyond a season of cashing out. Presidents and governors took every opportunity to give land away—to the railroads, to town-platting developers, to mining conglomerates and timber syndicates, the quicker the better. A fire sale in Eden.

"The American Colossus was fiercely intent on appropriating and exploiting the riches of the richest of all continents—grasping with both hands, reaping where he had not sown, wasting what he thought would last forever," Pinchot wrote. "The exploiters were pushing further and further into the wilderness. The man who could get his hands on the biggest slice of natural resources was the best citizen. Wealth and virtue were supposed to trot in double harness."

Pinchot's maternal grandfather urged him to give up this forestry nonsense and come manage part of the family empire. *Old boy, you'll be rich beyond your dreams!* Instead, Pinchot went west to sleep on cold rock and wet ground, to eat dried food and whatever bony bird he could shoot from the sky or fish he could pull from a river—to get his first look at land he would champion for the rest of his life.

His trip took him by train to Arizona, to the San Francisco Mountains above Flagstaff, the snowy peaks that towered over Navajo country and the canyonlands of wonder. On to California, to the High Sierra, the Range of Light, granite summits fourteen thousand feet above sea level, and north among the sequoias and redwoods, the biggest trees in the world—it took ten men to embrace a single trunk. In the Yosemite Valley, he climbed above the falls, higher than any he'd ever seen, then clambered down the rock and jumped in and out of the torrent itself, more than a quarter mile of falling water. The moment was pure bliss: baptism in the land. He felt immensely happy, the gloom gone. What's more, he felt that he belonged. In the Pacific Northwest, he hiked past trees with a diameter the size of his dining room table in Manhattan, waded through a sea of hyper-photosynthetic green in the nation's temperate rain forest. All of it was glorious, inspirational, a great thrill, everything his forestry education had lacked. But as the train took him east, back to old money and New York and persistent questions of What next, young man? the self-doubt returned. What good was this epic of self-indulgent travel if he could not put his passion to some use? His life needed an animating force.

"Footless, useless, selfish, dumb, and generally of no use to anybody," he wrote at the end of his first trip out west. "Rotten as usual," he noted five days later, now in a deep funk. "This uselessness probably a result of so much gadding about & so many late hours after that very severe western trip. Anyway, am disgusted with myself most thoroughly."

Back in New York city, Pinchot hung a shingle outside an office on Fourth Avenue and Twenty-second Street: CONSULTING FORESTER. He may have been the nation's *only* forester. He had decided to create his own job. His reputation grew quickly, aided by his father's contacts. In the closing days of the nineteenth century, when American cities decided to build a park they went to Frederick Law Olmsted or his two sons. And when the subject was trees, Gifford Pinchot was the expert. But Pinchot was not content to be a consulting caretaker. His free time was spent in the wild, where his dreams took flight.

It was on a hike in the Adirondacks in the fall of 1892 that Pinchot first met the most famous naturalist in America—John Muir, the wiry, engaging Scot with a Santa Claus beard and liquid blue eyes, full of spring. What Buffalo Bill meant for cowboy shows, John Muir was for serious lovers of the outdoors: a celebrity whose picture could evoke a man of action.

Muir was one of eight children, who moved as a boy with his family to Wisconsin. There, he worked a farm; the knuckle-scuffing task of turning hard midwestern ground gave Muir an affinity with beasts of burden, he said later, helping him empathize with all living things. His early life showed no mark of greatness or ambition. He studied botany at the University of Wisconsin for a time, then kicked around the country for the better part of a decade, from factories in the flatlands to swamps in Florida. At age thirty, suffering from malaria, he sought the sunshine of California. That same year, 1868, he first saw Yosemite—its three-thousand-foot-high granite flanks, its soft light, its symphony of waterfalls. He stayed in the area for the next six years, working odd jobs, mostly as a shepherd. He developed his views on the land by observing, taking copious notes on the active geology of his adopted state, and by submission. He could write in clear, often witty, usually passionate prose, and his byline soon became one of the nation's best known. By marrying, in his forties, into a family of means northeast of San Francisco, he found himself with a Victorian home on a vineyard and orchard, and the financial comfort that allowed him to roam. And roam he did—kayaking waters choked with icebergs, walking uncharted ground in Alaska, summiting glacier-draped volcanoes in the Pacific Northwest, hiking in the Adirondacks and all over his beloved Sierra.

A few days after meeting Muir in upstate New York, young Pinchot sent the naturalist a gift: a large hunting knife. Muir had no
use for it—he foraged, yes, on many of his trips in the wild, but
never took so much as a fish hook—to Pinchot's astonishment. Muir
said all he needed was to "throw some tea and bread in an old sack
and jump over the back fence." He was Huck Finn with shoes and
a notebook. A few months later, at a dinner party at Pinchot's parents' home in Gramercy Park, they found they were kindred souls.
"I took to him at once," Pinchot wrote. Muir became a friend and
mentor, starting when Pinchot was twenty-seven, and Muir was
nearly twice his age.

"You are choosing the right way into the woods," Muir wrote
him not long after the dinner party, where Pinchot had told him
about his solo excursions outdoors. Others considered it strange for
a man of Pinchot's standing to take monastic trips to the wilderness.
Not Muir. "Happy man," he wrote his acolyte. "You will never regret a single day spent thus." Muir liked this odd patrician in part
because he was such an eager follower—at first. In Pinchot, he saw
someone "who could relish, not run from a rainstorm," as he wrote.
Just like himself.

Of course, there was calculation and some cunning on both sides.
Pinchot's family wanted Gifford to connect with the influential
Muir, a man whose company was sought by everyone from Ralph
Waldo Emerson to New York Police Commissioner Teddy Roosevelt.
Muir, who had just started the Sierra Club in 1892 as a voice for the
California range, could always use the Pinchot money and perhaps
this bright young forester to further the cause. Together with a few
other men who were starting to talk of ways to protect the land,
they formed a conservation caucus that could barely fill a Union
Pacific caboose. Fellow travelers included Olmsted, who was one of
the first to insist that it was America's duty to put aside "great public grounds for the free enjoyment of people"; a German-American
forester, Bernhard Fernow, who headed the government's first division of forestry even though he had no land under his jurisdiction;

and the Boston botanist Charles Sargent. Small as the group was, their ideas were contagious, and well placed.

On several trips in the West, Muir and Pinchot bonded under the open sky. They spent nights along the rim of the Grand Canyon, slogged up snow-coated peaks in the Northwest, tramped through the Bitterroots in Montana, sometimes moving at a clip of twenty miles a day. Pinchot's eccentricities were becoming more pronounced, even to the quirky Muir, who liked to lash himself to a tree to better understand the feeling of wind in a forest. During a rainy trek to Crater Lake in Oregon, a hollowed-out caldera high in the Cascade Mountains, Muir noted, "All slept in tent except Pinchot."

Pinchot and Muir did more than share hiking trips, of course. In 1896, they toured the West as part of the National Forest Commission, trying to help President Grover Cleveland decide what to do with big parts of Montana, Idaho, Washington, Oregon, Colorado, California, Wyoming, and Arizona Territory. Muir was an observer, Pinchot a leading voice of the commission, having already established himself as a pioneer voice for public forestry. They crossed the Bitterroot Mountains and thrashed through the deepest woods of Idaho, in the Clearwater River country, perhaps the wildest part of the contiguous United States—certainly the most inaccessible. In Oregon they toured the narrow green walls carved by the raging Rogue River and visited a nearby valley, the Umpqua, thick with salmon, steelhead, and coastal elk. Along the way, they spoke with hunters, homesteaders, and assorted wanderers. They ran into railroad men plotting new routes through the wild and speculators scouting for timber. Pinchot broke off and went by himself for a time, as usual most comfortable when alone. Curious. Where did he go at night? Later, Pinchot rejoined the commission when they got to the Grand Canyon.

Muir and Pinchot were supposed to spend the evening at a hotel with other commission members, but they peeled away, pitching camp at the rim of the rainbow-colored gap in the earth—"the greatest sight this world has to offer," as Pinchot called it. That night, he felt "awestruck and silent." Not so with the gabby Muir, who often conversed with flowers. He talked until midnight without interruption, his blue eyes reflecting the fire's glare, telling stories and filling Pinchot with his wilderness philosophy. More than anything he tried to get Pinchot to let down his guard, to put aside his formal training for a moment, to allow nature to get inside him. "We all travel the Milky Way together, trees and men," Muir had said. Before dozing off, Pinchot caught a tarantula. Muir would not let him kill it. "He said it had as much right to be there as we did."

After returning to the East, the forest commission recommended that two national parks be created, Mount Rainier and Grand Canyon, and told President Cleveland he should establish a number of forest reserves for other lands they had seen. Muir had envisioned such protection for years, but the idea was heretical to Congress and the biggest landowners of the day, the natural resource syndicates. The disposal of public land was a one-way proposition — to commerce, to settlement, to profit, with only a few exceptions. After much publicity about the beauty of Yosemite Valley from people such as Olmsted and the landscape painter Albert Bierstadt, President Abraham Lincoln had signed a bill in 1864 giving a tiny portion of the valley to the state of California — the early stirrings of the national park idea, though no such words were used.

But grazing and all manner of commercial use continued. In a similar vein, Yellowstone, the world's first national park, was established in 1872 as a playground and tourist destination to help the railroads. Throughout the rest of the public domain, the railroads had already been given more than one hundred million acres; logging was unrestricted, the trees taken for free. And anyone could establish a mining claim on land not yet staked by another. The suggestions that Pinchot and Muir brought home in 1896 appeared to be dead on arrival. But Grover Cleveland, a Democrat and the only president to serve two nonconsecutive terms, had a mischievous side and just a few months left in his last tour of the White

House. The president had been granted the power to set aside certain forests, in a sort of limbo status, by a single clause in an act of 1891 — something that Congress apparently thought was inconsequential. Cleveland used that power on February 22, 1897, Washington's birthday. Nobody in the capital saw it coming. Ten days before leaving office, Cleveland established twenty-one million acres of forest reserves, among them the Olympic and Rainier in Washington, the Flathead and Lewis and Clark in Montana, the Bitterroot and Priest in Idaho. The biggest of them all straddled Idaho and Montana, more than four million acres in the northern Rockies. Congress moved promptly to make sure the reserves were stillborn, passing a bill to nullify protection for any public land. But on his way out the door, Cleveland vetoed the bill. Pinchot was delighted to be in on the brawl.

"It put forestry on the front page all over America," Pinchot exulted. His chosen profession was obscure no more.

The new Republican president, William McKinley, inherited the reserves and the controversy. He immediately suspended Cleveland's order. The woods became the domain of the General Land Office in the Interior Department, a backwater of patronage hacks, industry shills, and timekeepers. There were no forest rangers, no agents to patrol the land, no professionals. Logging, homesteading, mining, and property jumping continued as if nothing had happened. McKinley turned to Pinchot for guidance, asking him to tour these orphan forests one more time to help him decide what to do. Pinchot was appointed "confidential forest agent," a spy with a green eye. The job paid ten dollars a day plus expenses. His charge was to get another look, take plenty of notes, and for God's sake keep quiet and don't stir up any trouble — no reason to rouse the land barons or their supporters in Congress.

By now Pinchot knew who owned the West — the "feudal overlordship" of the woods by a many-tentacled timber trust, the two railroad monoliths that controlled all rail transport in the upper half of the continent, and Homestake Mine in the Dakotas and other northern states. The law in these colonies was company law. But, just given the chance to breathe nothing but outdoor air for a couple of months, Pinchot jumped at the opportunity: up at 3:30 many mornings, hikes with mountain men and guides who added to his fishing expertise. He'd found his calling. He took a steamboat up Lake Chelan in Washington, which looks like Lake Como in Italy — "a beautiful trip up this most lovely lake" — and crossed into the North Cascades near the Canadian border, the American alps. At Priest Lake in Idaho, Pinchot awoke one morning to take in the dawn. Suddenly, gunfire rang out; a bullet just missed him, fired from across the lake. Pinchot rowed furiously across the water and went face-to-face with the errant shooter. In Idaho, he also saw up close what fire could do to a forest. Entire mountainsides were left scorched and skeletal by earlier burns around Priest Lake. It spooked him, sickened him, and stayed with him, as if he had seen a dead body for the first time.

"Of all the foes which attack the woodlands of North America, no other is so terrible as fire," he wrote in a little primer outlining his views of forestry at the time.

Back in Washington, Pinchot's report was buried. But McKinley was impressed by the young man's energy, and found his family connections useful. He named Pinchot his forester, head of a tiny division with no power. Cleveland's reserves would stand for now, but with no manpower to protect them. They were reserves in name only. *Well, it's a start,* Pinchot told friends. He was given a back office in a brick building with a staff of ten. He had no land to manage, no oversight, no authority. On many days, it was humiliating: the big timber owners "held us in amused toleration or open contempt," he wrote.

He was invited to speak at garden clubs and universities, a harmless gadfly with some compelling ideas, and *thank you very much, Giff.* So by the time thirty-three-year-old Gifford Pinchot laced up his boxing gloves to face Teddy Roosevelt in the governor's mansion in 1899, he was a forester without a forest.

As a boxer, Roosevelt was predictable. Not for him would there be lightning-quick footwork and bouncing on his toes. He was a windmill of fists, with occasional uppercuts. The strategy was simple: throw it all at the opponent at once, overwhelming him. "I believe in going hard at everything" was his stated philosophy of life. Pinchot the boxer was classically trained, as with most things in his upbringing. He played it safe, using his height, keeping his distance from the flailing pug of a governor. Teddy landed a couple of glancing blows, nothing serious. Pinchot took his time to size up his man, taking in his moves. When his opening came, he hit Roosevelt hard several times. The governor was stunned, head snapping back. He staggered, swooned, tried to recover. A roundhouse round followed from Pinchot. *Snap! Snap! Boom!* Dazed, Roosevelt fell to the floor. Match to Pinchot.

Raised to be modest, keeping his thoughts to himself unless asked, the American model of Edwardian class, Pinchot still allowed himself to gloat—in private, of course. Before the year's end, Pinchot was back at the governor's mansion for a rematch—"boxed and wrestled with T.R. before dinner," he wrote, as if recording the day's weather. He and Roosevelt would maintain a brotherly, often tortured relationship for the rest of their lives, the needy and mysterious Pinchot, the ever-confident Bull Moose. It was unequal, as good friendships should not be, master and slave. They climbed rocks, swam icy channels, played tetherball on the roof of Pinchot's house and tennis on the White House grounds, rode horses at full gallop over dirt trails. But Pinchot never forgot his triumph in the governor's mansion. "I had the honor of knocking the future President of the United States off his very solid pins," he wrote.

Nineteen months later, an anarchist shot President McKinley at the Pan American Exposition in Buffalo, on September 6, 1901. Roosevelt was summoned from the Adirondacks, where he was on a hiking trip not far from where Pinchot had gone for his winter climb. He rushed to Buffalo to be at the side of the bleeding president. T.R. had served a single two-year term as governor, and then ran as the number two man on the Republican presidential ticket in 1900. The party bosses in Albany felt the Siberia of the vice president's office was a way to get rid of Roosevelt.

For a time, it looked as if the badly wounded McKinley would recover; Roosevelt was told he could rejoin his family back in the woods. He had just started to descend Mount Tahawus when a guide approached him in the fading light with an urgent telegram: McKinley had taken a turn for the worse. Roosevelt raced downhill, reaching his base cabin in the dark. After changing horses three times in a charge over primitive mountain roads, Roosevelt made it to a train station by dawn. There, he heard the news: McKinley was dead. That afternoon, eight days after the gunman fired at McKinley, Theodore Roosevelt took the oath in Buffalo; at forty-two, he was the youngest president, and the only native of New York City to hold the highest office.

"It is a dreadful thing to come into the presidency this way," Roosevelt told a friend, "but it would be a far worse thing to be morbid about it."

Though he said publicly that little would change, in private Roosevelt wanted to steer the Republican Party away from big business and toward becoming "a fairly radical progressive party," as he wrote in his memoir. To do that, he would need Gifford Pinchot. A week before Roosevelt moved into the White House, he huddled with Pinchot, telling him to stay on as forester—and as a presidential adviser. Pinchot could be his voice on many things. He could write his speeches, help him with hostile senators. And in turn Roosevelt would try to get Pinchot oversight of the reserves, some real land, and a corps of foresters to protect it. Roosevelt urged him to be expansive, idealistic, not some spectral bureaucrat in a back office. The world was open to them. Everything they had talked about in the past—keeping the public domain out of the hands of the trusts, a model for the world—was within their reach and their power. Think of it: he could be a forester *with* a forest—the chief forester at that, in charge of the world's largest public forest. It was vaporous talk in 1901, but enough to win Pinchot, just thirty-six years old.

"We dream the same dreams," Roosevelt later wrote to Pinchot; more than that, he added, they shared "a peculiar intimacy."

2

Roost of the Robber Barons

I F WILLIAM A. CLARK was not the meanest man in Montana, he was certainly the richest and the most hated. He was also a United States senator from the Big Sky State, a position he had initially purchased with bundles of crisp $100 bills handed out to legislators in monogrammed envelopes—W.A.C. stamped on the fold, $10,000 per vote. Clark was a sunken-faced gnomish man with a paintbrush beard and eyes that cut with a slicing stare. He had set out to corner the copper market at a time when the world most needed that commodity for two of the biggest advances in civilization: the telephone and harnessed electricity. Clark purchased cops and courts, newspaper editors and ministers, grand juries—any source of opposition or fair play. Because senators were then chosen by state legislatures, he didn't have to pretend to care about average citizens. He was above the law, because the law was easily bought, a commodity cheaper than the source of his wealth. Mark Twain hated Clark, even losing his trademark sarcasm when trying to describe him.

"To my mind he is the most disgusting creature that the republic has produced since Tweed's time," Twain said of Clark. "He is as rotten a human being as can be found anywhere under the flag." None of this made Senator Clark blush. Who was Mark Twain but a bankrupt has-been, now in his dotage? Clark judged a man's worth by the base measurement of material accumulation. And by his value system, everyone in the Senate, and of course every writer, was beneath him: he was worth at least $200 million at a time when there were barely 4,000 millionaires in the country. As for these moralists in the Roosevelt administration with their progressive agenda, who were they fooling? Wake up and smell the new century!

"I never bought a man who was not for sale," said Clark, shrugging off the high-minded.

The soul-darkened senator sat a few feet away from President Roosevelt at a dinner party in Butte, Montana, on May 27, 1903. The president and the Copper King despised each other—no surprise. What each held dearest in his heart could not have been more different. "There is not in the world a more ignoble character than the mere money-getting American, insensitive to every duty, regardless of every principle, bent only on amassing a fortune," Roosevelt said just before he became president. To him, the West was a place for restoration and a proving ground. To Clark, it served no greater purpose than his life ambition to become the world's richest man. Clark and his allies derided Roosevelt as an outsider who didn't belong in the West.

Making his way home from a long tour of the West, Roosevelt had reason for an additional bounce in his step. Whenever his train pulled into another depot in the Rockies, he would take a sip of mountain air and wave with a proprietary sweep. At times, his bronchial troubles bothered him in the high altitude, a price he didn't mind paying for spending time on the sunset side of the country.

"At heart," he told people, "I am just as much a Westerner as an Easterner."

The day before arriving in Butte, Roosevelt had stopped in Wallace, Idaho—a triumphant visit, and not just because thousands showed up to welcome the president. For on May 26, the president learned that his leading political opponent, Senator Mark Hanna, had given up the idea of challenging him. Hanna had called Roosevelt "that damned cowboy" and was horrified that he seemed to be taking the Republican Party on a different course.

But by the spring of 1903, it was clear that the country loved the cowboy, and Hanna, in failing health, could not stop him. In Wallace, Roosevelt made an appeal to the shared humanity of all Americans, a common plea in an era when the angry poor and the predatory rich were at each other's throats. Just a few blocks away, in a big house on a manicured street in Wallace, lived one of Roosevelt's most powerful opponents—Senator Weldon Heyburn, a fellow Republican and chief ally of Clark. He fought Roosevelt on the major ideas of the Progressive Era, from the eight-hour workday and child welfare laws to direct election of senators. But most vociferously, Heyburn hated the idea of national forests, vowing to his last breath to kill the principles that were just taking root with the first rangers in the West.

Chugging through Montana, Roosevelt had been approached by the mayor of Butte. All of Butte—the "richest hill on earth," the source of Clark's wealth, the biggest city between Minneapolis and Seattle—wanted to see Teddy, the mayor explained. The town was more often under martial law than playing host to a president. And it was also the center of timber and mining opposition to Roosevelt's forest reserves—Clark's kingdom. The Copper King used the newspapers he owned to destroy Roosevelt's "green rangers" before they could become part of the western landscape, painting them as sissies and interlopers who were in the woods on some kind of college-boy holiday. Still, Roosevelt's celebrity was enough to put public rancor aside for an evening.

The president no sooner arrived at dinner than he spied his rival, along with half a dozen or so underlings of other barons who had been carving up the West in mockery of Roosevelt and his choirboy chief forester. Teddy could feel the hatred in the room. "There was Senator Clark with his Iscariot face," he wrote. Nearly two years into his administration, the president had been barnstorming the country and wrestling with Congress, trying to keep some of the very people who sat at this dinner from getting further control of the land. In his first message to Congress, he said preserving the nation's forests and fresh water amounted to "the most vital internal question of the United States." It seemed an odd, even esoteric selection for the top issue of the day. But as Roosevelt persisted, it became clear this would be a defining feature of his presidency. In the new century, he wanted Americans to look with fresh eyes at the natural world. For people who saw the woods in purely utilitarian terms, he offered this: "There is nothing more practical in the end than the preservation of beauty," he said in an address at Stanford. "I feel most emphatically that we should not turn into shingles a tree which was old when the first Egyptian conquerors penetrated to the valley of the Euphrates."

To Clark, Heyburn, and many others, these assertions were laughable. They dismissed Roosevelt's crusade as nonsense. Roosevelt's task was to persuade people not just to cherish their natural heritage, but to understand that it was their right in a democracy to own it—every citizen holding a stake. In an era of free-for-all capitalism, it was revolutionary to insist, as he did, that the "rights of the public to the national resources outweigh private rights." Gifford Pinchot may have penned that line for his boss. Roosevelt liked it enough that he repeated it throughout his presidency. "The forest reserves should be set apart forever for the use and benefit of our people as a whole and not sacrificed to the shortsighted greed of a few," Roosevelt said in his first annual message to Congress. Some small ranchers and family-run logging outfits that were muscled out of good grazing land and forests by the big syndicates also wanted a green sheriff in the people's woods. But high-minded talk of preserving land for future generations and common folk was not something rattling around saloons in the West or town halls on the Great Plains. It was an argument made by two Ivy League patricians against a clique of self-made titans with an oversize sense of entitlement.

What Teddy and Pinchot had first spoken of on that winter night in Albany of 1899 had blossomed in the White House. Ideas take on their own trajectory, but they die without people to carry them into the corridors of power. Following his words with action, Roosevelt created the nation's first wildlife refuge, Pelican Island in Florida. His executive power, he discovered, while not on par with that of creation, certainly could do the opposite—keep species from going out of existence. "Is there any law that will prevent me from declaring Pelican Island a federal bird reservation?" he asked. "Very well, then I do so declare it." And with that, one of the signature birds of the Southeast had its nesting home written onto the map. Roosevelt used executive decrees to add considerably to the forest reserve system, building in huge initial chunks on what Grover Cleveland had started in the last months of his presidency.

Following Pinchot's lead, Roosevelt became close to John Muir, whose charisma and love a good fight matched the feistiness of the president. Muir saw wilderness as a tonic for a frenzied era, a place to escape the "stupefying effects of the vice of over-industry and the deadly apathy of luxury," as he wrote in an influential book. "Thousands of tired, nerve-shaken, over-civilized people are beginning to find out that going to the mountains is going home; that wilderness is a necessity and that mountain parks and reservations are useful not only as fountains of timber and irrigating rivers, but as fountains of life."

In that sentiment, he and Roosevelt were one. During the same spring 1903 trip that took him to Montana, Roosevelt met up with Muir in California. They fled from the clamoring press on a four-day trek through Yosemite—the president having taken the naturalist's advice to heart by going to Muir's favorite fountain of life. It was a proven Muir lobbying tactic: he had escorted one of the most influential editors of the day, the urbane urban dweller Robert Underwood Johnson, on a similar camping trip to the Sierra in 1899. The editor promptly became a crusader, joining voices that led to the federal government's creation of Yosemite National Park one year later—a move that finally gave it special status well beyond what Lincoln had provided a generation earlier. Roosevelt and Muir slept under the stars, high above the valley, waking one morning to four inches of fresh spring snow. Muir was fearless. In all his wandering, he had fallen only once, down a steep slope in the Sierra, knocked unconscious. When he came to, he blamed the stumble on a recent trip to the city—too much time among the nerve-shaken and overcivilized had thrown off his mountain stride, he explained.

Roosevelt professed to genuinely love the older man's company, a carryover from schoolboy days, happiest when he was trying to interpret the natural world with a brilliant mentor. With Muir, he delighted in pointing out birds during the day, and watching the sparks of a campfire rise to the heavens at night. Muir, in turn, was mesmerized by a president, twenty-five years younger than he, whose thoughts mirrored his own. He told reporters he fell for Roosevelt, this "interested, hearty and manly" leader. And he also fed Teddy's rage over plunderers of public land. "I stuffed him pretty well regarding the timber thieves," Muir said.

Roosevelt needed no prodding to remind him of his biggest failure to date. "Forests and foresters had nothing to do with each other," he lamented, echoing Pinchot's almost daily complaint. Without a corps of rangers, the land went unprotected and the decrees that set it aside were largely meaningless. Outside the reserves, the bulk of the public domain remained open for the taking by the copper kings, timber barons, and railroad magnates who dominated the economy and controlled much of Congress. The railroads alone had nine of the eleven stocks listed on the precursor to the Dow Jones average. Their 240,000 miles of roads were destiny in iron, determining what towns would flourish or fail, what ports would grow or languish as backwaters, what products would ship cheaply or face high costs. In the West, the railroad's subsidiaries and contractors cut indiscriminately in the reserves, converting whole forests into miles of underground wooden ribs for mines and aboveground ties for transportation.

The titans were accustomed to getting land for free. The Northern Pacific Railroad, now controlled by James J. Hill and J. P. Morgan, had been given more than 40 million acres by the government as an incentive to build a transcontinental route not long after the Civil War. The Northern Pacific's main competitor, the Union Pacific, controlled by E. H. Harriman, was given 11.4 million acres as a lure to build its line. Between them, the two railroads were handed a piece of the United States nearly equal in size to all of New England. But it was not enough. They sold off much of the land to ranchers, speculators, and city builders, and then took their timber at will from the reserves.

These western landlords swapped properties the way European dukes divided the spoils of a medieval war. The stocky Hill, known as the Empire Builder, was at the peak of his powers and his bluster. "Give me enough Swedes and whiskey and I'll build a railroad through hell," he boasted. He lived in a St. Paul mansion, next door to Frederick Weyerhaeuser, whose German-American family had clipped the choicest white pine from the upper Midwest. One day Hill made a proposition to his neighbor: Hill's railroad would sell 900,000 acres of prime western forestland to Weyerhaeuser for $7 an acre. Weyerhaeuser countered: How about $5? They settled on $6 for one of the largest land sales in the country. Weyerhaeuser paid about a dime per tree, on average, for lush forests around Mount Rainier, Mount St. Helens, and elsewhere. Weyerhaeuser then gobbled up other forests in Idaho to create Potlatch, a 400-square-mile timber empire that would own everything within its borders—towns, people, roads, forests, water, land—the western feudal ideal. Potlatch built the world's biggest sawmill, ready to cut all that Idaho white pine into dimension lumber at a rate of 350,000 board feet a minute.

Not to be outdone was J. P. Morgan, the lonely anti-Semite with a three-hundred-foot yacht and a taste for showy European art. Though he had a grotesquely mottled nose, Morgan could sniff a bargain. He had bought a controlling interest in the Northern Pacific during one of the periodic panics that plagued the railroads. Hill had also bought a big position. Looking to end all competition at the turn of the century, they merged with their chief rival, Harriman's Union Pacific. The new monopoly, the Northern Securities Company, controlled all rail traffic for one-fourth of the United States. Everyone from sheepherders in Nevada to drugstore merchants in small-town Minnesota had to go through the trust to make their living. Freight rates went up. Protests followed. The imperious Morgan now owned the country, critics claimed. "Whenever he doesn't like it," said William Jennings Bryan, the populist presidential candidate, "he can give it back to us."

Roosevelt too was incensed. The trusts had pushed him with double-fisted arrogance, which roused his scrappier instincts. Morgan thought he could strike a quick deal. "If we have done anything wrong, send your man to my man and they can fix it up," he said. But there would be nothing short of open war in the courts. The titans howled. E. H. Harriman warned a Roosevelt aide that the president could not stop them; the trusts would crush him. "He said that whenever it was necessary he could buy a sufficient number of senators and congressmen or state legislators to protect his interests," Roosevelt wrote a friend. "And when necessary, he could buy the judiciary."

At the same time, the Rockefeller family started shopping out west. William Rockefeller, brother of the Standard Oil founder, John D. Rockefeller, bought into the world's largest copper company, Anaconda, also known as the Snake, just down the road from Butte. This was the smelter and mining complex originally owned by Marcus Daly, the best known of the copper kings. The Irish miners, at least, loved Daly because he paid well and was one of them—a native of Ballyjamesduff in the Ulster county of Cavan. After he died in 1900, the world's biggest copper mine and smelter, along with two company towns, fell to Rockefeller's hands, and turned the ever-opportunistic Senator Clark—once Rockefeller's fierce rival—into his water carrier in Congress. The family already

controlled the nation's oil supply. Now William Rockefeller wanted
to build a third rail line, the Milwaukee Road, from the Midwest
to Puget Sound, a way to gain access to the riches being shipped in
from Asia. But to get from the flatlands to the inland sea, the line
would have to bore through the Bitterroot Mountains, the heart of
the Coeur d'Alene reserve.

John Rockefeller was perhaps the richest American who ever
lived. Morgan and Weyerhaeuser were not far behind, each with
a net worth roughly equal to that of Bill Gates, the Microsoft co-
founder, in contemporary dollars. Rockefeller had more than four
times the wealth of Gates, his stake at just under $200 billion, when
adjusted for inflation. As to Roosevelt's view of these men, he was
rarely discreet. He called them "the most dangerous members of
the criminal class, the malefactors of great wealth," in his best-
known phrase, uttered during a sharp economic downturn. And he
was more cutting when he really wanted to be dismissive.

"It tires me to talk to rich men," he said. "You expect a man of
millions to be worth hearing, but as a rule, they don't know anything outside their own business." When Standard Oil donated
$100,000 to Roosevelt's campaign, the president asked that it be re-
turned. It was somewhat jarring, to say the least, that Roosevelt,
from a wealthy New York family, and Pinchot, who had inherited
a chateau with twenty-three fireplaces, had turned so vehemently
against their class, envisioning the national forests as a way to "help
the small man make a living rather than help the big man make a
profit," as Pinchot said frequently. But once engaged, they never
looked back.

The dinner crowd in Butte was liquored up by the time food was
ready to be served, buzzed on "every kind of whiskey," Roosevelt
recalled. As he had asked that his guests be a cross-section of
Butte, there were more than the usual Irish who dominated the
town. Blacks, Chinese, Cornish, Italians, Greeks, Swedes, and Ger-
mans—all had a seat, in addition to pinch-faced Senator Clark and

his allies. Mayor Pat Mullins summoned his waiters: "Boys, bring on the feed." Then he ordered that the window blinds be lifted so that people on the street could look inside and see what Butte had corralled. Gifts were presented. One in particular touched Roosevelt: a pair of silver scales from black miners at the table. "This comes in the shape I appreciate—scales of justice held even," Roosevelt said. He went on to discuss the bravery of "colored troops" who had served with him in Cuba. Visibly moved, he turned to the miners and said the scale—this gift—made him want to help blacks get "a square deal." A pact, of sorts, was born at the banquet table: the simple phrase "a square deal" would be at the heart of the Roosevelt social contract.

Clark was not impressed. In a huff, the senator retreated to his manse in Butte—three stories, thirty-four rooms, stuffed with Tiffany glass lamps—fortified in his resolve to thwart Roosevelt at every turn. Since buying his Senate seat, he had rarely been home in the northern Rockies. Clark preferred the forest of chateaux in New York with the other titans now carving up the West. J. P. Morgan had a house at 219 Madison Avenue. The Astors, the Fricks, the Goulds, the Whitneys, the Harrimans, and the Carnegies each had a stone showpiece nearby. Clark started with a home on Fifth Avenue, a few blocks from Morgan. But after visiting the world's fair in Paris, he was determined to build a royalist fantasy in Manhattan. He created a 121-room palace on Park Avenue at Seventy-seventh Street. And so for the duration of his only term as a senator from Montana, Clark's principal residence was a Gotham fortress with thirty-one bathrooms—a different commode for every day of the month.

After the dinner in Butte, there would be no truce, no letup, no middle ground. Roosevelt had to be stopped. Clark used his Senate seat to block every effort at conservation, and he used his newspapers to echo his interests and applaud his opposition to Roosevelt. At the same time, his wealth grew with a plan to start a town in the Mojave Desert built around a pit stop for a railroad he owned—Las

Vegas, Nevada. The town took off, and the railroad was sold to E. H. Harriman, putting Clark within reach of becoming one of the richest Americans ever. Clark was the voice of brute wealth and blunt strength—might over right, the way copper kings did their business in the West. And, as his papers told it, he was heroic to take on this radical young president. His allies, such as Herschel Hogg, a congressman from Colorado, relied on ridicule: these conservationists were "google-eyed, bandy-legged dudes from the East and sad-eyed, absent-minded professors and bugologists," in Hogg's memorable phrase.

So long as there were no trained professionals to watch the woods and grasslands, big money prevailed. Clark could rest easy. The General Land Office existed for one reason: to transfer public property to private hands—in Clark's mind, the perfect government agency. It was staffed by bureaucrats who neither knew nor cared for wild land in the West. As for Pinchot's main request, Clark was consistently defiant: he would never agree to transfer the reserves from the land office to a forest service. As to the larger argument, he sniffed at calls from Roosevelt and Pinchot to leave something behind for the future.

"Those who succeed us," said Clark, "can well take care of themselves."

Everything changed in the next year, with the 1904 election, when Roosevelt at last won his own full term—a victory that would literally be landscape-altering. "It's all colossal," his firebrand daughter, Alice, wrote in her diary. Indeed it was: Roosevelt won by the largest margin of any presidential candidate to date, taking thirty-three of the forty-five states—something he could not keep from broadcasting. "How they are voting for me!" said Teddy as he skipped through the White House on election night. "I have the greatest popular majority and the greatest electoral majority ever given to a candidate for president," he wrote his son Kermit.

The public knew that this energetic leader was no mere keeper of the dead President McKinley's name. His Republican Party stood for public ownership of natural resources, among the pillars of the progressive cause. At a time when the gap between rich and poor was never greater, Roosevelt called for a national inheritance tax on wealthy families. And looking to remedy a situation where 26 percent of all boys aged ten to fifteen spent their days working full shifts away from home, and less than 5 percent of all workers had graduated from high school, Roosevelt asked for wholesale changes in child welfare laws. He said people had a right to a safe food supply, to regulation of prescription drugs. And for the sake of future generations, he called for a broad range of measures to protect land and wildlife. He was eager to slay any foe. "I felt his clothes might not contain him, he was so ready to go, to attack anything, anywhere," wrote the muckraking journalist Ida Tarbell.

"We are the heirs of the ages," Roosevelt said in his 1905 inaugural address, signaling that he intended to use that inheritance.

In one of the first orders of business after Roosevelt's landslide, Congress agreed to transfer the reserves to Gifford Pinchot's fledgling agency, and gave him a small budget to train rangers who would have stewardship of the forests. The General Land Office, that hidebound bureaucracy, service station for the syndicates, was pushed aside. Outmaneuvering Clark and Heyburn, Roosevelt promised that legitimate homesteaders would be allowed to claim 160 acres of land within national forest boundaries if they could prove that it was right for farming. There was not much arable land for homesteading in the reserves, but this move silenced critics who said the president was sealing off the land from opportunity.

With the transfer, the newly named United States Forest Service was created in 1905, with Pinchot as the first Chief—a job "worth more to me than all the treasures of all the pirates of history," he wrote. His domain was sixty million acres. Having fulfilled his promise to his friend, Roosevelt now gave Pinchot simple marching orders: "It must not be forgotten," he wrote to him, "that the forest reserves belong to all the people." Pinchot felt the same way; if anything, he was more militant in his belief that the essence of Progressive Era ideals could be manifest on the land, guided by his new agency. Pinchot and Roosevelt also knew that they had only a short time to prove their worth. Congress was skeptical, and the leash was short; legislators could kill the Forest Service simply by defunding it.

"The transfer meant a revolutionary change," Pinchot wrote. "We had the power, as we had the duty, to protect the Reserves for the use of the people, and that meant stepping on the toes of the biggest interests in the West. From that time on, it was fight, fight, fight."

To win that fight, he now took on a greater one—against something as old as the earth itself. Fire was an enemy, a force feared by settlers, loggers, ranchers, and outdoorsmen. "Fire has always been, and seemingly will always remain, the most terrible of elements," said Harry Houdini, perhaps the most popular entertainer of Pinchot's age, who knew a thing or two about tricking an element. The natives had used fire for selective purposes. But the new stewards of this land wanted nothing to do with it. Wolves had been wiped out, erased like the bison herds that once blotted the landscape. The grizzly bear was nearly gone. What remained in the wild to stir primordial fear was wildfire. Organized firefighting was an oxymoron at the time. Pinchot promised to bring a plan of attack.

Pinchot's thinking had evolved from five years earlier. He knew then, though he seldom said so in public, that wildfire was part of nature, even essential. He knew that some species in the West *needed* fire to proliferate—"gaining ground by the action of its enemy," as he said. But he put the science aside and chose to believe the words he used to sell Congress on his big idea.

That was the pact, the price of existence for his rangers. Certainly, he could count on people being terrified. Some still brought up two disasters: the Peshtigo fire of 1871, which killed 1,182 people and burned more than a million acres in Wisconsin, and an 1894 fire in Hinckley, Minnesota, where 413 people perished. Big cities—San Francisco, Seattle, Chicago—were leveled in the hot sweep of a night, and it was the same story in midsize burgs. In the way that people anthropomorphized it, fire was the final menace of the frontier, as if the land itself were sloughing off all attempts at establishing order in the woods. And now, at long last, here was a protector, green-shirted insurance from Gifford Pinchot. So even if he didn't believe it in his heart, perhaps the only way Pinchot could bring his grand vision to life was to promise that his foresters could whip fire.

Pinchot the missionary now professed that wildfire was akin to slavery—a blight on the young country, but something that could be wiped out by man. While nature could never be conquered, it could be tamed, tailored, customized. "I object to the law of the jungle," Pinchot always said, a philosophy that applied to predatory capitalism as well as the unruly extremes of the physical world. He assured Congress that his legion of rangers—men he would select himself, stamp with progressive principles, and train in the finishing school of the wild—could manage fire. And in controlling fire, they could win the confidence of skeptical westerners. One simply had to apply the principles of the newborn study of forestry to the reserves. Of this, Pinchot professed to have no doubt.

The moody, self-lacerating young man was no more. The man who had been greatly influenced by the book given him on his twenty-first birthday, *The Earth as Modified by Human Action* by George P. Marsh, had changed. Here was a titan in his own rank, lord of the outdoors. His deference to the complexity of the world seemed gone. He certainly knew his place: at the top.

"The first duty of the human race is to control the earth it lives upon," he wrote, flexing his muscles as a forester with a forest. But in a short time, a wildfire would make a mockery of Pinchot's certainty.

3

The Great Crusade

ELERS KOCH WAS JUST a few years out of college when Gifford Pinchot summoned him into his office and asked him if he wanted to scout an area nearly half the size of the Louisiana Purchase. On the Chief's office wall was a map of Montana and Wyoming—a big land pushed to the sky, the Continental Divide running through it, forests of tamarack, pine, fir, and aspen, high rock covered with snow for all but a month or so each year. Koch knew it well. He was a Montana boy, the son of Danish immigrants, raised in the Rockies. He grew up fishing in the Gallatin River and hiking in the Crazy Mountains.

Koch had been laboring for the fresh-minted Forest Service in Washington, D.C., going over land surveys in a small brick building at 930 F Street. Once a month on Friday night, Pinchot would have a dozen or so of the young foresters over to his palatial family home at 1615 Rhode Island Avenue, where he lived with his parents and an Irish maid who had been with him since age eleven. Sometimes President Roosevelt would drop by. They ate baked apples and cream, talking up the big dream in the wood-paneled library. Later, a select few would sneak down to the basement with Pinchot for marksmanship with pistols, the target placed in front of a steel wall; in Pinchot's home shooting range, it was rare for anybody to beat the Chief.

Koch liked his time in the capital. Still, the summers were hazy and steamy and there were no big mountains to climb, no horizons without end. Here was a way to go home, back to Montana. By executive decree, Roosevelt was adding millions of acres to the new forestry system, as fast as the land could be surveyed. At the same time, Pinchot was trying to transform an office with a staff of ten and no forests into the largest public land agency the world had yet known. He set about building his corps, first pruning the deadwood from the old land office—relatives of senators, people who had never seen a forest, "human rubbish," in Pinchot's words—then handpicking his men as if they were knights.

Koch was one of the first to be chosen. He had met Pinchot one summer on Mount Rainier; Koch was a teenage student assistant, and Pinchot spent several nights there as part of his forest commission tour of the West. In the crowd of old cedars around the volcano of Rainier, Koch stood out, in part because he was the only westerner among nearly two dozen Ivy Leaguers. Pinchot saw something in the boy from Bozeman. In turn, Koch was mesmerized by Pinchot. He had never met anyone so charismatic, so full of passion for the outdoors. When the chance came for Koch to do graduate work at Yale, studying at a new forestry school endowed by Pinchot family money, he jumped at it. If possible, Pinchot wanted the Forest Service to be manned by westerners, but first they had to have his imprint on them, and that usually meant the Yale School of Forestry.

Koch had never been to the East. Everything was new to him— the people, the dress, the social rituals. He learned to smoke a pipe and mix a martini, habits he would find useful at Koch family dinner parties in Missoula. This inaugural group of American forestry students, about twenty young men in all, was special, and they knew it, stamped from the start for greatness. At Yale's bicentennial in 1901, they dressed in Robin Hood costumes, parading around campus in green tights and hoods for all the old Yalies to see—uniformed brothers of the woods. It was New Haven, Connecticut, but it could have been Sherwood Forest.

Also in the class was Bill Greeley, who had come to Yale by way of Stanford and the University of California. When other students went out for nights of chugging ale and chasing women, Greeley stayed back and studied the cellular structure of poplars and deconstructed Bible verses. The son of a Congregational minister, he found the fullest expressions of creation in the intricacies of the natural world—the church of the outdoors. Like Pinchot, he'd been taught to "see God in nature," as the founding forester put it.

Greeley finished at the top of that first Yale forestry graduating class of 1904, which meant he was an easy pick to be another of Pinchot's knights of the woods. Pinchot told Greeley he was being tapped to be part of the "Great Crusade"; he could shape boundaries of land his great-grandchildren would one day walk through, a legacy that appealed to the responsibilities Greeley felt as part of his Christian faith. Indeed, he soon started calling himself "a forest missionary." He was flattered to join such a select group. Pinchot and his acolyte took a train out west, where they surveyed land in California, terrain to be included in the rapidly expanding national forests. They spent long days on horseback in country without trails. "My admiration for the boss grew with every mile," Greeley wrote. "I got to know Gifford Pinchot as men can know each other only in camp and on the trail."

Returning to Washington, back inside the building on F Street, they reviewed the same ground by map, drawing boundaries. If the land passed muster, it would be included in a new round of forest reserves, by Roosevelt's executive order. Most of Pinchot's early rangers performed a task similar to Greeley's, and they did it at a sprint.

"There was no time to lose, and G.P. was sending his young men to ride the forests and mountains of all parts of the West," Koch recalled. "I doubt if there has ever been such a wonderful job in the world as the early days of forest boundary work. One was given a state map of say California, or Montana or Wyoming, with an area of a few million acres roughly blocked out in green. One proceeded to the nearest point by rail, and then rode all summer, seeing thrilling new wild country every day."

In years past, wars had been fought and rivers of blood shed for far less land than that which was under consideration by the select group of "forest arrangers," as they called themselves. Never before had the fate of so much territory been determined by a small, mostly unarmed group of tree specialists. They were in on the creation, transforming by surveys, mapping, and suggestions areas larger than some eastern states. Thereafter, to all succeeding generations of forest rangers, the arrangers grew in legend. Anything a modern forester did was small by comparison, and how could it not be?

Pinchot was known as the Chief, or G.P. And his charges were called Little G.P.s. They bought into the Chief's vision that working for the Forest Service was the most noble thing a young American could do for his country in the new century. Like the other G.P.s, Bill Greeley worshiped the Chief, this patrician who could "outride and outshoot any ranger on the force." Teddy Roosevelt moved him in the same way. He went to see the president speak one night in 1905. Midway through his speech, Roosevelt put aside his prepared remarks. He went silent for a few seconds as he moved away from the podium. Unleashed, Roosevelt strode across the stage, looking out at his audience. "I am against the man who skins the land!" he bellowed. That was all Greeley needed to hear, and *bully for you, T.R.*

A few years out of college, Greeley was summoned down the hall by Pinchot to look at another of the Chief's maps. This one showed an even bigger part of the Rocky Mountain West than had been presented to Koch—all of Montana, much of Idaho and Washington, and a corner of South Dakota covered with pine. The Forest Service was breaking down its domain into regions. This was a map of the largest, Region One—forty-one million acres, twenty-two national forests in four states. How would Greeley like to be in charge of all of it, based in Missoula with Elers Koch? *All of it?* Yes. He would be regional forester. It was a dream job, of course, though it didn't pay much. Greeley packed for Missoula.

The two Yalies were joined in the Rockies by a third man from

Sherwood Forest, William Weigle. He was also one of the first forestry students to be schooled at Yale, and had completed an office rotation under Pinchot in Washington, D.C. Whereas Greeley was pious, Weigle could tell a joke, a dirty one at that; he was equally at home in a roadhouse saloon and a New Haven classroom. A big redhead with a hound-dog face, Weigle was known for his toughness and his pragmatism. Smart, yes. But people knew not to push him. With these qualities, Weigle was thought to be a perfect fit for the most wide-open, challenging forest in the system, the Coeur d'Alene, headquartered in Wallace, Idaho.

When the Chief offered him the job, Weigle knew Wallace only by reputation. It was a battleground, as most Americans understood, for one of the biggest labor wars in the nation's history: sabotage, bombings, and hijackings of trains led to a massive roundup of miners, who were held in a makeshift jail for months without basic legal rights. The class war around Wallace was the focus of world attention at the turn of the century; who was America to lecture people about democracy when it held hundreds of its own citizens in a pen without habeas corpus? When the ex-governor of Idaho, Frank Steunenberg, was assassinated in 1905, the man who confessed to the killing said he was simply a pawn in a larger conspiracy. A trial in Idaho, with Clarence Darrow on the unions' side and the great silky voiced orator, and later senator, William Borah on the other, was a spectacular show, ending in triumph by Darrow and the union officials accused of complicity in the governor's assassination. Any federal official, even one from a progressive administration, was suspect.

Things had settled down some since the assassination, Weigle was assured. People in the Coeur d'Alenes were back to moving precious metal out of the ground. And the woods were full of timber thieves, even with the Forest Service as the new sheriff in the land. Weigle took the job. The Yale School of Forestry, its graduating class dispatched across the continent, was in place in the Rockies. Koch had charge of the Lolo, Bitterroot, and Missoula national forests. Weigle ran the Coeur d'Alene. And overseeing all of it was Greeley.

"It was a wonderful thing to have a government bureau with nothing but young men in it," Koch said.

Though a degree from Yale was not required, Pinchot wanted his foresters to be able to write well, for the numerous reports that their enemies in Congress would be second-guessing. But as someone who had spent many summer days in the high Rockies without trail or road to guide his way, Pinchot also required aspiring forest rangers to pass a rigorous test, lasting two days, that showed they could survive on their own in the woods.

Most of them would be riding solo in a region they called the High Lonesome. They had to know how to navigate by compass and by the stars, how to cut wood and do basic carpentry, how to saddle a horse, how to tie a knot for lassos, how to throw a rope, how to shoot, how to cook. What's more, the food had to be more than gruel. As Pinchot said, one test was to cook a meal, the other was to eat it. Many of them would have to build their own cabins and their own outhouses. The written test would usually weed out illiterates, Pinchot recalled, and the practical test would cull people who could never shake their bookishness. One recruiting poster said, "Invalids need not apply."

As a complement to the Ivy Leaguers, the ideal hire was someone like Frank Herring, a cowboy who had worked with Roosevelt on his ranch in the Dakotas and then served under him in Cuba as one of Teddy's Rough Riders. In his crisp Forest Service uniform, pants tucked into high-top boots, a .44 holstered to his belt, and a silver-studded bridle, Herring made an imposing figure on his bay horse. Tough-nutted western men like Herring were often ill at ease around Bible-quoting college kids like Greeley. What they had in common, among other things, was miserable pay—$900 a year for an assistant ranger, barely half of what a grade school teacher makes in today's dollars. Rangers had to supply their own horses, their own saddles, their own rifles and hobnailed boots. At the same time, Senators Heyburn and Clark plotted to keep the Forest Service on a diet that would ensure malnutrition, if not starvation, slashing away at the budget and seizing on any excuse to humiliate the service.

At first it hardly mattered. Pinchot and Roosevelt had their way. Morale was high, Pinchot believed, because his boys had a great purpose: they were fighting to level the field for average Americans in the West. "The Forest Service stood up for the honest small man and fought the predatory big man as no government had done before," he wrote. "Big Money was King in the Great Open Spaces, and no mistake. But in the national forests, Big Money was not King."

Pinchot made frequent excursions out west for inspections and to make speeches in places packed with his enemies. On a trip to Idaho, he chose to go directly to Wallace, the lair of his chief antagonist, Senator Heyburn. His visit reinforced his view of Heyburn as a bought politician, owned by "the great lumber syndicates," he reported back to Roosevelt. One state over, in Montana, Pinchot scolded Greeley for letting those syndicates get away with too much timber cutting at giveaway prices. Logging was permitted in national forests—these weren't parks or pockets of pristine wilderness. But it was supposed to be limited, orderly, at a pace that would not deplete the timber supply or threaten the health of a forest. "The chief expected us to be supermen," Greeley wrote.

Out in the field, Pinchot would break away for time on horseback or foot with one of his young knights. Some forest rangers even thought of him as a prophet. "He made us all—rangers and fire guards and Mexican boys building trail—feel like soldiers in a patriotic cause," said Greeley. In the Southwest, a researcher for the Forest Service named a newly discovered tree after the Chief, *Juniperus pinchotii,* a subspecies of the fragrant high-desert juniper. But for all of that devotion, all the inspiring nights spent at the mansion on Rhode Island Avenue, all the weekends when forest recruits were invited to Grey Towers, all the time together in the wilderness, all the evangelical speeches, Pinchot was not a friend — he could not be. In the woods, he would often sleep alone, far removed from camp, which was as off-putting and antisocial to the rangers as it was to John Muir during earlier outings. Why did he go off by himself? One ranger who called him Pinchot, leaving out the Mister, was harshly reprimanded. "He was always the aristocrat, and his affability contained something of patronage," Koch wrote. "One never forgot that he was Gifford Pinchot, the Chief, and no one ever dreamed of taking any liberties with him."

Around Washington, Pinchot was the subject of clingy gossip. He was rich, attractive in a gentlemanly way, powerful, one of Roosevelt's closest confidants. He knew everybody — leading authors, Supreme Court justices, European royalty, bishops, diplomats, and sports heroes. He played tennis with Teddy on a regular basis, and when they weren't on the court, or in a boxing ring, they went for brisk walks through Rock Creek Park. Who else could say he had skinny-dipped with the president in the Potomac? In turn, what Roosevelt liked about Pinchot, he wrote, was his "tireless energy and activity, his fearlessness, his complete disinterestedness, his single-minded devotion to the interests of the plain people, and his extraordinary efficiency."

But . . . people talked. *Why wasn't Pinchot married? Good God, the man still lived with his parents! What did he do inside that enormous house on Rhode Island Avenue? Or at Grey Towers? And that distant expression of his: What could he be thinking?* Women certainly found Pinchot handsome and mysterious, a lethal combination. Ethel Barrymore, the actress, one of the first celebrities of the twentieth century, sat next to him once and said he was "dreamy looking." At Yale, he had been voted the best-looking man in his class, and the press in the capital dubbed Pinchot "the most eligible of Washington beaux." Alice Roosevelt, the president's eldest daughter, herself a magnet for romance and spicy speculation, said

Pinchot was "very appealing to the ladies." So why didn't he date? Why did he prefer to be alone? Word had it the man was celibate, a priest of the outdoors following some strange vows of his own making. Was there really no one to share the years with Gifford Pinchot?

Oh, but Pinchot did have someone: the love of his life. Laura Houghteling was a woman of high spirits, blond-haired and alabaster-skinned, a woman to whom he revealed every detail of his heart and mind, a woman who believed, as he did, that they were twined for eternity. The problem was that she was dead. By 1905, Laura Houghteling had been in the grave for eleven years, and yet Pinchot carried on a vigorous spiritual love affair with her—the biggest, best-kept secret of his life, which came out in full, more than a century after her death, only because of the scholarship of a researcher, James G. Bradley.

Pinchot fell in love with Laura at the compound of one of the world's richest men: George Washington Vanderbilt, grandson of Cornelius, heir to a shipping and rail fortune. A shy, soft-spoken wisp of a person, Vanderbilt harbored one great dream: to build the biggest country estate in America. In the Blue Ridge Mountains of North Carolina he found his site, and purchased 125,000 acres just outside Asheville. There, a thousand workers labored five years to construct the Biltmore Estate, a French Renaissance mansion. Biltmore was nearly a thousand feet across; the walls enclosed 65 fireplaces and 250 rooms, many of them filled with masterpieces by Renoir, Whistler, and others. The skinny little heir was a collector of name art and trophy experts. He hired Richard M. Hunt, the nation's foremost architect, to design Biltmore, and Frederick Law Olmsted to mold the landscape. Hunt also did Grey Towers. To oversee the woods, Vanderbilt turned to Pinchot.

The game preserve, as Vanderbilt called it, was modeled after the kind of feudal European grounds that Pinchot found repulsive. When he arrived in 1891, he was appalled at the stark contrast between one-room cabins tucked in the Appalachian hollows and this fortress of limestone—"a devastating commentary on the injustice of concentrated wealth," Pinchot said. The locals were shoeless, toothless, and highly suspicious of Vanderbilt. Nevertheless, Pinchot eagerly took to his task of running the Biltmore Forest, trying to apply some of the ideas he had learned at Yale and l'École Nationale Forestière. And it was at Biltmore that his romance with Laura Houghteling blossomed.

Pinchot was riding his horse through the woods one day when he crossed paths with Laura. They had met on earlier occasions; both were from socially prominent, wealthy families, though they had never before gotten to know each other. She was a stunning woman by all accounts—luminously pretty, smart, assertive, a lover of poetry, and deeply spiritual. Her home was in Chicago, but she spent summers in North Carolina because the mountain air was said to be good for her tuberculosis, growing worse with each month. Both twenty-eight years old, Laura and Giff rode and read together, had picnics in the woods, and spent long afternoons talking about his insecurities and his dreams, her ambitions and her troubles. The illness was always there, which only brought Pinchot closer to her. Friends noticed that he seemed less gloomy, less full of that youthful dread he had carried around for so long. He was in love as he had never been before. They were soon engaged. But it was a doomed affair. By 1894, Laura's illness became grave. "Laura had a bad night," he wrote in late January. On the first day of February came "a good report from Laura." A week later, February 7, she was dead.

Pinchot dressed in black, head to toe, for the next two years. The loss of Laura forever changed him. But it was not the end of the love affair, not by any means. One relationship was gone; another started up without her body. "Her passing," Pinchot tried to explain to his parents, "was nothing more than a temporary separation." Barely a month after Laura died, an apparition—variously described as a light, or later, as the full woman—revealed itself to Pinchot. He recorded it as a medieval mystic would write about a miracle.

"My Lady is very near," he wrote on March 18, 1894.

"My Lady has told me beautiful things," a month later.

Laura was in the ground, buried, but Pinchot talked as if she were in the room with him, in church, in the woods, on the train, at dinner. He spoke with her—not just to her—walked with her, showed her things, all in spirit, of course, though you would never know it from his diaries. Two months after Laura's death, Pinchot was back at Biltmore—"to church, where I sat with Miss Houghteling." At Grey Towers, "my lady was nearer than ever this afternoon." The ghost joined him on a train in Europe, at night before he dozed off, sometimes at meals. He read books to her, ran his ideas and speeches by her, craved her approval, checked opinions and policies with her.

New Year's Day, 1895: "My Dearest spoke to me, saying she wants to be with me as much as I want to be with her."

Two years after Laura's death, Pinchot stopped wearing black. His mood improved. He was buoyant, a skip in his step. In love! And newly married—to Laura. She appeared often in that spring, in glowing light, Pinchot feeling the mystical hand of Laura and God at the same time. They were as one, which perhaps was a way for Pinchot to fit this paranormal experience into his traditional Protestant upbringing. The union was now sealed. "In God's sight, my Lady and I are husband and wife."

This did not sit well with the other woman in Pinchot's life, the very much alive Mary Pinchot, his aristocratic mother. Her son, the oldest of three children, was her favorite. Mamee once told a reporter that it was "the paramount blessing of my life that I am Gifford Pinchot's mother." He had a special calling, she always told him, "a higher and noble mission to fulfill." This mystical "wife" was too much. "It is not right in this world to live in the past or with the dead," she said to Gifford with a mother's directness and no small amount of jealousy.

But the pull was too strong; regarding Laura, Pinchot could not please his mother. A full eight years after Laura's death, there she was, bright as ever. "Thank God for the light," he wrote in 1902.

Even as one of President Roosevelt's top advisers, Pinchot continued to converse regularly with the spirit. He also haunted the house where she had lived in her final days, an Italian-style manse at the corner of Connecticut Avenue and R Street. That was always "our house." At times, he was frustrated when he tried to summon her and the spirit would not appear. Those days he called "dark" or "cloudy." Later, he simply blamed himself, saying he was "blind" or "can't see." Typically, his diary entries reflected a schedule packed with the most powerful people in the United States, and then, almost as an afterthought, he would write a cryptic line: "Not a clear day." Other days, she all but sipped soup next to him—"bright days," he labeled them.

When he needed help, Pinchot consulted psychics and attended secret séances. Some of the associates at these sittings, exploring the mystical edge as was popular at the time, warned Pinchot to be careful; a man with his high profile should not be known as someone who communed with the dead. He must be discreet, visiting only the best mediums. "If I were in your position, I should, while avoiding promiscuous séances, try mediums of good character," an editor friend from London advised him.

Laura remained his ghost lover for nearly two decades. She was nearby when Pinchot faced his enemies in Congress, and with him in the Rocky Mountains during nights when he slept alone. Clearly, these solo excursions were attempts to commune with her. To look at another woman was to risk a slight of his lady, and so he never courted anyone else for twenty years. In order to be at his best for Laura—frozen at twenty-eight while Pinchot aged—he felt he had to stay in top spiritual shape. A regular churchgoer, he kept up a routine that matched his athletic pursuits—a sort of aerobics of the soul. And when he lapsed, he tortured himself. "I keep falling behind the advances I have to make," he noted. "My soul doesn't grow." The spirit joined him at Grey Towers and at Rhode Island Avenue and possibly even in the White House.

• • •

A more full-bodied companion was the president. Ideas that would shape American life for a century were hatched in Rock Creek Park, which Teddy and G.P. treated like a big backyard. New advisers were taken to the Crack, a fissure in a rock wall on the west bank of the creek, and shown how to climb. "If you made it, you belonged," Pinchot wrote, only half in jest. Well before the triathlon era, these excursions often involved a fast walk, a quick climb, and a swim. Out for a stroll once in late November, Roosevelt and Pinchot found themselves ankle-deep in mud at dusk. Roosevelt pointed to an inlet of open water. He removed his hat, put his valuables atop his head, and put the hat back on. Then he waded through the muck to open water and swam to the other side, in darkness. Pinchot trailed him. Back home, his mother helped him with his wet clothes.

"Drenched!" she said. "You've been out with the president."

On another trip, they found themselves at a dead end, facing the Potomac. Pinchot and Roosevelt stripped and dove in. Their companion, the French ambassador, hesitated on the bank before taking off his clothes, leaving him naked but for his gloves.

"Why do you wear gloves?" Roosevelt asked the ambassador as he swam toward them.

"We might meet ladies."

More often they went by horseback, striding over trails that braided the park. "Met President and rode with him" was a Pinchot diary entry on a winter day early in Roosevelt's first term. "Fine gallop." Often, Pinchot packed his .38 pistol, acting as an extra guardian for his friend. Roosevelt occasionally referred to Pinchot as one of his "faithful bodyguards."

A perfect day for Pinchot was one with at least three activities with Roosevelt. One July day at Roosevelt's Long Island home, Sagamore Hill, in Oyster Bay, Pinchot wrote a speech with Roosevelt on western issues in the morning, lunched with him and several cabinet secretaries at midday, played a lengthy set of doubles tennis (Pinchot and T.R. beating their opponents, of course) in the afternoon, followed by woodchopping before dinner, and then, just at sunset, an evening sail. Men less fleet-footed fell by the wayside, no matter their power. Pinchot remembered a walk where a top aide had to drop out "because he was too stout to stand the pace."

For all of that, their friendship was not one of equals. Somewhat jealous of others in Roosevelt's inner circle, Pinchot craved his respect and time. A Roosevelt ventriloquist on many issues, Pinchot would write pitch-perfect speeches that the president delivered with little change in the words. "T.R. told me he favored my material for his speeches more exactly than that of anyone else," Pinchot wrote, glowing like a schoolboy who had just charmed his mentor. But they also had that "peculiar intimacy," as Roosevelt had called it, which Pinchot cherished. "Long talk with T.R. in P.M. & fine intimate talk of men and things."

It was during a solo horseback ride on a February day in 1907 that Pinchot said he was struck by an idea that would bring together all the things the Roosevelt administration was trying to do in the natural world. Forests, wildlife, clean water, and man's role in the midst of it, trying to shape the land through irrigation and fire suppression in the arid West. Pinchot wondered, "What was the basic link between them?" It was on the back of his horse, mulling these thoughts, that Pinchot says he invented the idea of conservation as an overarching theme.

"Suddenly the idea flashed through my head that there was a unity in this complication," he wrote in his memoir. "To me it was a good deal like coming out of a dark tunnel. I had been seeing one spot of light ahead. Here, all of a sudden, was a whole landscape." It was a philosophy of the land, grounded in Pinchot's study of forestry, but more sweeping, with a moral, spiritual, and political dimension. "The earth, I repeat, belongs of right to all its people, and not to a minority, insignificant in numbers but tremendous in wealth and power." He took his idea to Roosevelt. "And T.R., as I expected, understood, accepted and adopted it without the smallest hesitation. It was directly in line with everything he had been thinking and doing. It became the heart of his administration."

Indeed, Roosevelt soon took to using the word "conservation" in his speeches and his proposals to Congress. Whether Pinchot and Roosevelt actually invented conservation is debatable. It takes many currents of thought, some from distant places, to form a river, and one of those most surely came from Pinchot's mentor, John Muir. In 1901, the naturalist published a powerfully argued book, *Our National Parks,* a popular cry for true preservation. A dog-eared copy found a prominent home in Roosevelt's library. But Pinchot and Teddy were the first to advance conservation for what it was: an executive branch agenda brought to the country with the full force of the bully pulpit.

Using conservation as a rallying cry, Roosevelt took ever more vigorously to the task of expanding the national forests and national parks, and creating more wildlife refuges and other protected lands. And with the public behind him, he was emboldened. On a trip to the Grand Canyon, he declared, "Leave it as it is. You cannot improve on it. The ages have been at work on it and man can only mar it. Keep it for your children, your children's children, and for all who come after you." Along with Mount Rainier, the canyon was given the initial protection that would eventually lead to national park status. These designations infuriated the syndicates, for they had significant mining and timber claims on both places.

At the same time, to show he was serious about public land belonging to the public, Roosevelt vigorously prosecuted timber thieves and cons, helped in no small part by investigative work from Pinchot's rangers in the field. He even put a senator—a fellow Republican, John H. Mitchell of Oregon—in prison for his role in a land scheme. Mitchell had been found guilty of taking bribes from timber companies in return for helping to process phony land claims. During his first year behind bars, he died—from complications of a tooth extraction.

Congress balked. Not only had the president done the unthinkable—putting Senator Mitchell, a twenty-two-year veteran of Washington's power corridors, away to rot in prison—but he also was moving far too quickly with this conservation business. A national monument here, ten million acres of new national forest there, and in between, wildlife refuges, plans to force western stockmen to pay for grazing, and timber companies to pay for logging in the national forests. The most powerful voice in the House, Joseph Gurney "Uncle Joe" Cannon of Illinois, joined with Heyburn and Clark in the Senate to stop Roosevelt.

"Not one cent for scenery!" declared Cannon, perhaps the most potent Speaker of the House in the history of Congress, a man whose government service dated to an appointment from Abraham Lincoln. Cannon had a Mennonite beard and small eyes; he was no friend of Roosevelt's despite their shared party affiliation. Nor was he owned by the trusts. He was prickly, moralistic, and did not like to be crossed. In his mind, Teddy Roosevelt was a radical.

In the Senate, the pushback was just as strong from fellow Republicans, led by Heyburn. With a triple set of jowls and a permanent scowl, the senator from Idaho was easily mocked by cartoonists and editorial writers. One profile said he was the most humorless, least liked person in the Senate. With a world view formed by his strict Quaker upbringing and the jungle capitalism of the West, where he had used his law office in Wallace to enrich mining syndicates, Heyburn had stood in the way of nearly all Roosevelt's progressive initiatives. He opposed the eight-hour workday, saying people should toil from sunup to sundown and to hell with the clock. He opposed direct election of senators; that would have kept Heyburn and Clark from office, were they to face the people. He opposed child welfare laws, saying it was the employer's right to hire anyone of any age. His reach and pettiness extended to young constituents in Idaho, rejecting a student who had won a debate prize named for Heyburn because "he does not seem to have learned enough to become a Republican," as Heyburn wrote in a scolding letter. When Congress took up the innocuous task of creating a national commission on fine arts, Heyburn blocked it, saying he despised "the artist's temperament."

He reserved a special wrath for Pinchot, regularly calling him before committees to explain the Forest Service and its budget. He questioned him as aggressively as a prosecutor would go after a man on trial for murder. When it came out that Pinchot was working without a salary and distributing to his clerks the money that should have gone to him as Chief, Heyburn tried to get the appropriation withdrawn. The very idea of forestry was a joke — it had no bearing in science, the senator believed. "Forestry," Heyburn said at one hearing, "has been fostered as a policy to uphold the leisurely, lazy dignity of a monarch," a reference to a man he called Czar Pinchot. To this remark, several senators hissed.

"Geese!" Heyburn shot back. "Geese! Hiss! Don't try that with me. I'm too old to be scared by that process."

After years of back-and-forth clashes with little to show for it, Heyburn and his allies finally came up with a way — they thought — that would stop Roosevelt. In 1907, an amendment was tacked onto a spending bill, a bit of dynamite in a small package. The add-on took away the president's authority to create new national forests in a huge part of the West without congressional approval. Every tree in the public domain in that area would be subject to the whim of key members of Congress like Heyburn. At the same time, Heyburn took to the Senate floor for a marathon attack, questioning whether the Forest Service had a right to exist, implying that it was a treasonous agency, unsanctioned by the Constitution.

Roosevelt felt cornered. Not so with Pinchot. To the forester, the Senate amendment was no defeat; it was an opportunity — but only if they acted quickly. The president had a week to sign the bill, and it had to be signed because it kept the government in operation. Pinchot had an idea. Why not use the seven-day window to put as much land into the national forest system as possible? Just go full bore and do in a week's time what they might normally do over the course of four years.

Roosevelt loved it. He asked the Forest Service to bring him maps — and hurry! — a carpet of cartography, every square mile in the area Heyburn was trying to take away. A messenger ran into agency headquarters with a two-word command from the Chief: "Get busy!" For a week, a huddle of Little G.P.s worked nonstop to outline valleys and rivers, mountain ranges and high meadows, ridge after ridge of forestland that might qualify. The floor of an entire room in the White House was covered with maps; Roosevelt, on his knees with Pinchot, went over individual sections, recalling hikes and hunting trips on land where he had mended a broken soul.

"Oh, this is bully!" said the president, in full nostril-snorting charge on the floor. "Have you put in the North Fork of the Flathead? Up there once I saw the biggest herd of black-tailed deer."

At the end of the week, Roosevelt issued executive proclamations covering sixteen million acres of land in half a dozen states, bringing them into the fold of the national forest system. And then he signed the bill that prevented him or any other president from doing such a thing again.

"The joke was on them," said Pinchot.

Heyburn and his allies seethed. "The opponents of the Forest Service turned handsprings in their wrath," Roosevelt wrote, "and dire were the threats to the Executive." A Senate delegation marched over to the White House to demand a change. In advance of the meeting, Roosevelt summoned Pinchot. Caught up in the euphoria of their triumph, they started laughing, loudly enough that the senators could hear them as they approached from the hallway. Heyburn was apoplectic, steaming. These new national forests were nothing but "midnight reserves," he said in a rant to the president. After the meeting, he arranged to cut off any funds that would allow the Forest Service to publicize them. By his reasoning, if the public did not know they existed, then perhaps they wouldn't exist at all.

But the forester and the president now had most everything they wanted. In just a few years' time, they had tripled the national forest system, to nearly 180 million acres. They had introduced a new term to the public debate—conservation—and it was here to stay. They had shifted oversight of public land from patronage bureaucrats to professional foresters. In battle, Pinchot seemed to be at his most exuberant. Work was joy; the thrust and parry over ideas gave it life. "I am very happy tonight," he signed off his diary just after the midnight reserves were created.

Embedded in Idaho and Montana, in Colorado and the Dakotas and Wyoming, in Washington, Oregon, and California, in the territories of Arizona and New Mexico and Alaska, were hundreds of Little G.P.s, keepers of the conservation dream. Their job was to make sure the land was in good shape, to convince people who lived nearby that they could prosper with national forests as their neighbors, to prevent the agents of timber companies from stealing public resources, and to fight fires.

Fire was the less formidable task, Pinchot believed. He already had a rough plan in place, a new gospel for the Little G.P.s. "The one secret to fighting fires is to discover your fire as soon as possible and fight it as hard as you can and refuse to leave it until the last ember is dead," he told the *New York Times*. And the first two summers of the Forest Service under Pinchot seemed to bear him out. Only one-tenth of one percent of Forest Service land burned in each of those years—a huge confidence booster that had Roosevelt feeling sure of the rangers' ability to control wildfire.

"It had a great task before it, and the Forest Service has proved that forest fires can be controlled," the president wrote Pinchot in late August 1906. Pinchot had set up the monumental task: ensure that nature could be subdued even as it was preserved, an inherent contradiction. And Roosevelt now gave him a passing grade on this earth-changing score. Still ahead was the sizable job of wresting control of the land from the syndicates, who vowed continued defiance of the forest rangers, and convincing average people that this land was theirs. The challenge was to show homesteaders, grubstakers, immigrants, and others that the Forest Service worked on their behalf.

"Finally, a body of intelligent, practical, well-trained men, citizens of the West, is being built up," Roosevelt wrote. But as the Little G.P.s would soon find out, many a poor man had a different idea in a land that was wild in all ways.

4

Deadwood Days

I N A T H I C K E T of dark Montana woods just downslope from the Idaho divide, a town sprang up with one prostitute for every three men and a murder rate higher than that of New York City. Carved inside a national forest, the village of Taft frightened most anyone not used to humanity with its raw appetites exposed. You could buy the basics in Taft: a woman, a man, a horse, a place at a card table or a spin of a roulette wheel, a fat steak for $1, a quart of whiskey for $1.25, a bunk for 25 cents. One nearby shop advertised "shoes, booze and screws," and they weren't talking about hardware. It was an easy place for an outlaw to hide, because everyone in Taft provided camouflage; a decent man would stand out like cactus on an ice floe. People drifted into town by day and just as easily faded away at night, never to be seen until the snow melted in the spring. During one thaw, eight bodies were found. A reporter visiting from Chicago described Taft as "the wickedest city in America."

The townsfolk took their amusement wherever they could find it, and so they didn't miss a beat when the churchgoing, well-fed secretary of war, William H. Taft, came for a visit in 1907. At the time, the town was nameless — just a sheltered place in the woods to get a bunk and a boff or to sleep off a hard night. Secretary Taft, who was on the shortlist to succeed Roosevelt as president, lectured the whores and saloonkeepers, the fugitives, timber thieves, claim jumpers, and cardsharps about morality and their wretched ways. This town was a blight on the idea of national forests. This sewer of sin was a defiance of how American settlements had been founded, dating to the Puritans' "city upon a hill." From atop their tree stumps, people cheered, whistled in approval, and hoisted their jugs. *Here, here!* And then, just after the future president left, they decided to name their town for the big man. That spring, there were eighteen murders in Taft.

The town of Taft was part of the public land domain of Elers Koch, the twenty-five-year-old supervisor of three national forests and a fresh-minted Little G.P. Pinchot never told him his empire would include some of the most openly lawless places in the country. Pinchot always looked past the gambling dens or the mining claims to the trees. "The forest is as beautiful as it is useful," he wrote in his *Primer of Forestry.* "The old fairy tales which spoke of it as a terrible place are wrong."

He had not visited the open sore of Taft, Montana. When Koch and his crew of young rangers first showed up in town to have a look, the saloons, card dens, dance halls, and whores' cribs were going full throttle. "The bars were lined with hard-faced dance hall girls," Koch wrote, "and every kind of gambling game going wide open." The rangers spent the night, but were unable to sleep because of the din. Koch got out of bed, dressed, and went down to one of the saloons. He dropped a coin in a slot machine—and it hit! As his winnings flowed out, painted women were instantly drawn to the forest supervisor. "One big blonde in a very low-cut dress had her arm tightly around my neck," he said. Koch ordered up drinks for the house, on him, and then gathered his coins, ducked under the arm of the blonde with the free-flowing cleavage, and made a retreat for his bunk. Welcome to Lolo National Forest.

Koch hired crews of seasonal rangers to go with his full-time assistants. They strung telephone wire, built trails, rescued hunters and hikers. In the winter, they snowshoed deep into the forest,

traveling for days at a time on little but tea, sugar, raisins, and hard-
tack. They felled dead, standing trees for firewood and tried to stay
warm wrapped in wool blankets—years before anyone had sleeping
bags. Koch learned to read the sky and the human heart. He made
some mistakes. One hire of his set up shop in the remote forest with
his wife and daughter. Not long into this arrangement, the ranger's wife showed up at Koch's office in tears. Her husband had been
sleeping with their little girl, the wife said—incest. Koch called the
ranger in and told him he knew what he'd been doing. The man
twitched, and Koch grew nervous looking at the gun in his pocket.
Koch slid a resignation letter across the desk.

"Sign that," he ordered. He kicked the man out, then reported
him to the authorities.

His colleague just over the ridge in Idaho, Bill Weigle, had a
bigger problem: inside his national forest, the Coeur d'Alene, were
three towns animated by debauchery and lusts of all kinds. The
worst was Grand Forks, where muddy streets thick with filth and
feces were lined with burned-out stumps of big cedars, like nubs on
a half-shaven face. Saloons were held together by rough-cut planks,
with canvas-walled cribs out back or on a second story for quick paid
sex. If a wagon broke down in the middle of the street, it remained
there until somebody burned it or picked it apart for scrap.

The Little G.P.s were horrified and perplexed by what they
found in the people's land: instead of honest homesteaders they confronted land thieves, instead of Pinchot's vaunted Little Man Who
Would Be King they found whiskey peddlers, instead of enlight-
ened merchants they found six varieties of pimps—all operating
in open defiance of the U.S. Forest Service. One man cut a swath in
the woods just outside Taft, a half acre or so, and opened a bar with
a few whores. He did this under the eyes of several rangers. A flummoxed ranger sent a telegram to Missoula, no idea how to proceed.

"Two undesirable prostitutes established on government land,"
he wired. "What should I do?"

Another ranger wired back: "Get two desirable ones."

• • •

The railroad that William Rockefeller financed—the Chicago, Milwaukee & Puget Sound Railway, called the Milwaukee Road for short—was going full bore, trying to cut through the solid vertical flank of the Bitterroots, straight into the wild heart of the Roosevelt reserves. Other magnates were moving on the mother lode of white pine, the largest uncut forest of that species in the world. In just three counties of northern Idaho, seventy-two sawmills were in operation. To the west, a rail line serving Potlatch—Frederick Weyerhaeuser's company town, the biggest timber complex in the nation—was moving farther into the forest on land purchased at a huge discount from the bigger railroads. All of this took place in an area where, just a few years earlier, a human being could have wandered for days without bumping into another. Idaho had not even two people per square mile at the start of the century—the entire state meeting the census classification for "frontier." Montana was similar. They were the least settled states in the nation, along with Nevada.

For sheer percussive onslaught, nothing could top the Milwaukee Road, the nation's sixth transcontinental route, using a right of way that preceded the forest designation and gave the railway power to move through the reserves. The line hired thousands of men to dynamite holes in the granite, to sluice away gravel, to cut timber for ties and trestles, some of them running three hundred feet above the forest floor. No railroad had ever spent as much, $75,000 per mile, to lace ties across the Rockies. The toughest section—entirely roadless, with steep peaks, enormous snowdrifts and blizzards in winter, raging floods in spring, swarms of mosquitoes and yellow-jackets in summer—was in the high mountains shared by Idaho and Montana. To cross that stretch of merely twenty-two miles, workers would need to build twenty-one bridges and sixteen tunnels. But flush with Rockefeller money, the Milwaukee Road had the cash, and so the once empty reaches of the Bitterroots clogged with people rushing to make money off the latest boom in the West. By day they clawed away at the mountains, by night they indulged their cravings in towns newly sprouted in the public woodlands.

In the Coeur d'Alene National Forest, a prostitute robbed and poisoned to death one of her customers. Trying to destroy the evidence, she burned down the building. The fire spread. By evening, Grand Forks was a smoldering heap and the whore had disappeared. Required to hold an inquest, people in the town hauled the bent and blackened shell of her bed out to the rutted byway in the center of the ruined town. The charred body was still on the bed. In Grand Forks it was just another entertainment; people pulled up seats atop beer kegs to have a look, jugs in hand. The town was rebuilt within a week, this time as a tent village. As darkness settled in with the evening, gas lamps lit up canvas walls and music poured into the woods from fiddles. The roar of laughter and brawling, the screech of off-key tunes, and the ring of gunshots fired at random filled the national forest.

It was a struggle, to say the least, for Bill Weigle to control Grand Forks. From Yale and Washington, D.C., he had been dispatched to a state with two time zones, a state where it was nearly impossible to travel from north to south without leaving it, a state with an odd boundary only 45 miles wide at the top that expanded to 479 miles at the bottom, a state where forests covered 82 percent of the landmass.

At first Weigle had politely informed merchants that they were selling liquor and lust on government property—a violation of federal law, *gentlemen*. They laughed at him; that is, those who didn't ignore him or threaten to kill him. Weigle had a ribald sense of humor and found the towns darkly comic at times. But he also had his orders. From Wallace, he wired pious Billy Greeley in Missoula: What should we do? Weigle felt helpless. There was nothing in Pinchot's little manual that rangers were required to carry—the *Use Book*—on how to tame a town that made Deadwood seem sedate. Nor had anyone at the Yale forestry school prepared the rangers for this. The Bible-quoting, bespectacled Greeley, who had once considered a career teaching the word of God, told Weigle he had no choice but to close the saloons and arrest the operators. This was a public forest! Not some haven of piracy in the high Rockies. Weigle sent a ranger to put the merchants on notice.

"Upon our return, we found most of the saloons still running full blast," recalled Joe Halm, who had been hired out of college in 1909 by Weigle to help patrol the Coeur d'Alene. "This went on for several weeks and we became extremely unpopular. When one saloon was closed, another sprang up next door under new management." Halm and two other men tried to arrest a saloonkeeper; the barkeep fingered a shotgun, threatening to kill the rangers. They backed away, muttering to the owner a promise to return in the morning with a warrant. As forest supervisor, Weigle felt duty-bound to make the arrest. He rode all night from Wallace. Just before dawn, Weigle assembled a posse of six armed forest rangers. They galloped into Grand Forks and took up positions outside the saloon. They banged on the door. No answer. Long, deadly silence. Weigle and another ranger then pushed open the door, walked in, and edged slowly forward, facing the bartender.

"Are you ready to go?" Weigle asked.

The saloonkeeper reached for a towel. The forest supervisor winced. The fear was that the man had a pistol under his cloth. Instead, he wiped his hands and surrendered. He was handcuffed, along with another saloon owner. There was no jail in Grand Forks. The closest lockup was through the woods and over the Idaho-Montana divide, at Taft—a long hike, too steep, rocky, and narrow for horses. It took the better part of a day for Weigle to guide his prisoners to Taft. Once there, they had a meal and a drink and then boarded the train for the biggest town in the region, Missoula. The prisoners were uncuffed for the ride, and Weigle settled into an easy conversation with one of them, the window open to let air circulate on a hot day. Weigle was a bachelor; he liked women and a drink; he looked like a lumberjack; with his pants up high-water style and his red suspenders, he looked like one of *them*. He could see why the townspeople catered to the tastes of roustabouts. But it was a public forest, this pragmatic Yalie tried to explain, not a grubstake. The bartender got up to stretch. In a flash he dove out the window into the passing woods. Weigle looked out: no sign of him as the train pushed on through the mountains. His prisoner disappeared, never to be seen in the Coeur d'Alene again. Later, Weigle found out that the man was an escaped convict with a long criminal record, currently wanted for several murders.

It was not just outlaws who had it in for the Little G.P.s. Timbermen were outraged at having to answer to kids just out of college—"Teddy's Green Rangers," in the derisive term of Senator Clark's newspapers. Home at last in Montana, Elers Koch hiked under cathedrals of big cedars, feeling a spiritual attachment to his beloved Big Sky Country. But he also had to sell off much of that same virgin forest to industry, as part of the new operating rules of the national forests. National forests were not parks or wildlife refuges; they were "working forests," as Pinchot said, there for the ages, but also not tree museums. Anaconda, a logging branch of the copper trust, tried to intimidate Koch, but he did have some power. He insisted that loggers leave the largest of pines standing as a seed source. A big upright tree in the middle of a ravaged, logged-over hillside became known as a "Koch Special." He was damn proud of them, despite the ridicule from Anaconda.

Everywhere, the woods were thick with timber cruisers—people hired by logging companies to stake out homesteads. Pinchot called them "as competent a body of land thieves as e'er the sun shone on." Homesteaders were pouring into the Far West; the twentieth century saw a frenzy of people seeking free land, more so than in the previous century, many from distant shores. But it was a different game in the forests. "Homesteading was not farming in those days, but just a subterfuge to gain possession of timber on land that has since proven worthless for farming," wrote Nancy R. Warren, who came to Idaho from Chicago in the boom years with her rel-

atively well-off family. The basic scheme was to find 160 acres, patent it with a shack that could be labeled a home on "agricultural"
ground, and then sell the land for a big profit to one of the timber companies, which were prohibited from homesteading. These
claims were neither homes nor farms, but in this way, big sections
of the new national forests were nibbled away and came under the
control of timber companies. In the Bitterroots, nearly 90 percent of
the homesteads were frauds set up by agents of industry, in the estimates of people on either side of the game.

A young woman, Ione Adair, hacked her way along a game trail
to find a piece of land in the heart of the Coeur d'Alene. Ione was
twenty-five years old, nicknamed Pinkie because of her shock of red
hair and freckled nose. When Pinkie set off to establish her own
homestead, people were making up to $8,000 selling their 160-acre
claims to timber companies—a fortune, equal to nearly a half-dozen
years at a good-paying job. Pinkie claimed her piece of ground in a
meadow above the St. Joe River, just east of the Montana border. In
her cabin, the walls were lined with unbleached muslin cloth, and
the mattress was stuffed with beargrass. She stored canned goods
in the attic, along with sealed sacks of flour and salt. Pinkie traveled with a .38 on her belt. The shack was inaccessible during the
winter, but in the warm months Pinkie made frequent visits. Once,
while she was eating breakfast on the steps of the cabin, a little man
surprised her from the brush.

"Oh—somebody's here," he said.

"Who are you?"

"They call me Dynamite. I'm working on the railroad—on the
tunnel. I do the drilling for the holes for the dynamite. I'd been living in your cabin while you were gone." She invited Dynamite in
for breakfast, though she kept her pistol strapped on.

Like other homesteaders in 1909, Pinkie Adair had no use for
Gifford Pinchot's rangers. The foresters had cautioned her about
making claims for profit on land not fit for legitimate homesteads.
She heard them out, then continued as if no national forest had ever

been established. She told everyone there was room enough in the upper St. Joe for a real homestead farm, and if the rangers thought otherwise, they'd just have to come after Pinkie. For the time being, they left her alone.

Trying to be useful, the rangers warned people about fire, and they attempted to enlist timber cruisers as lookouts. Of course, they were also trying to prosecute some of those same cruisers, but if they could be helpful in early fire detection, everyone could have a short-term benefit. Most of the land hunters had no incentive to help. If fire came to the forest, it was every man for himself. Plus, nobody in the new towns had ever seen a fire of any significant size in the northern Rockies, and they certainly had not been there long enough for a typical thirty-year fire cycle — a good-size burn every generation or so — which bred a sense of complacency. The timber in these mountains did not need protection, one Idaho newspaper editorialized in 1908, "because it was not subject to fire."

Deep in the emerald drainage of the St. Joe River, about thirty miles from Pinkie's cabin, the Forest Service was building a home-stead of its own — a ranger station — to win people over. With little money to build trails, roads, or lookouts, Bill Greeley was struggling to get control of the forty-one-million-acre expanse of national for-ests in Region One. His rangers were swallowed by the enormity of the place. "One man in such a tract of land, without roads, trails or a telegraph is absolutely helpless," said Ranger Emery Wilson, who worked for Greeley. It was bad enough that his men had to pay for their own uniforms, their own horses, their own food and supplies, but living conditions, for most of them, were primitive. Greeley and Koch had homes in Missoula — an oasis of culture in a fine valley cut by three rivers. Weigle lived in the mining town of Wallace. The other rangers were footloose for much of the year, living out of tents in the warm months. If Greeley could establish permanent ranger stations, he could put an imprint of the Chief in the woods, something to show that the Forest Service was not going away.

As the new century dawned, the valley carved by the St. Joe was still undisturbed, one of the nation's most isolated places. This tunnel of wild land was so remote that the only way to get to the upper St. Joe was by canoe. The Indians had a network of trails along the river, which they used to hunt elk and deer, and to fish. The big river pulled snowmelt in from an arc of broad-shouldered mountains, and it was flush with cutthroat and big bull trout that could rival salmon in size. Enormous trees, some more than five hundred years old, hugged the floor of the valley, and the upward slopes were thick with white pine as straight as a beam of sunlight. People who had poled upstream to have a look at the valley came away struck by its dreamy beauty and stillness. In this lost world, rangers started work on a shining outpost of the Forest Service in 1908.

The station would have to be built with scraps from the forest and detritus from railroad construction, using the manpower of Little G.P.s with their limited carpentry skills. Lucky for Weigle, he had just hired a local man, Ed Pulaski, as an assistant ranger — a man who knew nothing about the science of silviculture and probably could not find Yale on a map. But Ed Pulaski was just what the beleaguered Forest Service needed. He was nearly twenty years older than most of the Little G.P.s, a middle-aged master of carpentry, metal forging, riding, route finding, and other skills that had allowed him to survive in the Rocky Mountain West at a time when it was being fully opened up.

His father had immigrated to the United States from Poland, settling in Ohio. For most of his life, Ed was thought to be a descendant of Count Casimir Pulaski, the Revolutionary War hero who served under George Washington. *No sir*, he told anyone willing to listen, the count was only a distant ancestor. Big Ed was from the poor Pulaskis, without money or title. But people believed what they wanted to believe, and so he went through life as *that* Pulaski, even to some of his closest friends. At age sixteen he had left school in Ohio for the Rockies, tramping around the big hill of Butte, the copper lodes of Arizona, the Silver Valley of Idaho — the min-

ing tour, but he never hit it big. He worked as a plumber, a steam-
fitter, a blacksmith, an outfitter. He tried to join the Army to fight
in the Spanish-American War, but was rejected. He married once,
divorced, and then married again. Pulaski was respected around
Wallace and throughout the Bitterroots, something that could not
be said for most of Gifford Pinchot's boys. It was one of his selling
points, as a supervisor noted in his personnel file: "He is a very good
man in a district at the center of a community none too favorably
inclined toward the Forest Service."

For several months, the rangers hammered and sawed, cut and
felled, fitted and shaved, as the ranger station along the St. Joe took
shape. It had big windows, a broad porch, loft space for guests upstairs. It looked permanent. Soon the new station was home to a forest ranger, a married man with two young children. Next door, the
government built a post office and established the ranger's wife as
postmistress. A few other cabins rose in the cluster. To look at it now
was to see the shaping of a real town. Inspired, the Little G.P.s in-
corporated their burg and named it for Big G.P. At the new town of
Pinchot, Idaho, nestled in the St. Joe River valley, the Forest Service had made its mark, a brand on the raw hide of the Bitterroots.

But upriver, the railroad bosses had another idea. Soon the coal-
fired locomotives of the Milwaukee Road would come roaring
through—all fire and steel, sparks and combustion, chugging out of
a nearly two-mile-long tunnel in the mountains and wending their
way down until the road found the silent, sylvan valley of the St.
Joe. At a clearing next to the river, just upstream from Pinchot, railroad workers assembled in the usual pattern, brothel and bar first,
followed by a general store, a few hundred cabins, and a three-story
hotel whose chief attraction was a black bear purchased from a railroad employee. The chance to wrestle with the bear, on a bet, provided a little side income for the hotel. In this village, people ignored the nearby town of Pinchot, because they wanted their own
town with their own rules. Life was cheap, and death could come
and go like a spring shower. A typhoid epidemic swept through in

1908, killing dozens of construction workers. But the enterprise had its upside. The railroad's president, Albert J. Earling, and his corporate confidant and benefactor, William Rockefeller, said this new line would be unrivaled in the United States for speed, power, and modern touches.

When one of Earling's wealthy friends asked him if there was something he could do about his sons, a pair of hard-drinking, skirt-chasing, recent college graduates—the Kelley brothers, Spike and Bill—Earling recommended sending them out west to get in on the bonanza following his new rail line. The Kelley brothers showed up in the St. Joe Valley, cartons of liquor, raccoon coats, and fine possessions in tow, and took to it like hounds on a rabbit hunt. They loved the bawdy life of the wide-open tent towns and the chance to make an easy buck. The brothers opened general merchandise stores in Taft, Grand Forks, and the new town taking shape next to Pinchot. Spike Kelley was the most industrious. He oversaw construction of a two-story mansion across the river from the other cabins—the biggest house in the valley—and hired servants from among the Japanese who had also moved there. When the manse was finished and fitted out with antiques, Spike disappeared for several months. He returned with the socialite daughter of a California judge—his bride, Mrs. Spike Kelley. She arrived on the St. Joe with eighteen trunks.

The town of Pinchot had to go. The Milwaukee Road was coming through, and they wanted the land on which the new ranger station had been built. They had their legal right of way, awarded in an earlier land grant. Worn down, the fight drained away, the Forest Service retreated. And so Weigle's rangers took their hammers, saws, and crowbars to the outpost they had so lovingly constructed in honor of the Chief, and tore it apart. Off came the roof, the porch, the well-crafted loft space, the perfectly cut timbers. They would move the station upriver to join the rowdies at the edge of the new town. The people there had no use for them, of course, and reminded the rangers of it daily. At the least, the rangers thought, the town, now with about 250 people, would keep the name of the founder of the Forest Service. Sorry, they were told: this cluster of humanity on the St. Joe River was now a projection of the very Gilded Age powers that Pinchot and Roosevelt had been fighting for nearly a decade. The name of the town would be Avery, after William Rockefeller's grandson. Pinchot, the town, was erased from the map. Pinchot, the man, would be the next to fall.

5

Showdown

O N ONE OF THE LAST days of Teddy Roosevelt's time in the White House, the president called in his handpicked successor to talk about plans to run the nation in the second decade of the American century. Despite his girth, William H. Taft was always the smaller man when in Roosevelt's presence, or so he felt. Roosevelt was the human volcano; Taft was a putting green. Roosevelt sucked the air out of a room; Taft tried to be invisible. Roosevelt barked; Taft had a low monotone, punctuated by a random and annoying chuckle. Roosevelt burned two thousand calories before noon and drank his coffee with seven lumps of sugar; Taft was the picture of sloth: multiple chins, a zest for five-course meals and long baths. Sleeping Beauty was the nickname his wife, Nellie, gave him, and oh, how he loved to nap. But on the question of how and where to lead the country, they did not differ, the president believed.

Taft had spent the past three years observing Roosevelt's likes and dislikes, his private quirks and public persona. He took it all in carefully and then projected it back to him, hitting the right notes as Roosevelt probed him on his political beliefs. As such, he seemed to be the perfect successor. Roosevelt was full of energy, at the peak of his power and popularity, but he felt duty-bound to keep the

promise he had made to serve only two terms. More than any guiding philosophy, Will Taft simply was driven by the desire to please
the man he considered his closest friend. And so when Roosevelt
asked him to the White House in late 1908, after a campaign in
which Taft won with the full backing and expert advice of the still-
young Roosevelt, the incoming president again said all the right
things. Taft had won in a landslide, crushing the perennial Democratic populist William Jennings Bryan. For this meeting in the old
cabinet room upstairs Roosevelt invited Pinchot along. The three
men talked late into the night.

Roosevelt was convinced that conservation and the rest of the
progressive agenda would have a central place in the Taft administration. No need for the big man to be bold; just keep the ship
going forward, even keel. Fighting the trusts, holding firm to the
idea that natural resources belonged to the public, setting aside
unique pieces of land for future generations, trying to do something
about nine-year-old girls working twelve-hour days in cotton mills
down south — on all of these issues Taft would be solid. But Pinchot
thought otherwise. He considered Taft superficial, somewhat silly,
and malleable. He didn't trust him. Taft, in his view, "had successfully followed and chuckled his way through life."

The country was bursting at the seams, people buying automobiles and feathering the insides of gabled houses, on a roll with the
downturn of 1907 behind them. In Pinchot's eyes, Taft had been
carried into office by the tailwind of T.R.'s popularity. Pinchot
thought of quitting. How could he work for a man he didn't respect? But Roosevelt talked him out of it, inviting him to come to
the White House to hear out Taft in the cabinet room. Their work
was not finished, the president reminded the forester; stay on for
the good of all the Little G.P.s if nothing else.

That night in the White House, Taft made a promise. "Then
and there Taft pledged himself to T.R., and incidentally to me, to
stand by and carry on the conservation fight," wrote Pinchot. "It
was no perfunctory promise . . . He bound himself, as completely as

one man can to another, to stand by and go forward with the T.R. conservation policy."

In his final months as president, Roosevelt tried to ensure that his policies had a permanent place in the country. That meant conservation was to be as lasting an American principle as free speech. Three weeks before leaving office, he requested that the world's great powers meet in The Hague to do an inventory of the world's resources. Far ahead of his time, and to the criticism of isolationists in his own party, Roosevelt tried to get the major nations of the world to come together and take stock of the globe they shared.

In barely five years' time, many of these same powers would be at war, in a drawn-out conflict of nationalistic frenzy with repercussions for the rest of the century. But for now Roosevelt wanted only to get other nations to see their rivers, their forests, their farm fields, their oil and coal, their wildlife as valuable assets that would not last if they failed to become good stewards. There was a limit to what the world could bear. His idea was not a complicated notion, he said — "all of this is simply good common sense." At home, Roosevelt's legacy was intact: he had added about 230 million acres to national forests, parks, wildlife refuges, and other lands managed for future generations — an endowment 50 percent bigger than all of Texas. In one of his last acts as president, Roosevelt presented a report on what conservation had meant for America — and what it could mean for the world. People living in 1909 were obligated to the future, he wrote.

"It is high time to realize that our responsibility to the coming millions is like that of parents to their children, and that in wasting our resources we are wronging our children."

In the final hours of his presidency, Roosevelt gathered his closest confidants for a self-congratulatory lunch, excluding Taft. He spoke of their achievements, how they had altered the American landscape, changed its politics, its view of itself in the world. Not all of their goals had been achieved, but the United States was a nation transformed — for the better, he believed. As a parting pres-

ent, Teddy's friends gave him a bronze lion; it brought him close
to tears.

Early on, there were clear signs that Congress would have its way
with Taft, simply because he so loathed conflict. With Roosevelt out
of the way, the spark-eyed, cigar-chomping Speaker of the House,
Uncle Joe Cannon, was back in full form, a force that Taft tried
first to avoid and then to please. Senator Heyburn was ginning up
complaints from powerful constituents in the West, preparing to
cripple the Forest Service with a thousand little blows. His bully
pulpit gone, Roosevelt left for Africa on a long-planned safari. "To
the lions!" his enemies toasted. Like a fresh college graduate who
has waited years to hit the road, T.R. lighted out for adventure in
distant parts of the big continent, with plans to make his way up
through Egypt, the Mediterranean, and much of Europe. He was
free. Pinchot hated to see him go. Two days before he left the White
House, Roosevelt penned a farewell to G.P.

"I am a better man for having known you," he wrote, "and I
can't think of a man whose loss would be a more real misfortune
to the Nation than yours would be. For seven-and-a-half years we
have worked together, and now and then played together . . ."

Not long after Roosevelt sailed for Africa, Pinchot headed out
west on a trip of his own. He found his rangers full of misery: the
budget cutbacks were killing them. No pay raises. No new funds for
roads, trails, telephones. No money to hire fire patrols in advance of
the perils of the dry season. All those restrictions came after a four-
fold expansion in the land the rangers had to oversee, and it was
taking its toll. With room, board, laundry, tools, the costs of main-
taining their own four-footed transports—it was a lot to cover on
a ranger's salary of barely $1,000 a year, the foresters complained.
Yale graduates, five years into service, were not making as much
money as a first lieutenant in the Army, whose pay was 50 percent
higher. Pinchot promised to take the fight to Congress. He would
stay on to keep his creation intact, to remind the rangers of their

sense of purpose, keepers of this great experiment. But when he returned to the capital after a month, it was as if the life had been vacuumed from the city.

"Washington was a dead town," Pinchot wrote. Without Teddy Roosevelt, the city was lifeless, apathetic. In the White House, where pets, games, and kids once filled the halls, where a rooster crowed in a bedroom, where a pony rode in the elevator, where the crack and snap of energy and excitement, of youth and purpose, filled every cubic foot, there was now nothing but the silent passing of time, Pinchot felt—which in itself was backward motion. The forester tried to give Taft counsel, but they clashed, opposites in every way. In the new Washington there was no more incongruous sight than the skeletal Pinchot, with all his nervous energy, and the spherical Taft.

Just before Inauguration Day, March 4, 1909, Roosevelt had offered Taft one last bit of advice: stay off the back of a horse, at least in public. He feared for beast and man, he said. And in fact, a horse had already collapsed under the weight of the man. Taft had shed some fat during the campaign, getting down to 280 pounds. But he started to gain it back almost as soon as the election returns were counted. Pictures of the new president shot from behind—"Aft Taft," they were called—made him look ridiculous, as he was.

Beyond the surface ridicule were much deeper concerns. The energy of the Progressive Era, the sense of taking on giants and bringing them down, of gleefully tripping up the "malefactors of great wealth," of changing the way America looked at its future, its land, the world around it—all had disappeared. Soon the nation would have another loss, with the death of Mark Twain. "It's a losing race," the writer said before he slipped away in 1910. "No ship can outsail death."

Pinchot fell into a deep funk. He grew moody and somber despite his outward vigor and cheer. He did not think Taft was evil or open to petty corruption. Nor did he think the new president was stupid. "Weak rather than wicked" was his view, though he kept such musings to himself. Pinchot's closest ally in town was the secretary of the interior, James Garfield, son of the assassinated twentieth president and a Roosevelt holdover like Pinchot. Garfield had been along on many of the rigorous walks in Rock Creek Park and swims in the icy Potomac, when the grand ideas of conservation were hatched. He also shared Roosevelt's and Pinchot's disdain for the gilded rulers of American industry who maneuvered around G.P. during his years working for Teddy. In one of Taft's first acts as president—and a surprise, at least to Pinchot—he let Garfield go, and replaced him with Richard Ballinger, a former Seattle mayor and lawyer with ties to some of the biggest land barons in the West. Ballinger believed that the conservation crusade had gone too far, a view secretly shared by Taft. Pinchot was stunned.

"A stocky, square-headed little man who believed in turning all public resources as freely and rapidly as possible over to private ownership," Pinchot said of the new secretary of the interior. And regarding Ballinger, Pinchot did not keep his comments to himself.

Compounding Pinchot's woes, he had more trouble summoning Laura, his dead lover. Oh, she was there when he faced his nemesis in Congress, fighting for the Forest Service against the blunt scorn of the swollen-faced Senator Heyburn. "I felt my Lady's help," he wrote after numerous appearances in the hot seat. But during the first year of Taft's presidency, Laura started to fade. She had been his refuge, confidante, and spiritual wife. But the apparition had grown dimmer, its appearances less frequent, with each passing year; by 1909, the flesh-and-blood Laura had been gone for fifteen years. No more did Pinchot write of "bright days" in which Laura was clear as a chatty seat-mate at dinner. Now it was mostly "cloudy days" or worse. "A blind day," Pinchot wrote, night-after-day. About this time, Pinchot may have started to think of seeing other women. His friend in the psychic world, the London editor W. T. Steadman, advised Pinchot that he owed it to Laura to let her know if he ever gave his heart to someone else. "You should at least be able to get in direct touch with her mind to know her wishes," he wrote Pinchot. The forester's long spiritual affair with the lovely, deceased woman of his youth was nearing an end, it appeared, just as the man who gave life to his biggest ideas had left the country.

On top of everything else, Pinchot now had a troubled relationship with his mentor, John Muir, the man who had done even more than Roosevelt to get Americans to rethink their ideas on the land. Muir seemed dismissive of Pinchot's gloomy year. They drifted apart, and then began to feud at a distance. Muir thought Pinchot had become drunk with power and his status in the Roosevelt administration. "P. is ambitious," Muir wrote, "and never hesitates to sacrifice anything or anybody in his way."

Pinchot wanted the land to work for the people. His was a practical conservation, forged from the daily struggle with his adversaries—the art of the possible. Muir saw the land as sacrosanct, best when left alone, without human shaping. He seldom dirtied his hands in the muck of politics. "I care to live only to entice people to look at nature's loveliness," Muir said, floating above the conflict. It was a debate, mostly abstract, that they could have on civil terms. It turned personal after business interests in San Francisco pressed to dam the waters of the Tuolumne River in Muir's temple of Yosemite National Park. Muir believed it was an abomination, a high crime against nature, to back up the river in the Hetch Hetchy Valley so that San Francisco could outgrow its water shortages. In 1905, Muir had taken his case directly to another hiking friend—Roosevelt, who seemed sympathetic. But then the earthquake of 1906 gave fresh urgency to the case for helping San Francisco, with many people left homeless on the hills of a burned-out city. Pinchot favored the dam, which would provide a humanitarian lift, he believed. And from there the argument simmered off and on for years between two of the founding voices of conservation, the fate of Hetch Hetchy undetermined for the rest of the Roosevelt presidency and into the new president's term.

Taft was emboldened by Pinchot's woes, but he knew he could not fire him without causing a storm among Roosevelt loyalists. Despite his promise to Roosevelt that night in the White House, Taft believed the conservation movement had gone too far too fast, and that too much land had been put in the public's hands. Roosevelt and Pinchot were radicals, he said in confidence to his brother; they were crusaders. They had steered the Republican Party into territory where Taft was clearly uncomfortable. In private, he dismissed Pinchot as "Sir Galahad" and agreed with the forester's many enemies who derided him as "a millionaire with a mission." Of course, Taft had competed with him for the affections of Roosevelt; both the new president and the Chief adored T.R. But Taft thought Pinchot's ardor was over the top—"sort of a fetish worship," he said. He mocked Pinchot in a letter to his brother in 1909: "G.P. is out there again defying the lightning and the storm and championing the cause of the oppressed and downtrodden, and harassing the wealthy and the greedy and the dishonest."

Out west, the Little G.P.s felt overwhelmed. Prosecutions for fraudulent homesteads were few and time-consuming. It would take a single ranger months to make a case against someone who tried to claim part of the national forest as his own. On fire patrol, the rangers were even more short-handed, and volunteers to help with the watch were scarce. A killing could be made in these public lands, but not by befriending the Forest Service. With the opening of the Milwaukee Road in 1909, the iron muscle of modern industry came to the Bitterroots, the trains charging through, all roars and thunder, whistle yelps bouncing off the rock walls of the mountains. In the first summer of the new line, the train also proved to be an iron fire-starter—a serious problem for the undermanned Forest Service. From his headquarters in Wallace, Bill Weigle sent a man to do nothing but follow the tracks all day on a velocipede, putting out small fires. He could not keep up. Suddenly, as if an immigration starting gun had gone off, people poured into Montana, Idaho, and Washington—a growth spurt like no other in the history of the Northwest. Nancy Warren, the Chicago transplant in Idaho, had been rhapsodic over the beauty of the area. Now she saw a different side. "The possibilities of profit soon mounted to millions in terms of money and board feet. Everyone was elated at the sight of so much raw material for monetary advancement," she wrote. "The timber companies were planning a monstrous cut."

At the least, Weigle, Greeley, Pulaski, Koch, and other rangers expected a bit more support from their government. During a meeting in Missoula, the foresters spent all day commiserating about low pay and constant harassment from Heyburn and his monied clients in the woods. "It's a well-known fact that on several occasions Senator Heyburn has solicited complaints from residents of the Coeur d'Alene against the Forest Service," one ranger wrote in a letter to Greeley. Heyburn was working several angles to crush the national forests. He had drawn up a bill, not yet announced, that would take millions of acres out of public land and give them to private interests—a complete reversal of the Roosevelt agenda. The best forest rangers were tempted to leave. "The spirit of the young men in the service is kept alive only by the ideals of leaders in forestry and the optimism from youth," wrote one forest supervisor. "But there must be a living wage."

They would get no help from Congress. Pinchot pleaded with the president to take on the enemies of the Forest Service. In desperation, Pinchot again paid some ranger expenses with money from his own pocket. But even a man as rich as Pinchot could not fund the service on his own. And Taft, wincing at conflict as someone blinking in the dawn sunlight, did not want to go after Heyburn or the Speaker of the House. "He is an amiable man," said one senator, referring to the new president, "completely surrounded by men who know what they want."

Less than a year into Taft's presidency, a scandal engulfed Pinchot's nemesis, Ballinger; it would split the Republican Party. The interior secretary, whose duty was to oversee an empire of public land on behalf of the American people, had once backed a syndicate as it tried to take control of coal in a part of Alaska that was later added to the Chugach National Forest. When a federal official complained that the coal deal was a fraud, like one of the homesteading schemes of the timber industry, Ballinger fired the whistleblower rather than move against the syndicate. The fired official went public, creating a furor — page-one stories for nearly a year. Pinchot called Ballinger a crook and urged the president to get rid of him. Taft advised the forester to lie low, and promised that he would look into the matter and listen to all sides. Privately, he fumed, and seemed flummoxed. He backed Ballinger, and he did not know what to do with Pinchot, the most public link to Roosevelt. "He is a good deal of a radical and a good deal of a crank," Taft said of Pinchot in a letter to his brother. "Still, I'm glad to have him in my administration."

Beyond the Alaska coal deal, Ballinger was now showing his true colors — as a traitor to the progressives, Pinchot believed. "You chaps who are in favor of this conservation program are all wrong," Ballinger said in a speech. "You are hindering the development of the West. In my opinion, the proper course is to divide it up among the big corporations and let the people who know how to make money out of it get the benefits of the circulation of money." This was what Pinchot was up against, what the saintly Muir could never understand: the wolves were at the door, working with the president to undo all that Roosevelt had accomplished. They wanted to hand public lands over to the very people Roosevelt and Pinchot had battled for the past decade.

Defying Taft, Pinchot took his case to the public. But first he touched home and tried to rally his base. In the summer of 1909, he met as usual with a large group of students from the School of Forestry at Yale, encamped at the Pinchot family estate of Grey Towers. They spent their nights in tents, but often were invited to cross the moat surrounding the castle and share dinner with the Chief inside the forty-two-room chateau. After dinner, it was songs around the piano or speeches in front of a huge bonfire outside. Pinchot told the young foresters that his fight was their fight — a battle for the land itself, and the future. Posing with the students, Pinchot looked grim, gaunt, grey, and out of place with a bow tie on a hot summer's eve. He tried to summon Laura from the mists, but the spirit was absent.

Then he went west for a series of incendiary speeches, vowing not to quit and urging Americans to stand on behalf of their birth-right. Nothing brightened his mood like a battle, and he fed off the energy of westerners who shared his views. In Spokane, Pinchot and Ballinger found themselves in the same room before a large gathering of farmers dependent on government irrigation. The audience members sat on their hands for Ballinger but gave Pinchot a five-minute standing ovation. These people were his "Little Men," and they loved him — or so he felt.

"The great oppressive trusts exist because of subservient law-makers," he told the farmers in Spokane. It was a direct slap at Ballinger, seated a few feet away, and at Heyburn. "I stand for the Roosevelt policies because they set the common good of all of us above the private gain of some of us," he said. The speech landed him, again, on front pages of newspapers across the nation. It was conflict! Defiance! The feud was on! Furious, Taft called the for-ester to the woodshed at a meeting in Salt Lake City. Their face-off was tense, precisely the kind of confrontation that Taft could not stomach. Pinchot gave little ground, telling the president he had "no confidence" in the interior secretary. And, he vowed, he would not resign. Now Pinchot was truly on his own. He knew he was in-subordinate, and was surprised Taft did not fire him on the spot.

"As President, he should never have approved my aggressive and defiant statement," Pinchot wrote later. "And as a man he was in honor and in duty bound to stick to his word, given to T.R. in my presence." But Taft did not have the nerve to fire him. Fresh stories were breaking every day on the Ballinger affair, and it would look bad to ax the face of Roosevelt's conservation policies at the very time when Taft was being accused of caving in to the trusts. "Are the Guggenheims in Charge of the Department of Interior?" was a *Collier's* headline.

The scandal threatened to make Taft a one-term president. There was a stirring among progressive Republicans, called Insurgents, of turning against Taft—very early in his term for a party mutiny. Pinchot appeared to have the public, or at least the press, on his side. Taft was portrayed as a bulbous buffoon, easily manipulated. There were snide remarks about the huge new bathtub he had installed in the White House; it was said he got stuck in the old one. Consuming meals of roast turkey and lobster, ham, cakes and pudding, a hefty steak for breakfast every morning, and salted almonds at all times, he ballooned beyond the 330-pound mark, and his shirt buttons strained on his vest when he sat down. He fell asleep in the middle of a meeting with Cannon, snoring loudly, to the Speaker's annoyance.

What Pinchot had going for him, in addition to sympathetic press coverage, were his Little G.P.s—"probably the best-trained body of men and women in the government today," as the *New York Times* noted in a story about his legacy in the heat of the controversy. "Wherever you find a Forest Service man or woman, you find a devoted believer in Gifford Pinchot. He is the Little Father of his people and they know it and will show it by the most faithful and loyal service that Uncle Sam gets from any of his employees." But the *Times* warned Pinchot to be careful, and to back off, or he would soon find himself out of power.

"Mr. Gifford Pinchot, the savior of the country's forests, is wrong," the paper concluded. "Unless he rights himself speedily, he may cease to become a member of Mr Taft's administration, despite his great services to the Nation."

Exhausted after more speeches similar to his exhortation in Spokane, Pinchot took refuge on a little island off the coast of southern California. At the height of the biggest battle of his public life, he decided to disappear for a few days, perhaps to summon Laura, to be alone with nature and in pursuit of a big fish. He missed T.R. and wished that he were in Africa with him. "We have fallen back down the hill you led us up," he wrote to Roosevelt, who was then in Khartoum. "There is general belief that the special interests are once more substantially in full control of both Congress and the Administration."

On a day infused with the winter sun of California, Pinchot took a fishing rod and a small skiff to the sea. He trolled most of the morning, ate a packed lunch, and continued through the afternoon. A few hours before the sun set, his line snapped taut, the reel disengaged, and Pinchot was jolted to one side of the skiff. Fish on! The swells of the Pacific rolled in, rocking his small craft. He fought and reeled, tugging and giving back much of the line to the fish. Near dusk, his arms ached and his back was stiff but the fish was nowhere near to being landed. At one point, his line went briefly slack, and the surface water broke with a loud splash. He saw then that he had hooked a man-size marlin. It leapt well above the surface, a stirring encounter. "High out of the water sprang this splendid creature," Pinchot wrote, "his big eye staring as he rose, till the impression of beauty and lithe power was enough to make a man's heart sing with him. It was a moment to be remembered for a lifetime." Forester and fish fought for two and a half hours. Near the end, Pinchot was eight miles from land, and it was dark. At last he brought the fish close enough to spear and haul it into the boat. The marlin weighed 168 pounds.

Back in Washington for the new year, Pinchot geared up for congressional hearings on the Ballinger affair. The story dominated the news and preoccupied the Taft administration. Pinchot was rested and ready for battle; he not only felt renewed, he felt more than ever that the country was with him. Taft could not bear the thought of another year with a chief forester in unbridled defiance. And then Pinchot pushed him to the edge. He arranged for a letter to be read in Congress that was openly critical of the president, saying his boss had misinterpreted the facts in the Ballinger imbroglio. The next day's headlines—"Forester's Letter Creates Sensation" was typical—foretold the logical outcome. On January 7, 1910, just as Pinchot was leaving the family home on Rhode Island Avenue to go to a dinner party, he was approached by a messenger with an envelope, a long, formal letter from the president. Pinchot, dressed in evening clothes, silk hat in hand, hastily read it. He turned to his mother.

"I'm fired."

"Hurrah!" she replied, clearly relieved.

In his letter, Taft wrote, "By your own conduct you have betrayed your usefulness as a helpful subordinate of the government."

For Pinchot's enemies, the firing was received like news of a large inheritance from a rich uncle. Syndicates that fought for free grazing on millions of acres of public land were holding a national meeting in Denver at the time. They had battled Pinchot for nearly a decade. In the forests of Colorado and Arizona, they ran rangers out of the woods, hiring killers in some cases to threaten their lives. When that didn't work, they tried to bribe the Little G.P.s, reasoning that it was still cheaper to pay off a ranger than pay a grazing fee. The convention was interrupted with a bulletin, read from the podium: Pinchot is gone! Great cheering and whistling broke out, lasting several minutes.

It took a few weeks for the news to reach Roosevelt in Africa. "We have just heard by runner that you have been removed," he wrote to Pinchot. "I cannot believe it. I do not know any man in public life who has rendered quite the service you have rendered; and it seems to me absolutely impossible that there can be any truth in this statement. But of course it makes me very uneasy." With time to reflect, Roosevelt was more than uneasy. He was angry. Pinchot, he said in his letter, was a fighter who stood for good causes. Taft was jelly. "You were the leader among all the men in public office—and the aggressive, hard-hitting leader—of all the forces struggling for conservation," he said in his letter to Pinchot. He had started to think of Taft as a "puzzlewit," as he put it later, and wondered if he had made a terrible mistake in choosing him. Yes, Pinchot, his friend since they boxed together in Albany, the man with whom he built the conservation dream from scratch, had all but

asked to be fired. And no doubt Pinchot could be too zealous, too eager for a fight, too full of his own self-righteousness. A *pain!* But for
Roosevelt, the forester always had a special place: Gifford Pinchot,
he told a friend, was the true keeper of his conscience.

When Pinchot arrived at Forest Service headquarters the day after his firing, some rangers were weeping. Others expected him to
bivouac inside this fortress of foresters, forcing Taft to remove him
at the barrel end of a gun. Pinchot acted the gentleman. First he met
with top associates and urged them to stay on and fight for the life
of the Forest Service. "You are engaged in a piece of work that lies
at the foundation of the new patriotism of conservation and equal
opportunity," he told them. "You are creating a point of view that
will in the end control this and all other nations." Next he spoke to
a larger group, rank-and-file forest rangers, black and white, jani-
tors and executive assistants, about three hundred people in all, a
very boisterous, defiant crowd. When Pinchot started to talk, the
ovation was so loud and sustained that passersby outside thought an
entire government agency was in revolt. "Don't let the spirit of the
service decline one-half inch," Pinchot said. "Stay in the service.
Stick to the work."

In the northern Rockies, the late winter of 1910 was one for the records. Storm after storm rolled out of the Gulf of Alaska, over the
mountain hurdles in the western Pacific Northwest, and into the
Bitterroots. Furious blizzards dumped snow over the whole range,
from the lowest valleys to the highest peaks, sometimes a foot a day.
The towns of Wallace and Grand Forks, Taft and Avery, continued
their honky-tonk ways, their squeals muffled by heavy snow. Ten
feet of it covered the valley where Wallace was built.

In late February, the weather warmed, and rain and higher temperatures made the snow heavy and prone to movement. A tug of
gravity, a shrug and a roar, brought the snow down. The avalanche
was loud enough that it shattered windows in a school hundreds of
feet away. The slide rolled over a big rooming house, killing a fam-

ily and several boarders. The Forest Service was called to the rescue. The rangers came and dug out the house buried by snow. To the west, in the Cascades, trains were smothered and swept away in another slide, killing dozens of people. But in early spring came a dramatic change, as if a switch had been turned off. Bluebird days were the rule.

Where was the spring rain? The snow melted early, all of it. Creeks withered and stilled, the forest leathered and baked. Pine needles and twigs on the floor cracked underfoot, dry as sun-crisped bread chips. The shiny cars of the Milwaukee Road screamed through the heart of the Bitterroots on the way to Puget Sound for loads of silk, making another generation of Rockefellers rich on a gamble that looked as if it was going to pay off big. Whenever the forest supervisors, Koch in Missoula and Weigle in Wallace, heard whistles in the woods they thought of showers of sparks trailing the trains and landing in a very dry public forest.

They had other concerns, of course. With the founder ousted, the Forest Service was in extreme peril. "We used to call you our Greek god," a Forest Service colleague wrote to Pinchot. "None of us had any idea how much of Jove's thunder there really was in you, but I assure you that you have made us proud of you time and again. We have grown to like your thunder and its loudness, too, because that has always told us the lightning has struck something!" The Little G.P.s felt orphaned and glum without the Chief. "I feel as if attending a funeral," one regional forester wrote of an upcoming meeting. "I hope somebody in Congress can be brought to see the other side of the shield." Another forester wrote a memo summarizing "the complete demoralization of the service" and a "widespread state of unrest." Senator Heyburn and others were closing in for the kill, backed by newspaper owners who had long hated the Forest Service and Roosevelt's idea of land preservation. "It is criminal folly to preserve the forests merely to placate Gifford Pinchot," one newspaper, a mouthpiece for the corrupt Senator Clark, had editorialized on the front page. The national forests "are an expensive and useless burden to the public," another paper wrote that summer, adding that "this Pinchot troop of foresters now infesting the West should be called in, paid off, and abolished. If they are not a nuisance, they are of no practical use."

And then smoke started to fill the woods. There had been no rain since early spring, a drought worse than any in nearly a generation's time. Typically, mornings were windless. In the afternoons, parts of the sky darkened with the formation of thunderheads, followed by lightning strikes and claps of thunder echoing through the canyons—dry storms, all sound and fury from the sky, but no water. It did not take much for these electric forks to light the forests. Greeley, the northern Rockies supervisor, soon had his hands full dispatching men to put out numerous spot blazes, as they were called. This became all part of a day's work—a dozen men with shovels dashing after an acre or two on fire, trying to corral the blaze before dark. By midsummer, lightning-sparked fires were breaking out every day: a pile of brush here, a hillside of pine there, a meadow of heat-withered grass smoking through a week. It was a nuisance and wearing, but the rangers took to it stoically. If this was the cost of keeping the Great Crusade alive, so be it. But they were afraid, many of them, for the first time since joining the service. A single question dominated talk: What if it all blows up?

PART II

What They Lost

6

Summer of Smoke

U P AT FIRST LIGHT on the half-lidded side of 5 A.M., Ed Pulaski grabbed his shield, his gun, his knife, his compass, and his leather-bound book of notations, laced his tattered boots, packed some food, and set out for another day of fire patrol. Every morning in July 1910 dawned with smoke to chase. Pulaski would round up a small crew of civilian firefighters, find the blaze, then try to contain it within a hand-dug perimeter. It was very primitive and wearing — dig and snuff, dig and snuff — swatting firebrands, struggling for footing on steep slopes, the picks and shovels snagging on roots, the crew coughing on dust and haze, their clothes crusted with sweat-sticky grime.

Just now, in the dim light before most of Wallace began to stir, drunks staggered home to bed and miners loaded with dynamite trundled off to extract silver from inside the mountains. Even during the longest days of the year, the sun did not find the town, a triangle set in a deep crease of the mountains, until well into the morning. At times Pulaski could imagine the valley before the railroads, mines, and sawmills — the way the South Fork of the Coeur d'Alene River cut through the mountains on its meander west, the blue-green rise and fold of the forests, summits of salt-and-pepper granite holding the alpenglow at day's end. Though he was not a

Little G.P., never knighted at Yale or the Pinchot castle of Grey
Towers, and not one of the original "forest arrangers" who had
drawn the boundaries, he shared the ousted Chief's love of the High
Lonesome as it once was—empty, wild, unpredictable. Some nights
in open meadows he could see Halley's comet streaking across the
sky, with its blaze and tail of light that made so many people remember 1910 as a year of wonder—and fear.

Pulaski had gone west on his own as a teenager, rode horseback over country still in the hands of Indian people, and slept on
ground never touched by a fellow human. Now the conveniences
of early-twentieth-century America had found the isolation of Pulaski's home. Backfiring, stuck-in-the-mud Model T's were all over
town, causing trouble. "Automobiles—a Menace," one headline had
it. Many families had a telephone, which they used for six calls a day
on average, the overhead lines cluttering the sky. The river close to
town was a paradise lost, a wasteland of mine tailings, tree stumps,
discarded barrels, and assorted bits of garbage, from rusted tin cans
to torn scraps of clothing. Pulaski was considered a local, a man of
the people, but he was blunt and seldom diplomatic at a time when
the Forest Service needed every friend it could get. At a Chamber of
Commerce luncheon he was asked what measures were necessary to
prevent thoughtless visitors from setting the woods on fire.

"None," Pulaski answered. The room went cold. "The residents of *this* city have less respect for the forest fire laws and are
more trouble than any tourists." That was not what the bankers,
shopkeepers, saloon owners, and mine operators of Wallace, Idaho,
wanted to hear from their public servant.

But Ed Pulaski was at an age where he didn't care what people
thought about him. Ten years earlier, when he tried to enlist in the
Spanish-American War, the Army told him he wasn't needed. Too
old, even then. He shrugged it off, returning to odd jobs, cutting
railroad ties, packing supplies for store owners, working shifts at
the mills, crafting tools in his little blacksmith shop. He had been
hired by the Forest Service in 1908. Listing his qualifications to be a

ranger, he cited practical skills: "Built house and barn at Montgomery Creek. Worked in woods in Owyhee Mountains." Most rangers were young; he was in his forties. At six foot three, with rugged good looks, he was compared, later, to Gary Cooper in earnest middle age. They were college kids, these rangers taking up posts in the Rocky Mountains; Pulaski had dropped out of school at sixteen, making his way west with pockets stuffed full of letters that a wandering uncle had written years before about opportunities in the big land. This West was magical, full of chance—the young Pulaski had only to reach into his pocket for one of the letters, his reinforcement when he felt low. Other foresters tended to be single men; Pulaski was on his second marriage by the time he was hired. Other rangers sometimes made literary allusions, scientific references, or political observations in their reports. Pulaski wrote elliptical, meat-and-potatoes prose, first in his four-by-six-inch book—stamped E. G. PULASKI, U.S.F.S. on the outside—and then more formal notes to his supervisor in Wallace, Bill Weigle. In two years as a ranger, he had built trails, hung telephone lines, constructed cabins, and smothered numerous small fires, often with nothing but shovel and ax.

What Pulaski lacked in formal forestry training he made up for with practical knowledge of the woods. Never cut cottonwood for firewood: the ax will twist up and bind like a comb in witch hair. You can always tell a grand fir, growing into three centuries, by that Christmas tree fragrance, and the Indians relied on gum pinched from the tree's resin blisters for healing. Those scrubby little Pacific yew trees most everyone overlooked—same thing, healing powers. A slice of yew made a great archery bow or canoe paddle as well. And on summer afternoons when warm air rises from the valleys and heated slopes, the sky may look as clear as infinity itself, but it can quickly turn on you. The air cools as it rises, forms thunderheads, and inside those clouds, positive charges collide with negative charges. When it doesn't produce any rain, what follows is trouble.

• • •

By July 1910, Pulaski was feeling worn down by the stale hot breath of summer and the constant little flareups—fires started by coal-burning trains, fires started by mine operators, fires sparked by lightning. There hung in the air that summer a personal question of just how long he could continue humping over brush and loose rock in the Bitterroots, pursuing flame fourteen hours a day.

The woods had been sylvan and lovely during Pulaski's first summers married to Emma, his second wife. He built a house in Wallace with a broad porch and a second-story dormer, snug against the mountain walls that rose so sharply from town. In the center of Wallace, four-story buildings of brick and stone were rising, and no fire would ever penetrate their walls, the owners boasted. Pulaski had to make do with planks and the polish of good paint; it was all he could afford. He knew he wasn't going anywhere on a salary of $80 a month. He wasn't a full ranger—he was an *assistant*—and if the Little G.P.s wanted to put him in his place, they had only to remind him of that. After so many false starts, Pulaski was at a stage in life where he wasn't going to find his own mother lode in the valley that had made so many other men rich; a government job in the woods was just fine.

That summer, Pulaski could not get over how quickly the green had been bled out of the Bitterroots. The heat, the domino of days without rain—everyone remarked on how strangely dry it was. The combined rainfall for June and July was not even one-tenth of an inch, a mere whisper of rain. The wind sucked moisture from the forest, blowing hard in the afternoons, leaving all that standing timber as if it was just hung out to dry. Balsamroot, blossoming big butter-colored flowers in late spring, had wilted early; the mountain meadows, the puffy white balls of beargrass, the sprightly lupine and Indian paintbrush—all had faded quickly. Spring was so easy, so warm, no rain or chill. And then summer came without advance notice, wildfires in April! Nobody had seen that before. By late July, the big flume at the edge of Wallace, source of the town's drinking water, still carried a clear trickle of runoff down from the mountains, but it was a withered little spray, barely enough to slake the town's thirst.

Fire was on everybody's mind. When? How big? How bad? Bill Weigle could not walk the streets of Wallace without some miner, railroad boss, or timberman stopping him with a poke in the chest: *What happens if the woods near town catch fire, Bill? Are we going to be trapped here?* They had their investments now, their hold on the forest. And yet few of these people in the woods or in town were willing to lend a hand to help the Forest Service defend the land. Leave it up to the green rangers, they said with a shrug. Hadn't they promised to protect the woods? Weigle would go into a lunch counter at midday, make a few jokes and choke down a meal, then snap his suspenders a few times in a cajoling effort before dozens of able-bodied men. The red-headed ranger gave his talk: *The situation is urgent, boys. We need to save Wallace, not just the woods outside of town.* He left with nothing to show. Nothing! Not a man. "While there are plenty of idle men in Wallace or vicinity, they refuse to accept work of any kind," he told reporters in late July.

So when Weigle sent a message to Pulaski, saying he needed him to abandon one fire and turn his attention to another one, a gnarly little blaze threatening someone's private clutter, it was an insult. Enough! Rangers were openly suspicious of these fires: they heard numerous stories that the blazes had been deliberately set—as a way to clear land, to get title, to ensure that a patch of woods not remain for long as part of Roosevelt's reserves.

Truth be told, some rangers already had their fill of these button-popping towns and their dirty, clanking, pushy timber and mining start-ups in the mountains. Five years into the formal foundation of the Forest Service, many still feared for their lives. A ranger had been killed by a hunter in Montana in 1907; the killer said he mistook the forester for a deer, which nobody in the service believed. "We never knew when a bullet might meet us in a thicket or on the trail," Joe Halm recalled. He was a rookie ranger, just out of Washington State College in Pullman, paired with Pulaski for his first

year on the job. Adding insult, was what happened over the ridge
in Avery, where folks had just taken down Gifford Pinchot's name
on the town, about the same time the Chief was fired. That was the
ultimate snub, and a power grab too. The eastern rich kids working for Rockefeller's railroad, the Kelley brothers and their buddies,
made it clear they did not need the piddly-ass United States Forest
Service. Spike Kelley had his mansion on the St. Joe, his Japanese
servants, his new bride, and all the fine antiques that arrived on the
Milwaukee Road. Up above the St. Joe Valley, nestled amid thick
woods where the towns of Taft and Grand Forks squatted, saloons
were roaring again, as if the bust that Supervisor Weigle had put together never happened. It was summer, peak season, and thousands
of people were in the mountains for one reason: to squeeze money
from the place as quickly as they could push themselves. It was the
people's forest, by God, just as Gifford Pinchot said, and folks intended to get something while the getting was good.

"The will to grow was everywhere written large, and to grow
at no matter what or whose expense," Henry James wrote of a decade when people rushed to fill the last of the nation's empty places.
In barely a hundred years' time, the United States had gone from a
fledgling set of former colonies with 2.9 million people to an ocean-
to-ocean country of 91 million. This first decade of the twentieth
century exceeded all others for the volume of new people, the nation adding 16 million residents to its forty-six states and two territories by decade's end. Passed over for years, no states grew faster
during this spurt than Idaho and Washington. Their populations
doubled in less than a decade. Idaho went from 162,000 to 325,000,
and the biggest city in the region, Seattle, tripled—from 80,000 to
240,000.

Pulaski told his boss he would try to get to the mine and their
little fire, but he was tired to the bone, reluctant to start fresh on another flareup. "I have about all the fires I want for a day or two,"
Pulaski wrote to Weigle, not trying to disguise his disgust.

As it was, conditions were so dry and hot that Pulaski could never really leave one fire to tend another. A ranger could feel it: the woods wanted to burn. The great challenge of the summer was to hold down the fires until the fall rains came to close out the combustible season. August looked as though it was going to be an eternity. Time and again, Pulaski had to circle back to make sure a patch of ground he had worked over did not reignite. These little fires would smolder for days, only to be kick-started anew by a sneeze of wind. The towns in the Bitterroots had telephones and telegraphs, after the rangers had spent the spring of 1910 stringing wire between Avery, Grand Forks, Taft, Wallace, and other towns. But outside the villages, communication was primitive. Foresters often went days without contact.

Unlike the transients in town, the Pulaskis weren't planning to go anywhere when the summer ended. They liked the valley in north Idaho, and could see spending the rest of their lives there, maybe downriver from Wallace, away from the racket of mining and logging. On soft Sunday afternoons in the wild upper reaches of the St. Joe, Emma would wash her hair and lie in the sun while her husband and his dog hunted birds. Once she was taking a nap on the grassy bank of the river when a group of natives came upon her. The Indians startled Emma, scaring her to death. When Pulaski returned, he had a good laugh over his wife's fear. He had friends among the Coeur d'Alene tribe. The St. Joe served as summer fishing camps for them, he explained; they were looking for big bull trout—seven pounds or more—that moved upstream when the weather got hot. The Indians could remember years when their homeland caught fire; sometimes they set blazes themselves to clear a patch of land. Cresting the ridge not far from here, a hundred or so years earlier, Lewis and Clark saw land that had been burned deliberately to open up the country, and the Indians entertained them at night by setting fire to tall trees.

This year, the Indians' world had been taken away from them: their 600,000-acre reservation, to the west of the Idaho panhandle's national forests, had been opened to settlement by Presi-

dent Taft. The Coeur d'Alenes were a Salish-speaking people, the
Schitsu'umsh—the Ones That Were Found Here. French trappers
had given them another name, Heart of the Awl—Coeur d'Alène
—because they had a reputation for hard bargaining. Early on,
the Indians had welcomed black-robed Jesuits into their land, and
a mission had been established at the mouth of the St. Joe. The
Jesuits showed them how to grow lowland crops, to supplement a
diet of camas and bitterroot bulbs, deer, elk, birds, and huckleberries
with farming. The tribe had been promised, by treaty in 1887, the
vast headwaters of the Spokane and Clearwater rivers—most of the
Idaho panhandle. But with ten thousand or more new people clawing at the land, and the upstart Milwaukee Road bringing in hundreds by the day, the pressure was too great. "Why are you in such a
hurry?" Chief Joseph of the Nez Perce had wondered as he watched
Idaho and Montana fill with Anglo settlers.

Taft's proclamation meant a fresh bonanza for the settlers in
the twentieth-century West. Indian families would get small individual allotments, most of which were quickly bought by speculators. To everyone else would go the big drainages of the St. Joe
and Coeur d'Alene rivers that bordered the national forests. By May
1910, 167,000 people had registered for a lottery to get a piece of the
newly opened reservation. The selloff was ritualized by three little
Indian girls outfitted in tribal gear who picked names from a big
bowl—the winners getting their choice of land to claim from the
Ones That Were Found Here.

To the Forest Service, the latest homesteaders from the Indian
lottery only added to their headaches—more sourdoughs who didn't
know jack about the woods stumbling around the forests, carving
out their piece. It meant fires from timber clearing; it meant disputes over title and surveys; it meant more scouting, trading, and
speculating of fraudulent homesteads. When the year started, it
looked as though sorting these land disputes would be the primary
task of a strained Forest Service. But by July, everybody was on fire
duty. A few of the Little G.P.s, some of the Indians, and a handful of

old-timers said these woods *needed* fire—could not flourish without
it. Take a look at a stand of lodgepole pine, a veteran of the woods
would try to explain: eighty, ninety, one hundred years old, starting
to show some wear. It'll live another thirty years at most, but the
trees must have fire to carry on the species. The cones stay on limbs,
tight and closed, until the heat of a big fire comes along and opens
them up, starting the next cycle of life again. In that sense, lodgepole was like the Pacific salmon that made their way to the Continental Divide on the Idaho-Montana border—giving it up at death,
in the high Rockies, for the next generation.

On July 26, the night sky over the Bitterroots exploded—not an
isolated thunder boomer or two clapping around the valleys, but a
rolling, continuous, full-throated electrical storm. It sounded like
breaking glass amplified a hundredfold, and could be heard in the
higher reaches of three states. The fireworks spread across the range,
one supercharged bolt after the other. Entire mountain flanks came
to life with the pulsing skeletal arms of the storm, shooting down
crooked until they hit a big rock outcrop or grounded into the blunt
edge of a summit.

 The next day, hundreds of wildfires were reported to Supervisor Weigle. And that was in the Coeur d'Alene alone. There were
twenty-one other national forests in the northern Rockies region,
and they all had fires. Glacier National Park was burning. The Cabinets, north in Montana, were ablaze. Slopes above Priest Lake had
been torched. The Kaniksu National Forest, in Washington near
the Canadian border, burned out of control. Same with the Pend
Oreille, the Kootenai. The Lolo, under the watch of young Elers
Koch, was so choked with flame the fires were visible from Missoula, causing a stir in the town. South in the Clearwater drainage,
along either side of the wild and tricky Lochsa, and farther south
around the River of No Return—fires all around. Most of the land
was roadless, inaccessible by horse, vast and burning. Regional Forester Greeley sent a high alert out to his supervisors.

"Strengthen the patrol. Retain a strong guard. Keep on hand a strong force of experienced firefighters who can be brought together quickly and relied upon to do good work."

A few days later, he wired them again, ramping up the orders: Start looking for men, anywhere you can find them. Scour the mines, the logging camps, the hiring halls. Round up horses, mules, and supplies. Find cooks, horsemen, ditch diggers, packers, sawyers. The Forest Service may have been demoralized, defunded, adrift, and mourning the loss of its founder, but it was determined to save a big part of what had been set aside during the Great Crusade. The problem was, forest supervisors didn't have the money to pay for all these emergency services. And the men they did have knew little about fighting big fires. Could they raise an army on a promise, from communities where they were not liked, not trusted, ridiculed?

"I will be responsible for finding the necessary funds," Greeley wrote his rangers. He had never seen the woods so ready to explode. Low humidity, always a key indicator, "had dropped to the level of the Mojave Desert," Greeley noted.

The newspapers attacked the Forest Service again. The one thing it was supposed to be good for was fire protection, and here it did not seem up to the task. "The present fires are the first severe test to which Mr. Roosevelt's green rangers have been put and it clearly indicates that something is radically wrong," one paper said. People had no respect for a ranger. "They evade him, disobey him, play jokes on him. Probably he is a good-natured college boy who got his job through a pull, or is riding the reserve for his health and the incidental federal vouchers. It's a gay life, that of many of these foresters—until the fire starts." Another paper urged President Taft to "abolish the forester and put the soldier in charge of the timber wealth."

Smoke penetrated Wallace for the first time, and with it came a whiff of real fear, a quickening of the collective pulse. How were these rangers going to keep the town from catching fire? Did the Forest Service have a plan? A clue? Supervisor Weigle had scrambled to put a couple of things in motion even before he got Greeley's orders. Working with the mayor, fire chief, and police, he arranged for a general evacuation by train. The exodus would start when an alarm was sounded by Weigle, time to be determined. But people wondered about the routes in and out of town. Which way should the evacuation trains go, east or west? The wrong decision could lead into the heart of a fire.

Overall, the job of keeping fire from stomping Wallace fell to big Ed Pulaski. He knew the region better than anyone and could put a crew to task quicker than most. Some of the rangers, the Little G.P.s, didn't know what they would do with a troop of seasonal firefighters. Where would they sleep, how would they feed them, what was the plan of attack?

"Just bed them down anywhere," Pulaski told a fellow ranger. "The country's all vacant." The government would try to rustle up two hundred men for Pulaski, and if it wasn't enough, maybe the military could be brought in to help. But with two hundred men he should have sufficient force, it was thought, to knock down a string of fires not far from Wallace, a row of nasty flames, small but intense, whipped up by the big electrical storm of July 26. It would take a few days, maybe a week at most, to round up his crew — time enough to prepare for one big battle.

7

Men, Men, Men!

ELERS KOCH WENT into the saloons and sex cribs of Taft, Montana, without warrants or cuffs. This time he had his hand out, begging for help. As supervisor of the Lolo, he needed firefighters, following Greeley's order. He would take almost anyone: people without experience in the outdoors, immigrants from all countries, strong women for logistical chores. In Taft now, as in Wallace fifty miles to the west, smoke snaked into the bars and rooming houses, not yet heavy, but it didn't go away. People slept with it, ate with it, woke up to it, never quite got used to it. The sunrises were clouded by a veil of smoke; the sunsets were blood red.

After the electrical storm of July 26, 1910, nearly a thousand fires raged in the northern Rockies. This snapping horsetail of blazes was bigger than anything nature had yet thrown at the young Forest Service. If every ranger in all twenty-two national forests in the district were put on the fires, it would not be enough. Not by any stretch. The Forest Service needed at least five thousand people, in the most recent estimate of Bill Greeley, the regional forester—and maybe double that amount.

Although Greeley knew he didn't have the money to protect many areas, he acted as if he did. His first job, he told other rangers, was to save the people's land. Congress would surely reimburse him. Glacier Park, on the northern border of Montana, was ablaze when

Greeley arrived for a look, the fire scaring tourists and prompting many frightened letters and cards back east. To those who saw the harried Forest Service as a backward parade, all brass and fuss but no progress, Greeley tried to explain the strategy, such as it was. "The method most commonly and most successfully used is called backfiring," he told reporters. "This is fighting fire with fire and this is the way it is done: a trail is cut across a part of the fire, be-tween it and the direction toward which the wind is blowing—that is, on the leeward side of the fire. This trail cut right down to the mineral soil, and then fires are started at short distances from each other on the windward side of the trail, that is on the side toward the forest fire."

To many, it sounded counterintuitive. Start a fire to kill a fire? What did these soft-handed Yalies know about a burn running up a steep slope in Montana? What they knew, of course, was informed by Pinchot's belief that man could control fire. After all, the agency had "proved" that it could control wildfire, as Roosevelt had writ-ten in that early assessment, with satisfaction. Such an assertion did not seem out of place in a year when headlines proclaimed, "Cure for Cancer Is Found" and "Experts Declare Bald Heads Show Brains." A car had driven at sixty miles an hour in 1910, for more than twenty miles nonstop, and the government would soon double its fleet of airplanes—from two to four.

They had been lucky, the rangers now realized, that the first years of the Forest Service were largely free of big fires. This had allowed them time to fall in love with the land, to get acquainted with its storms and quiet periods, its seasonal quirks, to realize the enormity of what Pinchot and Roosevelt had entrusted to them. Most rangers had never been on a war footing, never looked up at columns of dark smoke and felt their throats tighten, never been asked to organize from scratch hundreds of men to march into a wall of flame-hissing trees. Supervisor Koch, the youngest of the Little G.P.s in charge of his own forests, felt protective about his five million or so acres, even proprietary. He understood—as Pinchot had preached on many nights at the family mansion, as Roosevelt had sermonized in his epistles on the outdoor life—that Americans needed wilderness to be fully alive. Needed it this year, as people poured into cities back east already saturated with humanity's opportunity refugees.

Overseeing three national forests was everything Koch wanted. After returning home to Montana, he had met a dark-haired woman from the old country, a Dane named Gerda Heiberg-Jurgensen, on a postgraduate visit. A friend of Scandinavian monarchs and other elites, she left a life of European sophistication to become a forester's wife in the Montana wilds. Koch considered her a full partner: she joined him on horseback, riding the High Lonesome, cleaning fish, sleeping many nights on hard ground. The first summer of her life with Koch, in fact, was spent in a Forest Service teepee, nine feet by nine feet, on the floor of the forest. With a broad floppy hat, knickers, and knee-high boots, she moved through the pathless expanse of the Lolo like a native.

They made a home in Missoula near a field of bunchgrass for Koch to graze his three horses. Any Anglo with an open mind could see why the Salishan natives had cherished this broad valley where Missoula was built, where three mighty rivers converged under mountains of thick forests, a temperate climate most of the year. The streets were mud in the spring and dust in the summer, but indoors, the Koch home was stocked with artwork and quilted pillows from Copenhagen, with a library heavy on poetry and history books. Koch was a Rudyard Kipling fan; he memorized long verse passages and recited them to pass the days in the Rockies. He also liked Robert Browning, and one of his favorites was:

> *Oh, the wild joys of living! the leaping from rock up to rock,*
> *The strong rending of boughs from the fir tree, the cool silver shock*
> *Of the plunge in a pool's living water . . .*

Koch was eager to apply all that he learned at Yale and the school of Gifford Pinchot to the land beneath the big sky. But early on, he found he had more pressing concerns: his Lolo National Forest was a frontier. The shortage of tools to fight fires had become the subject of can-you-top-this tales. When Koch complained about his lack of shovels and picks in the Lolo, Weigle countered that he had but two crosscut saws to keep fires from burning the town of Avery. Koch certainly had the bawdiest of towns, for Taft at one time had nearly 500 prostitutes among its 2,500 people, in the estimate of a journalist, and 30 saloons. By contrast, there was just a single drug-store and one grocery outlet. The hospital was portable, subject to the railroad's need to keep men patched up and vertical. One of the current patients was a man with a bullet lodged in his tongue. He'd been in a gunfight at a card table and had killed the player across from him, but not before the deceased got off a single shot through the chin. Koch had tried to keep his distance from the town, a fes-tering sinkhole in the middle of his national forest.

One of his first hires was Frank Haun, a seasoned woodsman, tough as bark, with intimate knowledge of the outdoors, but with a bit less caution than the college-trained Koch. Patrolling the woods one day, Koch and Haun stumbled upon a huge cache of liquor — cases of bourbon, Scotch, champagne, and rye, enough to supply a small town. Haun wanted to have a closer look, but Koch held him back.

"We better move on," Koch said. The decision probably saved their lives, for Koch heard later that a lookout, his rifle trained on the forest rangers, had kept guard over the cache with orders to shoot anyone who came near it.

Recruiting in the string of towns downslope from Taft, Koch found that people would rather chip away at a silver vein for twelve hours a day than go into the woods and stomp smoke. The money from the Forest Service was not bad, especially for someone out of work. In 1910, the average American wage earner took home $13 for a sixty-hour week. Koch was authorized to pay 25 cents an hour, so that same sixty-hour week, which most people worked, could bring $15. He had Greeley's promise that the government would back its word with cash, eventually. What kept men from signing up was fear of the unknown. They knew about danger in the mines. They knew about felling trees or laying railroad ties or blasting tunnels in the rock with explosives. But fire—that was a mystery predator in this part of the world.

In Missoula, scraping the bottom of the barrel, Koch grabbed anybody who disembarked from the train. At least half of the newcomers were drunk on arrival, he reported, and had no firm plans. But if a man stood upright in the morning light and had a blanket to call his own, Koch would put him in service to Gifford Pinchot's agency.

"Got a bed?" he asked one greenhorn.

"Yep."

"Bring it."

He noticed during his first days with these novice crews that they lacked basic outdoor common sense. "Punks, stew bums and pool hall boys," Koch called them. When they shivered at night, ignorant of ways to keep warm, Koch would make a huge bonfire to comfort his crews. Their talk late into the evening was mostly of the various jails they had known, and rumors of riches still to be found here or there. Many demanded payment up front. But Koch's Lolo forest was tapped out, same as Weigle's Coeur d'Alene.

The Forest Service was buying supplies on credit—food, mules, and axes. Koch did have a little savings of his own, just under $500, money he and Gerda had put away to raise a family. He'd promised her that life in a tent was temporary, and followed up on that when they moved into the fine house in Missoula. They wanted children, educated, with means enough to visit Gerda's relatives in Europe. But the heavier the smoke that settled on Missoula, the more Koch was nudged toward a hard decision. Should he use his own money to pay for fire crews? As one of the original "forest arrangers," Koch had a love of the Lolo that was deep and complicated—like his feelings for Gerda. He'd selected much of this land under Pinchot's guidance, and in that sense he had a bit of immortality, provided he could get through this season of flame.

Up on the front lines, his rangers were crying for help, working in ambient heat well above 100 degrees, trying to beat back flames but losing everything they'd gained whenever the winds picked up in the afternoon. To the east, as smoke settled in Helena and Great Falls around the front range of the Rockies, some rangers complained that they had stopped receiving their regular paychecks. Congress, a year earlier, had given the Forest Service authority to pay firefighters after the fact—basically, hiring on credit in a national emergency. But in practice, funds did not flow from Washington to the burning woods. "I was told there was no money to pay my salary," said one ranger, Albert Cole.

In the first week of August, Koch went down to his bank in Missoula and withdrew his personal savings. Gerda would understand: it was an emergency. He turned to his rangers, Haun, the skilled outdoorsman, and a twenty-two-year-old rookie, Ferdinand A. "Gus" Silcox, the dew of Yale still on him, filled with the gospel of Gifford Pinchot. Koch asked the older ranger and the kid to follow his example. Haun complained some: he was getting on in years and didn't have much to spare. He had a bit of a gut, unusual among the sinewy rangers. Koch poked him, kidded him about his extra load. *C'mon!* Gus Silcox pleaded poverty; he was just out of school, with the smallest of savings accounts. But both men gave in. Even after three years without raises, after Congress had ratcheted down the budget until it was a pittance, after the newspapers of the copper kings and timber barons had called for the Forest Service to be run out of the woods   after all of that, the rangers reached deep into their own pockets to try to save the land.

"Men, men, men! Is the frenzied cry of forest officials," *The Missoulian* reported on the third of August. "The available supply is now almost exhausted, or so it seems."

Finally, all the rangers had left were the jails. Early on, the Forest Service had considered prison labor, but delayed the move, hoping to build its fire lines from other sources. The service also floated a plan to have state legislatures pass emergency laws that required people to assist the rangers when a fire was imminent—essentially a draft, like forced military conscription. But it never got off the ground. The first week of August, Koch and Greeley arranged to get sixty prisoners released from jail in Missoula. That move, a very public release of criminals, started a chain of gossip, feeding a story that the firefighters rounded up by the Forest Service were the scum of the earth—criminals, bums, and foreigners—and should be shunned. Missoula added extra police officers, fearing the newcomers would raise hell in town.

By August 10, what had been one thousand fires was more than double that amount. The rangers sent another round of requests to the hiring halls of the West—to Bozeman and Butte, Denver and Rapid City, Albuquerque and Phoenix, Portland and Seattle. From Butte, several hundred miles to the east, came a trainload of broken miners who had been out of work for months. They were middle-aged, many of them, with bad habits, grumpy and prone to cutting corners. Koch and Weigle took them.

Among those who arrived from Butte was an Irishman, Patrick Grogan, a few months short of his sixtieth birthday. He was a sight when he stepped off the train—jowly, with a bindle of ragged clothes, and his dog. A dog! How could a man like this fight a fire? Grogan said he had done a little bit of everything in Butte: labored in the copper mines, put down railroad track, worked in restaurants. Butte was the most Irish city in America at the time, with more than one in four inhabitants tracing their ancestry to the island across the Atlantic. Many were famine Irish, the sons and daughters of those who had first left County Cork, Limerick, and Galway when a million people starved to death and another million fled their homeland. The stories—of hollow-bellied children with teeth stained green from eating grass, of old men shivering with tin cups outside castle doors, of British authorities turning away food aid from the harbor at Dublin—were ingrained in the Irish who settled in Butte. In the United States, they had been called flannelmouths and compared to apes and savages. How could a wildfire deter them? Grogan needed the money to help his large family back in Butte, more than a dozen children and grandchildren. He and his dog were not in the best of shape, not exactly ready to charge up a steep slope with ax in hand. But he could cook. Cook? *Surely, lad.* That was it, then. A cook in a fire camp was invaluable. Anyone who could feed two hundred people at a sitting, with little more than sacks of potatoes, onions, and sourdough for pancakes, was worth putting on the Forest Service payroll. Grogan was hired on August 6.

That same day, another electrical storm rumbled through the forests. It made the rangers shudder. August was the driest month since 1894. Every clap, every boom brought the potential for something horrible on a grand scale. And by morning, sure enough, the total number of fires had reached 2,500. Even after emptying the saloons, trains, jails, and hiring halls of men, Koch felt that he was not making progress. The Forest Service had less than one man for each fire burning in the northern Rockies. Koch was exasperated: one man per fire!

"For every fire we put out," he told the newspaper in Missoula, "a new one is reported. The rangers have been fighting fires steadily now for 10 days and they are about worn out."

At the summer house he rented in Beverly, Massachusetts, President Taft was immersed in his annual five-week vacation, one that was continually interrupted by the fire alarms out west. Telegrams from the Forest Service, from governors and congressmen, from big timber owners, had grown more pressing with each day of August. Five states had requested federal troops to fight wildfires. They implored him to do something quickly to intercede. Taft's agriculture secretary, James Wilson, who oversaw the Forest Service and had a strained relationship with Pinchot, had just returned from Montana. He feared that the collapse of entire western forests and many towns would happen on his watch. "I was confronted with the problem of either putting out the fires or being directly responsible for what would have been one of the worst disasters in the history of the country," Wilson wrote later.

Taft was in the second year of a troubled presidency, and had become ever more sensitive to the caustic criticism of him. The Great
Postponer, he was called, one of the less cruel nicknames. Pinchot
considered him a traitor to the progressive cause, and said so in public now that he was "freed for the larger fight," as he had told his
mother when Taft fired him in January. Indeed, Pinchot was giddy
in his liberation, full of fight. Taft had become "the accomplice
and the refuge of land-grabbers, water-power grabbers, grabbers of
timber and oil—all of the swarm of big and little thieves," Pinchot wrote. Much of the year had been dominated by congressional
hearings on Pinchot's charges against embattled Interior Secretary
Ballinger, which had grown to a larger rift. During testimony, Ballinger said he had felt duty-bound to thwart some of the Roosevelt-
Pinchot agenda, saying he had acted to stop "certain overzealous
persons from converting the public domain into a national preserve." This confirmed everything Pinchot had suspected of the interior secretary, and he took up the cause on behalf of his beloved
Forest Service and against the anticonservation forces with gusto.

For the most part, the press still sided with Pinchot. They mocked
Taft, with his multiple jowls and walrus mustache, his waddle and
his summer "yachting costume" of white pants and black jacket.
Taft dressed up in silly outfits and planted himself on a deck chair
of his yacht, the *Sylph*, in the morning and took long naps in the afternoon. A highlight of his day was a regular massage. As always, he
took refuge in food. He also suffered from gout, and like most men
in the presidency, seemed to age quickly. Friends noticed the deep
lines in his face, the folds of fat, and they urged him to diet or go
for daily walks. But exercise, he complained, made him moody; he
would rather eat, and say the hell with it.

Always, there was the shadow of Teddy Roosevelt. "When I am
addressed as Mr. President," Taft had said to Roosevelt shortly after the election, "I turn to see whether you are at my elbow." But
for most of 1910, Teddy could not have been farther from the big
man's arm. His trip abroad, now nearing its end, was triumphant,

judging by the speaking invitations, the glowing press from reporters who followed his every move, the letters home about big game
hunted or foreign dignitaries consulted. Privately, he referred to
Taft as a "flubdub," a "floppy-souled creature," and a "fathead."
The sacking of Pinchot had angered him. And as the Ballinger affair dragged on through 1910, Roosevelt came to believe that Taft
had betrayed all that he and Pinchot had started—as evidenced by
Ballinger's testimony and the near gutting of the Forest Service.

At last, Taft could postpone no more. On August 7, he wired his
war secretary, authorizing him to "lend every assistance possible in
suppression of forest fires." The government would send troops, a
total of 2,500, to the front lines of the burning West—an extraordinary commitment, given that the standing Army of the United
States comprised barely 80,000 men. In an era of invention and material expansion, a time that had seen innovations from Marconi's
wireless to telephones in every middle-class neighborhood, many
a well-stuffed parlor evoking the Edwardian Age of comfort, here
was a primitive, timeless battle of man against elemental nature.
It was a war and a reminder that this new country sprawling from
sea to sea was still trying to settle its surroundings. Blue-shirted soldiers armed with rifle magazines and revolvers would be put at the
call of the Forest Service. The rangers were relieved. Weigle said
his Coeur d'Alene would now have sufficient manpower to save the
town of Wallace.

"I'm mighty pleased to hear of the order of President Taft,"
Weigle told reporters. "We need the men."

The call came to the 25th Infantry while it was bivouacked at Fort
George Wright, in stifling barracks on a hill above the river in Spokane. It fell to the infantrymen to be the front line of the troop commitment, though fire duty was a first for the 25th. Part of an all-black
regiment established after the Civil War, these Buffalo Soldiers—so
named by the Indians for their hair—had done much of the government's dirty work while garrisoned in Army ghettos throughout

the West. In Texas, they fought the Comanche and Apache on behalf of white settlers who, in the state's post–Civil War constitution, had banned blacks from full citizenship. In the Dakotas, they were dispatched to clean up lingering problems with the Sioux Nation, whose members had been slaughtered at Wounded Knee. In Idaho, during the labor wars around the turn of the century, the black soldiers were sent to keep guard over militant strikers, on the assumption that white miners would never bond with their black captors. As labor strife spread from Idaho across the West, the 25th Infantry was called on repeatedly to put down civil unrest.

But the soldiers also strung telegraph lines, built roads, and constructed military forts. They were part of the bicycle corps, riding two-wheelers over bad terrain from Fort Missoula to St. Louis as a test. Other black soldiers served as the first park rangers, patrolling Yellowstone and Yosemite well before these reserves had a formal national park service. Using soldiers as rangers was not that much of a stretch: while putting together the Forest Service, Pinchot considered an idea to recruit all of his rangers from West Point. While on duty in California, the Buffalo Soldiers named a grove of giant sequoia trees for Booker T. Washington.

In the summer of 1910, the Negro troops were a curious presence in Spokane, a fast-growing city larded by riches from mining and railroad and timber interests, an hour from the fires by train. The city was undergoing its biggest growth spurt, with terracotta-surfaced bank buildings and stores rising downtown along the falls and mansions designed by renowned architects in the leafy cocoons of South Hill. New money was conspicuous. Blacks, on the other hand, were almost invisible—that is, until the troops arrived. In Spokane, the two battalions at Fort George Wright comprised the majority of blacks in the city. In Idaho, they would stand out even more: the state had only 651 African Americans among its population of 325,000 in 1910.

The call to the fire lines was a chance for the 25th to prove itself again, to its own men, to the rest of the nation, and to Teddy Roosevelt. They were still under probation of sorts, in the eyes of many. A few years earlier, a handful of soldiers from the infantry had killed a bartender in Brownsville, Texas, after they were refused service in town—a last-straw insult in a place where they complained about being treated like dogs despite wearing the uniform of their country. Books such as *The Negro: A Menace to American Civilization* were popular throughout the nation, not just in the South, and the sexual drive of black males was said to be uncontrollable when they were around young white women. Dark-skinned men were always "pulsating with the desire to sate their passions upon white maidens and wives," as the white supremacist senator from South Carolina, Ben Tillman, said at the time. Tillman was proud of taking away the vote from black men. "We have scratched our head to figure out how we can eliminate the last one of them," he said. "We stuffed ballot boxes. We shot them. We are not ashamed."

When questioned about the Brownsville violence, the soldiers closed ranks, refusing to name names within their division. Reaction was swift and strong, going all the way up the chain of command to President Roosevelt. Some of the same soldiers stationed in Brownsville had served under Roosevelt during the charge up San Juan Hill. He never forgot their valor, as he reminded the black miners who gave him the scale at that dinner in Butte. But he felt the soldiers were far out of line in Brownsville.

After several investigations, 167 men were dishonorably discharged from the ranks of the storied Buffalo Soldiers. Those who stayed with the 25th carried a load of resentment heavier than anything on their backs; all of them had been punished for the actions of a few. They were railroaded, they felt, betrayed by Roosevelt to appease southern whites. What happened in Brownsville was the largest summary dismissal in the history of the U.S. Army.

Going to Idaho and Montana to protect some isolated mountain towns was seen as a way to win back their honor. The soldiers who had served as makeshift park rangers were now back in the role of patrolling the land, this time enlisted to protect Roosevelt's greatest domestic policy experiment. They were dispatched to Wallace, to Missoula, to the Flathead Valley near Glacier Park, moving as always under the motto that had carried them for half a century: *Onward*. When they arrived, it soon became clear that the soldiers of the 25th Infantry shared at least one thing with the members of the Forest Service: none of them knew a thing about fighting a big wildfire.

For President Taft, his time away from Washington was supposed to be a tonic for his problems, but the fires kept intruding, even after he dispatched the troops. Newspaper cartoons showed a grotesquely obese figure in a yachting costume, ear cupped to the distant, burning West. The cursed Pinchot was never out of the news. "I have had a hard time of it," Taft wrote Roosevelt in one of his self-pitying moods. "I do know that thus far I have succeeded far less than have others." He had taken office with one of the bigger majorities in the history of the presidency — 321 electoral votes to 162 — and yet he felt that the country was not with him. When the press described him as "foggy" and "bewildered," he couldn't just slough it off. When *Collier's*, which broke the Ballinger story and stoked it for nearly a year, asked for an interview, Taft's response was intemperate. "Condemn them all to hell and eternal damnation!" he said. And the wealthy, who were relieved to have Taft in office after taking seven years of abuse from Roosevelt, had quickly grown tired of him. The railroad magnate James J. Hill, an informal Taft adviser, called him "a platter of mush."

Taft found a few moments of ceremonial relief, throwing out a pitch on opening day of baseball, the first president to do so. But he never mastered the public face, the bully pulpit, as Roosevelt had urged him to do. His political skills were abysmal. He couldn't bluff an opponent, nor could he scare one. Worse, for a politician, he could not remember names. Not yet halfway into his term, Taft sensed he was a failure. "There is no use trying to be William Howard Taft with Roosevelt's ways," he wrote his brother. The White House, he realized, was the "loneliest place in the world." Roosevelt would only make it lonelier.

8

Spaghetti Westerners

ORE THAN 5,000 MILES from the fires of the northern Rockies, a mother in the village of Rivara Canavese
opened a letter from her son in the faraway American West. Domenico Bruno had left Italy with his friend Giacomo Viettone to
find work in the United States. Every few months, the boys sent
money back to their families, enough to allow them to keep some
measure of dignity.

Tucked away in the foothills of the Italian Alps, Rivara was
nearly empty of its young men in 1910, like many places in Italy at
the turn of the century. Though it was only thirty miles from the
bustle and prosperity of Torino, the village had the feel of gloom
and yesterday on it. Through the ages, under a succession of rulers dating to feudal times, Rivara had existed primarily to supply
ore for European cities. People were poor, with little education, isolated from the outside world. The fortress walls of the Alps blocked
weather systems from the west and north, making Rivara a balmy
respite year-round. But with the mines nearly spent, wages fell to
bare subsistence, and those who did have jobs worked six days a
week. "We get old quickly," one miner said.

Word spread, through anecdotal stories and pamphlets circu-
lated by employment agencies in the United States, that a man
with a strong back and good work ethic could make a year's pay in

just a few months' time in America. Passage to the United States, in steerage, could be bought for $12, and it took little more than a week to cross the Atlantic. The copper mines of Arizona, the silver and lead havens of the Rocky Mountains—it was Italy, with gold on the streets! But these places were so remote, distant from the American cities that Italians had heard about. Where was Montana? Where was Arizona Territory? And what were the Bitterroot Mountains?

Domenico Bruno had left his home, like many in the village, with the intention of making just enough money to help his family and build his own nest egg. After that, he would return to Rivara, if not a rich man, then at least with enough of a stake to buy a farm in the Canavese Valley, with its good grass and alluvial soil, replenished by snowmelt from the mountains. His father was a farm laborer, an aging peasant no longer able to work, who lived off his small garden and help from friends. The family's other son, Pietro, had been drafted by the military and sent to Tripoli. It was up to Domenico to save the family. He said goodbye in 1907, a year when 285,000 Italians went to America.

Never before had so many people fled Italy for the United States. In that year, one in four immigrants came from Italy, a country that could barely feed its citizens as it tried to move, a latecomer, into the industrial age. By 1910, the high-water mark of emigration, Italy had given up more than two million of its people in less than a decade. Most of them were from the south, from Naples, with its corruption and crowded tenements, from Sicily and Apulia and other parts of the heel of Italy's boot—places where the soil was as tired and broken as the people, hopeless lands with dark suspicions. The north was considered more European, more prosperous, closer in identity and outlook to France, Germany, or Switzerland. One of the exceptions was the mountain valley northwest of Torino, the home of Domenico and Giacomo.

Most immigrants landed in Boston, New York, or Philadelphia, the docks thick with Sicilian dialect, which Domenico and his

friends could barely understand. The cities were filthy and dangerous, and "many Italians were dazed by the complexity of existence"
in these urban centers, the immigration commission reported.
Everyone heard the story of the twelve-year-old Italian girl, Ca-
mella Teoli, who was working in a factory where cotton was twisted
into thread when the machine tore off a big part of her scalp.

Domenico and Giacomo hopped aboard a train, finding work
in Rock Springs, Wyoming, a foul-aired boomtown six thousand
feet above sea level. Rock Springs was treeless, raked by cold winds,
populated by Finns, Chinese, Austrians, and Italians, each with
their own ghetto. The Italian miners lived in a cluster of shacks
near the railroad tracks north of town. The business of Rock Springs
was coal, with mines dating to the first transcontinental railroad in
the nineteenth century. Domenico missed the green hills of home,
the chestnut trees and balmy weather. But he was making money.
In that first year in America, he sent his family $70, a fortune in
the ragged village of Rivara Canavese. His friend Giacomo did just
as well: after eighteen months of work, he mailed $150 back to his
mother, who was blind in one eye and had five children at home
with her.

The Rivara immigrants heard about a place in Arizona Territory with better pay, six hundred miles to the southwest. Copper
mining was said to be cleaner than digging coal. On a hunch, they
headed for Morenci, where the Phelps Dodge Company ran the
town with ironfisted consistency. The company favored Mexican
and Italian laborers, who were cheaper and thought to be more doc-
ile than the Irish. What passed for law and constitutional protec-
tions in Morenci were thugs hired by Phelps Dodge. They main-
tained a three-tier wage system: one for trouble-free whites, one
for Mexicans, one for Italians. Such attitudes were typical in a decade when nine million immigrants came to the United States, and
one-third of the population was either foreign-born or a child of
someone born abroad. The Italian surge in particular angered those
who felt the nation was no longer recognizable, had lost its sense

of identity. And they hated all these strange languages spoken in shops, schools, and churches. The Immigration Restriction League, founded by Boston blue bloods with family ties to the old Tories of England, campaigned to keep "undesirable classes" from entering the country. They meant Italians, Greeks, Jews, and people from eastern Europe.

"The scum of creation has been dumped on us," said the nativist politician Thomas Watson. "The most dangerous and corrupting hordes of the Old World have invaded us." It was not just politicians who attacked Mediterranean immigrants as a threat to the American way of life. Francis A. Walker, president of the Massachusetts Institute of Technology, called Italian and Greek immigrants "beaten men from beaten races, representing the worst failures in the struggles for existence." Another educated expert cautioned Americans against "absorbing the excitable blood from Southern Europe."

In 1880, the United States had barely forty thousand Americans of Italian descent. In little more than a generation's time, there were more than three million, a wave that prompted calls to close the doors of passage to Italy. Aside from the Chinese, who had been rousted out of many western mining towns at the end of a gun or pitchfork, the Italians received "the roughest treatment of all ethnic groups," as one study found. During a congressional hearing on immigration restrictions, a building contractor told the lawmakers he never referred to his Italian workers as white men. "No, sir, an Italian is a dago."

In Arizona, Domenico was united with a lost uncle, Giuseppe Bruno, and another boyhood friend, Paolo Poletto. They joined a fraternal club in neighboring Clifton, La Società Fratellanza di Mutuo Soccorso, where they could drink wine made from California grapes, eat salted cod, and sing songs from the north. They also had their own saloon, run by the Spezia brothers. Despite a larger support group of his countrymen, Giacomo had trouble in Morenci. He loaned a friend money, was never paid back, and fell into a hole of debt. In 1907 and 1908, bad years for the American economy after a panic, he was not able to send anything home to his family. But in 1910, he started fresh, losing some of his bad habits and saving money with diligence. By the summer of that year, he had $280 set aside—enough for him to keep his family well for several years, or to buy that small farm in the Canavese Valley. It would not be long before he returned to the green hills in the shadow of the high Alps.

Domenico did even better: he mailed $80 in 1909, his best year yet, and was well on his way to surpassing that in 1910. But work in the copper mines was horrid, and the Italians grew tired of the war-zone atmosphere and the harassment from company guards. Morenci's other name, the one used by people who worked there, was Hell Town. People defecated and urinated in the streets. There was little fresh food. If you wanted a room in the company town, the rent was $18 a month, which could easily swallow up wages. Underground, conditions grew worse. Miners descended four thousand feet in rickety elevators, with limited oxygen. A man went down, every shift, not knowing whether he would make it back up. He felt swallowed by the earth itself, deep in that cold, dark intestine beneath Hell Town.

So it did not take a lot of convincing for Domenico and Giacomo to head north in the summer of 1910, north to the Rocky Mountains, where the government was looking for young men to fight fires. These boys had the mountains in their blood. The air would be clean, or at least fresher than in the Phelps Dodge pits, and they'd be surrounded by trees, just like back in Italy, even if many of those trees were on fire. When the call for firefighters came in late July, the offers of immediate work paying 25 cents an hour, the two best friends from Rivara jumped on the next train. And after that, word was, there might be steady work in one of the bright new cities of the Pacific Northwest or its primeval woods. "There are Indians and huge forests," one Italian wrote home. "We are told there will be steady work for at least 50 years."

• • •

Four months earlier, the squall that was Teddy Roosevelt had made landfall in Porto Maurizio, on the Italian Riviera, about 130 miles from the village where Domenico and Giacomo were raised. Roosevelt was trailed by an international press corps with rumors to stoke. Gifford Pinchot had sailed to Europe to meet his political soul mate after more than a year apart. At first he tried to stay out of sight, traveling under an assumed name. But the closer he got to Roosevelt, the more open he became, eventually shedding all inhibitions about what he and Teddy might be plotting. His presence alone spurred talk about a rift in the Republican Party. Would Pinchot and Roosevelt go after Taft, the man they had chosen to carry on their legacy? Did Roosevelt share Pinchot's view that his successor had betrayed the progressive cause? And if so, what did he intend to do about it?

Roosevelt had been mum on the president since leaving office, trying to make good on a vow to refrain from comment about Taft. He had traveled north from Africa, up from the Sudan and Egypt, made his way to Rome to visit the Vatican, and then intended to renew his romance with his wife on the Ligurian coast. The Roosevelts had tried to sneak into Porto Maurizio with little fanfare, arranging to stay at a villa in the hills above the sea. But Pinchot's pending arrival disrupted the plan. Tipped by the press, crowds gathered as soon as the ex-president and his family came to town. A parade was organized, and Roosevelt was made an honorary citizen of Italy. On the day of his reunion with Teddy, Pinchot walked through the village in the early morning, as if trolling for attention. His time away from the hothouse of Washington politics had done him good: at age forty-five, he looked fit, everyone said, and was full of vigor. Asked how he felt, he replied, "Like a cock!"

Roosevelt always did stimulate the adrenaline in Pinchot. On this visit, Pinchot intended to pour out his fury over Taft. He had seen his beloved Forest Service crack and begin to fall apart. The rangers were bereft, without money to fight fires or hold the network of stations together. Their enemies in Congress had just passed a law making it illegal for the agency to publicize itself, an attempt to undermine the constituency of support for the service and for conservation. Senator Heyburn went one step further: he said no federal money should be spent on forests, that it was a violation of states' rights. Worse, some of the land that Roosevelt had set aside had been turned over to private interests by Taft. The big man talked of conservation, but his actions showed otherwise. And his interior secretary, Ballinger, the administration's advocate for letting corporations have their way again with public land, was still in charge. Nor had the Alaska scandal knocked him from office. With every passing month of 1910, Pinchot's animus grew. Saving the Forest Service would require a Roosevelt Renaissance.

Pinchot was sure that Roosevelt would see things his way, saying, "On that road, T.R. was with us all the way. He knew the forests and he loved them." But Teddy was also starting to see a side of Pinchot that concerned him—the missionary zeal, the cocky certitude, the loose cannon. So long as he was someone's subordinate, Pinchot held his excesses in check. As a free agent, he was a different man, a Roman candle of self-righteous indignation. "G.P. is a dear, but he is a fanatic with an element of hardness and narrowness in his temperament," Roosevelt said in a letter to his son.

In Porto Maurizio, the men greeted each other with a round of robust back slaps and hail-fellow jokes. Walking among the olive groves and vineyards of the village, high above the azure Mediterranean near the French border, Pinchot was exhilarated. The final year of the Roosevelt presidency, he recalled, had given his life meaning. "Those were great days, days of the intensest action, and in them I did the hardest work of my life," he wrote in the rosy glow of hindsight. What they had created together, in Pinchot's mind, would outlive both of them—should it survive Taft's neglect. "The Conservation movement had grown from a series of disjointed efforts into the most vital single question before the American people," he said.

Pinchot intended to get Roosevelt to break his silence, and in so doing, cripple the Taft presidency. With the sea breeze blowing in their faces, the two men talked all day and well into the night—a marathon even for these two famously robust conversationalists. For Pinchot, the meeting went beyond his expectations. "One of the best & most satisfactory talks with T.R. I ever had," he wrote in his diary.

Roosevelt was left with a quandary: he wanted to honor his pledge of silence, but Pinchot had stoked his anger. When reporters pressed him for details afterward, he dropped a bomb. He would soon be returning the United States, and when he did so, he planned to go out west and make a major speech on conservation. The implication, of course, was that Taft had failed the country in what Roosevelt had started; it was up to Teddy to revive it. At least that's how the press and Pinchot interpreted it—a slap in Taft's face. "Most interesting report from home," Pinchot wrote a week later, from Paris. "Taft losing ground steadily." And in hindsight, it looks as if Roosevelt's decision to take on the man he had groomed for the highest office in the land was in fact made in the olive groves of Porto Maurizio. Pinchot said as much. "If you and I had made it to order, it couldn't be any better from our point of view," he wrote to his brother Amos.

"I finally have to admit to myself," Roosevelt wrote at the same time to his friend Henry Cabot Lodge, "that deep down underneath I had all along known I was wrong, on points which I had tried to deceive myself." Pinchot's gamble in Italy had paid off.

Domenico Bruno and Giacomo Viettone arrived in Wallace in the first week of August and found a town under a skirt of smoke. Still, it was better than the open sewage of Morenci. The Bitterroots *did* look a lot like home: steep green flanks, the town pressed into the narrowest opening in the valley. At dusk, with eyes half closed, it could be Rivara. But everywhere people scurried in anticipation of disaster. The military was in the valley now, the 25th Infantry, camped just south of Wallace. To some of the immigrants, the black troops were a curious sight. "It was here we saw our first negroes," one Italian miner wrote.

For now, Domenico and Giacomo had a vital role in the new country. Though a cartoon in that year showed a sleeping Uncle Sam in a country overrun by Italians—"Wake up, Sam!" was the caption—Domenico, Giacomo, and hundreds of other Italians were now working for the pride and joy of Gifford Pinchot and Teddy Roosevelt. Their small part of the Great Crusade, just like the Buffalo Soldiers', was to save the centerpiece of the dream of the two easterners. Pinchot and T.R. would do the speechifying, the political lifting, while these strong backs would hold the front line. The Italians were hired by Bill Weigle as part of his pledge to give Pulaski enough men to keep Wallace from falling to fire. The job interview took but a few minutes, and then they were put on a mountain crew. August 4 was their first day of work. They were sent over the ridge to join about fifty men under the overall direction of Pulaski. What they wore into the woods was what they wore when they arrived in town. They could expect to be on Uncle Sam's payroll for a month, maybe more, because their job was no small task: hold back the fires of August.

Teddy Roosevelt had returned to New York on June 10, to a tumultuous dockside reception, a spit in the eye of his enemies. "That spring," the Kansas writer William Allen White wrote, "the country was politically seething with the yeast of a progressive movement." J. P. Morgan's fondest wish for Roosevelt's travels in Africa—"I trust some lion will do its duty"—had not come to pass. Teddy was back, ready to stir the progressive pot. A ticker-tape parade was arranged, showering Roosevelt with the kind of attention usually reserved for an expedition hero or someone who had broken a world record. All Roosevelt had done was leave the country for a year. During his last months in Europe, he went to Sweden to pick up the Nobel Peace Prize he had been awarded four years earlier for helping to resolve a conflict between Russia and Japan. And he gave a speech in Paris, at the Sorbonne, that came to define his life philosophy—the Man in the Arena speech. Better for a man to fail, he said, even "to fail greatly, so that his place shall never be with those cold and timid souls who know neither victory nor defeat."

Certainly, Gifford Pinchot had not retreated into timidity since his reunion in Italy with T.R. He dashed off a short book, a call to arms, *The Fight for Conservation*, almost a religious cry. He predicted that America might one day, within this century, be a nation of two or three hundred million people. And what would his generation leave them? Their duty was to the future. To ensure that people in 2010 would have a country of clean water, healthy forests, and open land would require battle with certain groups, namely "the alliance between business and politics." It was, he said, "the snake that we must kill."

The book also showed that Pinchot had continued to see wildfire as a mere hindrance to controlling the garden of America's native ground. Still full of confidence when it came to how man should look at the land, he was completely dismissive of fire as a threat. "I recall very well indeed how, in the early days of forest fires, they were considered simply and solely as acts of God, against which any opposition was hopeless and any attempt to control them not merely hopeless but childish. It was assumed that they came in the natural order of things, as inevitably as the seasons or the rising and setting of the sun. Today we understand forest fires are wholly within the control of men." That was as far as he had yet gone—wildfires were now virtually a thing of the past, no longer part of the cycles of the land, because of the march of green-shirted arborists into the woods. As an act of hubris, Pinchot had all but invited nature to strike back. And in a few short weeks, it would.

Pinchot now plotted openly to bring down Taft. The wild, near-hysterical reception for Roosevelt upon his return had only galvanized him further. Roosevelt advised caution, telling Pinchot to hold his fire. He felt that Taft "was rather a pitiful failure" and that he "evidently is a man who takes his color from his surroundings."

The press played up Roosevelt's vigor around the Sagamore Hill house, in contrast with the brooding and slothful Taft. Roosevelt cut trees, walked, engaged in "great exercise," all subject to prominent news stories, while Taft could not get through a round of golf, as it happened, without spraining an ankle. What made news from the Taft family was a story of his college-age son hitting a blue-collar worker with his car, seriously injuring the man.

Three weeks after Roosevelt sailed into New York, the two men met at Taft's summer place in Massachusetts. The meeting was tense by some accounts, though the president assured reporters that everything was fine between the nation's leading Republicans. Taft's loyal press organ, *Leslie's Weekly*, reported that there was no rift. The Ballinger affair and the firing of Gifford Pinchot were not deemed "casus belli" for Teddy to take down Taft. Instead, the magazine noted, the two men chatted amiably while sitting on the veranda of Taft's retreat. A few weeks later, Roosevelt announced that he would soon be off on his speaking tour, slowly wending his way west. By August, just as Taft had ordered troops to the northern Rockies to fight wildfires, Roosevelt boarded his train.

WILL TEDDY RUN AGAIN?

The headline from a wire-service story in mid-August showed the grip that Roosevelt had on the country. His every inflection was parsed for larger meaning, ending typically with a question: What will he do? The Colonel, as he was called by the press, downplayed suggestions that he intended to attack Taft. What Taft was doing with public land angered him, but he kept it to himself. But just days after meeting Roosevelt, Taft issued a proclamation eliminating nearly a half million acres of land from the national forest system. Eliminating acres! Here was another stab at the Great Crusade. If Taft was trying to get the attention of the man he professed to love as the closest of friends, his slap at the Bull Moose just before his western tour would certainly do that. Roosevelt would have something to say about the fate of burning, orphaned national forests, about removing land from the public domain, about fighting the foes of conservation, but not just yet. He told reporters he was simply going out to the land he loved, land that had restored him, land where the conservation experiment was a living, breathing thing. Land that was about to blow up.

The aftermath, in the Bitterroot Mountains of Idaho, of what historians have called the largest wildfire in American history. *U.S. Forest Service*

A 1910 photo of Ed Pulaski, whose actions saved many lives. Badly wounded by the fire, he retired a bitter man. *U.S. Forest Service*

This tunnel above Wallace, Idaho, is where Ranger Pulaski and his crew took refuge on the night the forest blew up under hurricane-force winds, August 20, 1910. *U.S. Forest Service*

Ranger Joe Halm (right) after the fire. Halm was hired just out of college, and like Ranger Pulaski, he helped save many lives. *U.S. Forest Service*

Men standing amid downed timber after the Big Burn of 1910. The fire covered an area the size of Connecticut. *U.S. Forest Service*

A forest in ruins. Winds knocked down trees that had held to the ground for two centuries or more, and fire left others standing, but stripped of all green. *U.S. Forest Service*

On horseback, a forest ranger patrolled the blackened and still forest in the first days after the fire. Smoke from the Big Burn drifted as far east as Chicago. *U.S. Forest Service*

Burned, bandaged, and dazed, two firefighters posed for a studio photo in Wallace, Idaho, just days after the Big Burn. Many of the men who fought the blaze were immigrants or out-of-work city dwellers who knew nothing of fighting wildfires. *Barnard-Stockbridge Studio Collection, University of Idaho Library*

The gutted core of the town of Wallace after the fire.
Barnard-Stockbridge Studio Collection, University of Idaho Library

An iconic photo of President Theodore Roosevelt and John Muir atop Glacier Point in Yosemite National Park during their 1903 camping trip. Roosevelt was an immense fan of Muir's, and the naturalist felt a similar admiration for the president. *Library of Congress*

President Roosevelt in his element, giving a stemwinder. Both he and Gifford Pinchot reveled in conflict with the foes of conservation. *Library of Congress*

Young Gifford Pinchot, a close friend and personal aide of Roosevelt's and the first Chief of the U.S. Forest Service. *Library of Congress*

Teddy Roosevelt speaking outside a church in Rifle, Colorado, in 1905. At heart, he said, he was just as much a westerner as an easterner. *Library of Congress*

After leaving the Forest Service, Gifford Pinchot had a stint in Pennsylvania politics. Here, as a candidate for governor, he meets with two rangers. "I have been a governor now and then," he once said, "but I am a forester all the time—have been, and shall be, all my working life." *Library of Congress*

A typical lookout tower of the type constructed all over the West. After the Big Burn, the Forest Service vowed zero tolerance for wildfire, a policy doomed to fail. *Library of Congress*

A Forest Service fire patrol in 1914. The average ranger had to patrol 300,000 acres, usually on foot, but also on horseback or riding the rails. *Library of Congress*

Gifford Pinchot with his family. Much of his private life was a well-kept secret — mystical and mysterious, even as he moved in the highest reaches of power. *Library of Congress*

Grey Towers, the Pinchot family estate in Pennsylvania. Though Gifford Pinchot's grandfather made his fortune by cutting down trees, the family name later became synonymous with forest preservation. *U.S. Forest Service*

Pinchot out for a stroll. Like Roosevelt, he came from wealth and privilege, but he found his life's purpose in Progressive Era causes on behalf of public land and "the little man." *Library of Congress*

Roosevelt and Pinchot, political soulmates, on the deck of the steamer *Mississippi* during a tour of inland waterways. *Library of Congress*

9

Firestorm's Eve

THE FIRST TIME a shower of flaming embers pounded the streets of Wallace it changed everything for those who lived there. People could tolerate the ever-present smoke, though it wasn't good for children and the elderly, made eyes redden and throats scratchy and brought on a ragged cough. Some days it was so thick that Bill Weigle could not see more than two blocks down Bank Street. Other days, the smoke settled at different tiers, like a multilayered mist, and it took a scramble five hundred feet up the mountains to find a pocket of clean air. They could also put up with that mass of hot air that had been sitting on them like an oversize village bully, though it was oppressive, lingered far too long, and what a family wouldn't do for a cool breeze just one afternoon to break this siege. Some people said they didn't even mind the ash that fell from the sky, needles of fir and pine burned to dust, lighter than air, settling on rooftops and brown lawns. They put up with these low-grade tortures because shorter days told them summer was almost over, and they had lived through a humdinger, and soon the rains would come and wash the town clean.

The constant chatter of fire and heat would be replaced by talk about canning vegetables and hunting deer and checking to see whether Andrew Carnegie was going to make good on his promise to put a library in their town. That's what he said: a Carnegie library, a trophy home for books, built of the finest marble and timber, was coming to Wallace, Idaho. The town could count seven churches, two schools, nine doctors, twelve hotels, and two hospitals, but not a decent library. Carnegie had decided to give away his fortune well before the other titans of the age. His idea was to plant libraries—as gateways to knowledge and citizenship—across the country, as missionaries had put churches on the frontier. At a time when the very rich and the very poor were engaged in open warfare, Carnegie said, "It would be a great mistake for the community to shoot the millionaires. For they are the bees that make the most honey and they contribute the most to the hive, even after they have gorged themselves full." As people in Wallace wondered about the fate of their town in the third week of August, the word from Carnegie was confirmed: Wallace would get its library, from a very big honeybee.

The news passed with scant notice, because on August 19 that first big ember came whistling out of the sky and set fire to an awning at the edge of town, making it difficult to think of anything but wildfire moving steadily closer. The flying combustible consumed the cloth, and was put out before it spread. A few hours later, another volley came from beyond the ceiling of smoke and torched a canvas overhang in the middle of town. These flaming fusillades meant townsfolk were vulnerable to an unseen terror, something bigger, more distant, and less predictable than anything that had threatened Wallace over the past month. They meant that the people had to think seriously about getting out, or losing everything.

Within days, several hundred gathered what they could carry, by carriage or on horseback or in the compartment of a train, and fled. Insurance companies had been writing policies with a flourish, like ice cream vendors on the hottest day of the year. But that nineteenth of August, a Friday, they stopped issuing policies. The bet was no longer worth it; the smart money said Wallace would burn. Yet most people stayed behind, counting on a change in the weather that would end the shelling of fire from the mountains, knowing full well, as the *Seattle Times* reported in a long front-page story, that "should the wind become much stronger nothing can save the town."

When Emma Pulaski walked outside of town to greet her husband, and all the vegetation crunched underfoot, brown and crisp to the touch, she knew that everything and everybody in this pocket of people in the mountains had been reduced to fuel. One of Ed Pulaski's young charges, Joe Halm, the ex–football player who had been working the Coeur d'Alene for barely a year, said as much. He was a forestry student, full of fun, trained to see the woods without anthropomorphizing, but he felt a nervousness that matched the jitters of the town. "All of nature seemed tense, unnatural and ominous," Halm wrote.

Halm had been dispatched into the Coeur d'Alene forest, sixty-five miles from the nearest road or rail line, as far up the St. Joe River as a person could travel. A spotter from high on a peak had identified a fire near the headwaters of the river, on the evening side of the divide between Montana and Idaho. It took Halm's crew several days to hack their way through thickets of devil's club, nettles, and calcified scrub brush.

Halm was strong, with a body built by four years of varsity sports. He had set a hammer-throw record of 139 feet 3 inches at Washington State College, put a heavy metal shot 40 feet, pitched for the baseball team, and played two positions on the football team. He was known throughout the state as the kid who drop-kicked a winning field goal against a hated rival, the Huskies of Washington, on a rocky, muddy field in Seattle. On his way up to the St. Joe headwaters, he had passed deer and elk, black bears and birds—all looking to be in desperate retreat from the smoke and heat of the upper mountains. The forest floor itself was blighted, as he noted, "withered ferns and grasses covered by a hoar frost of gray ashes."

His crew found their fire lapping against alpine fir near a mountain wall and proceeded to dig a trench around it. After a few days, the blaze at the lifespring of the mighty Joe was contained. Halm's crew split up, some heading down the St. Joe for rest, others camping in an opening next to big pines and spruce for mop-up duty. Halm feared something catastrophic that night of August 19, but also — because his crew was so far in, so distant from any place to replenish their supply lines — he was worried about getting cut off should a fire start downhill. He had the mountain wall at his back, a sheer vertical scramble. It would be difficult to climb in the best conditions. And as good a shape as Halm was in, he knew he could not outrun a fire with the wind at its back.

Halm's boss in Wallace was also fretting over an exit strategy — but for an entire town, not just a fire crew. Bill Weigle had been working with soldiers from the 25th Infantry and the mayor on the evacuation plan for the three thousand or so residents of Wallace who remained behind. Like Halm, his concern was that people would get trapped. There were only two ways out of town: downriver, to the west and Spokane, or uphill, to the east and Missoula. Each of those exits was a narrow slot in the mountains. The passageways were funnels, and should one or both of them catch fire, they would force flame up the narrow byway like peas through a straw shooter. It was agreed that the two trains from two different lines that came through Wallace would evacuate all the women and children. The men would stay and fight for the town.

Weigle had his doubts. Despite pleading for assistance for a month, he had not been able to find enough men among the citizens to help his Forest Service fight the fires as they closed in on Wallace. What made the mayor think people would stay and fight now? Mayor Walter Hanson's answer was the lethal force of the law. To back his plan, the mayor was empowered to declare martial law; he would use the soldiers if needed. Hanson now ordered the men to be prepared to light a backfire, a way to scorch the ground ahead of any blaze coming down from the mountains. Anyone who refused to help, he said, would be put in jail—and there they might roast to death. The mayor was just twenty-five years old, and lived with his parents, and it's hard to say whether his words carried much weight.

Across the river, where the Sisters of Providence ran a hospital, was a problem. The four-story brick facility had about forty patients (some not long removed from surgery), fifteen nuns, a priest, and a doctor. A small bridge over the river was all that connected them to the main part of town. Another railroad, the Northern Pacific, had a branch line that ran close to the hospital and traveled east. But people feared that the line's big-timbered rail trestles would burn in the canyon crossings.

By Weigle's reckoning, the nearest big fire was five miles from the city, in the Placer Creek drainage to the south—a lumbering advance of flame pushed along by the prevailing winds from the south and west. Those breezes had died down of late; the air, slow and heavy, smelled like piles of wood chips that had smoldered for days. All told, the forest supervisor had 1,800 men on fires in the Coeur d'Alene—immigrants, vagabonds, prisoners, and soldiers, led by a handful of Gifford Pinchot's rangers. Weigle had sent one company of troops from the 25th south to protect the town of Avery and help it evacuate, should it come to that. The rangers had no love for the motley assortment of roustabouts in the Milwaukee Road watering stop, especially after they'd stripped the town of its name for the beloved Chief. Weigle sent another company out to take a look at the small fire a few miles away from Wallace, the blaze that threatened a cluster of cabins, blacksmith shops, and two mines near Placer Creek.

By August 19, the soldiers had been in Wallace for five days. Their first job was to try to induce rain from the skies. For sixty straight hours, they aimed dynamite and cannon fire overhead, but no relief came from above, no moisture. The papers called the men of the 25th "dusky dough boys," and marveled that they seemed so orderly, curious mainly for their singing and gambling at night.

"The men of the company surprised many Wallace people by their remarkably good behavior," the *Idaho Press* reported. The Swedes and Irish, Greeks and Italians, the felons let loose to fight fire — they crowded the saloons and caused many a fight. But the black soldiers kept to themselves, camped on a baseball field, occasionally playing craps with people from town who ventured their way.

In that year of 1910, Jack Johnson reigned as the heavyweight champion of the world, the first African-American boxer to hold the title. When he fought to retain his title on the Fourth of July, Jack London noted with approval in the *San Francisco Chronicle* that "the negro showed no yellow." London was one of the more tolerant writers. Many headlines called Johnson "the Dusky Fighter" and a wire-service feature told how happy he was with watermelon and fried chicken, using a shambling southern inflection in the story. "Mammy Greets Him with a Mighty Fine Chicken and a Watah-melon" was a subheading. And when Robert Peary claimed to have reached the North Pole a year earlier — a moon landing, essentially, in the age of geographic firsts — he "had with him a negro at the time of this great discovery," a leading magazine noted. But they never named the companion who shared this world-shaking feat, Matthew Henson. Whether blacks had the stomach for any kind of prolonged fight was a subject of much debate, bordering on ridicule. Looking for help to protect its own private timber holdings, the Potlatch Company of Idaho told an employment agency to send anyone but blacks. "If you cannot get white men, you may send five or six good Greeks or Italians" was their request. And the black soldiers had no sooner been dispatched up the Placer Creek drainage than four of their men disappeared. It didn't look like desertion, more like confusion. The tangle of smoke and burning brush, the lack of trails and clear directions, made it difficult to keep their bearings.

The soldiers would be better off helping defend Wallace, perhaps digging the fire line, Weigle decided. A search party was sent out for the missing men, while the rest of the company was sent back to

Wallace. Everyone in town expected Weigle — now — to have all the answers. He knew something of how different tree species reacted to blight and disease, and how a forest aged through the stages leading to decay, and about species diversity. But the course and character of a big fire? Heat? Intensity? Creation of its own weather? Not in the books. The pressure mounted on him and the other Little G.P.s. Weren't they supposed to be insurance against catastrophic wildfire? Hadn't Pinchot and Roosevelt promised as much? Wasn't that the main selling point — at least in the West — for putting so much public land in the forest reserves? Weren't these rangers both stewards and protectors? Common sense told Weigle that most of the timber at the edge of Wallace was green — second growth, coming up after the first citizens had leveled the big cedars to build the town. Because it was young timber, on downhill slopes, it should not catch fire easily should a swoop of wind come through. When the mayor asked him again for a prediction, Weigle was noncommittal.

"God only knows what's going to happen next," he said. "I don't."

Late on Saturday afternoon, August 20, Weigle rode up alone toward Placer Creek, past soldiers wandering in retreat amid the heavy smoke. He intended to get a quick look, to aid him in making his evacuation call.

Weigle's best ranger, Ed Pulaski, had divided his firefighters, about 200 men in all, between two sides of the mountain ridge separating Wallace from Avery and the drainage of the St. Joe. Because they had two towns to defend, it made sense to split them up — 50 men for the St. Joe side, 150 to keep the fires from spilling into the much larger city of Wallace. The ridge was ablaze over a distance of about ten miles, a series of persistent but still relatively small fires on its flanks. Men were dispatched in crews, each with a fire to control. At night, they retreated to a big camp for a dinner of beans, rice, potatoes, and meat.

Domenico Bruno and Giacomo Viettone were part of the crew sent to the St. Joe side of the ridge. The Italians had been on fire duty since August 4, and if working the flame-spitting ground of the northern Rockies was supposed to be easier than the deep mining pits of the Arizona Territory, they had been misinformed. The job was brutal—seventeen-hour days, circling fire, digging trenches, gasping on smoke, with little sleep. It was cold at night, and during the day they often became dehydrated and cramped. By August 20, the boys from Rivara Canavese had worked sixteen days in row, at a location within five miles of a place known as Dago Creek. They were making good money—more than $60 apiece for their labors in August, which could keep each of their families going for a year. But they had yet to see a paycheck. The fire suppression budget for the Coeur d'Alene National Forest was $30,000—for an entire year. With 1,800 men on fire duty, that year's money was gone in less than two weeks. What kept men on the front line going was the promise of a fat paycheck by month's end. A promise.

Their crew was international, the woods thick with a babel of languages from people forced to the edge of the new America because the cities were deemed less hospitable. "The Italians, the Hebrew and the Slav, according to popular belief, are poisoning the pure air of our otherwise well-regulated cities," the immigration commissioner, E. A. Goldenweiser, wrote of a prevailing view, based on a survey of ten thousand American households. Facing a fire, all men were equal. Serbs. Croats. Greeks. Italians from the north. Italians from the south. Austrians. Montenegrins. A Brit who had fought in the Boer War. Irishmen who hated the Brits. Two men from South Carolina with thick accents. Two fresh arrivals from Ohio, flatlanders disoriented in a vertical world. At least one Italian American, from a large family down in the valley, worked with Domenico and Giacomo; he could have told them it was easier earning money from a desperate Forest Service than finding stability down below. The Italians had a saying: "I came to America because I heard the streets were paved with gold. When I got here, I found out three things. First, the streets weren't paved with gold. Second, they weren't paved at all. And third, I was expected to pave them."

Their other mates included floaters from hiring halls, a handful of miners, and some men who had homesteaded on level ground inside the national forest. One of the homesteaders, Joe Beauchamp, had built a cabin and cleared two acres. He was middle-aged and had worked himself raw trying to scratch out his place in the woods. Beauchamp wasn't on the payroll of a timber company or a speculator looking to defraud the Forest Service; he wanted only to get his section in shape and be left alone. He joined the crew as a volunteer, fighting fire to save his home. But his little clearing also figured into the exit plan. If the fires on the ridge merged and leapt over the lines, the order was to retreat to Joe Beauchamp's. The ground was level, with big stumps and some fencing around his tiny cabin. A small creek ran nearby, bordered by towering trees, some nearly two hundred feet tall.

Pulaski was riding his horse hard all over the spine of the mountains, up and down, trying to keep the crews on task. Over the past two weeks, he had dutifully reported to Weigle new fires on either side of the divide, including a troubling blaze along the only trail leading to the beer-sodden tent town of Grand Forks on the Avery side of the ridge. These reports were forwarded along with others to regional headquarters in Missoula. Glacier Park was still burning. So was Yellowstone. The big Indian reservation in western Montana, home of the Flatheads, was on fire. Near Spokane, the woods of eastern Washington were ablaze, and the authorities had requested an additional thousand men. That was impossible; there were no firefighters in reserve. Throughout three states, ten thousand people were now on wildfire duty in almost two dozen national forests, spread out over an area nearly the size of New England. The frenzy and fear of planning the next stage of battle on a ridge above Wallace was duplicated all over the northern Rockies, each forest supervisor trying to craft something to protect the woods from flame and to project a confidence beyond their tender age or their inadequate knowledge of fire.

Pulaski's men were often short of energy during the long, draining days, and certainly short of outdoor skills. They had to be taught, like little kids, how to hold an ax, where to stand, to keep drinking water. A general in the woods, Pulaski strode on horseback along the lines of his crew, pistol strapped to his side. A big chore was simply keeping track of everybody. When head counts were taken, men were always missing or presumed lost. Some had walked away, without explanation or pay. The smoke was like a stale dream that hangs on through awakening into the bright hours of day. By August 19, it was clear to Pulaski that he needed to retreat to Wallace for more supplies. The men would go hungry if he could not bring fresh food. It was one thing to hold back a paycheck, but without a regular infusion of high-calorie stews, the Pulaski battalions could not fight another day.

He headed for Wallace that Friday night, the nineteenth. As he was coming into town, Pulaski couldn't help but notice the confusion and chaos. Neighbors he had known for years were straggling out, weighted down by their belongings. Others were in hurried retreat, carrying little but a suitcase or knapsack. Who could fault them? Survival was stronger than any altruistic impulse. Pulaski checked in with Weigle, then had dinner with his family. He looked like a beaten man, face blackened and coated, hair matted, eyes sunken. He did not mince words with Emma and Elsie: the town was going to burn. They had to take refuge. The family discussed the train evacuation, just like everyone in Wallace. The Pulaskis decided that mother and daughter would go to the mine tailings at the reservoir—essentially a berm, like a levee above a river that served as a buffer. The tailings would not burn; they were mine waste, set against impounded water, and a better risk than trains headed into flaming forests. The next morning, Elsie and Emma joined Ed in a buckboard ride, eight miles to road's end at the trailhead to Placer Creek. There Pulaski met his mule packer, loaded with fresh supplies. Ed turned to his wife, and as she remembered, he spoke but one sentence at their departure.

"I may never see you again."

Returning to Wallace, bumping along the dry road, dust kicking up and smoke heavy on the town, Emma Pulaski held back her tears. Glancing back, up at the mountains, she saw fire where her husband was headed, a snarl of uncertainty. When the sun was visible it was horrid—a feverish red ball. A black bear dashed across the road, frightening the horses, almost plunging the carriage into a ditch. The bear disappeared into the woods as quickly as it appeared. Mother and daughter rode in silence for a while.

"That was a black bear," said Elsie, who was eight.

"No," her mother said, "it was a big black dog." But back at their house, she changed her story. Better not to lie. Eighteen-inch-long embers, like flaming arrows fired from invading soldiers, landed on the Pulaski front lawn. The burning bark lit the grass, and had to be put out by hose. Their porch was covered with ash, warm to the touch when held in the palm of the hand.

"Mama, that was a bear—not a dog," Elsie said.

"It *was* a bear. I didn't want to frighten you, so I called it a dog."

"You look scared, Mama."

In the mountains, Pulaski rode seventeen miles that Saturday, following the steep trail that miners had hacked along the upper reaches of Placer Creek. On the way, he passed a couple of deep holes dug in the earth and supported by timbers—the burrowing of fortune seekers. Pulaski himself had spent some time prospecting in the upper reaches of the forest, always coming up empty. He recognized some of the mines, the claims of lucky bastards who hit a vein.

Now his doubt followed him up the path. Maybe he should have stayed behind to protect Emma and Elsie. How could he leave them? Yes, he was in charge of all these directionless lives in burning woods, these men from distant shores speaking languages he could not comprehend, but wasn't his first duty to his family? If he abandoned the crews now, and went back to Wallace to be with his wife and daughter, would anyone hold it against him? Up, up, up the trail he went with his fresh supplies, the horses balking at times in the stifling air and the swarm of smoke, the packers quiet and brooding. The relative stillness of the woods was broken by the crash of a flame-engulfed tree falling somewhere in the distance. And then came voices through the haze; it was unnerving. That Saturday morning had been calm, with winds standing down, quiet enough for Pulaski to believe, if only for a moment, they might get the best of this thing yet. His doubts he had to keep to himself. As he started to meet stragglers, people who had pulled back from the fire lines, he was given status reports: two miles of trench dug, men missing in the sea of smoke. He also saw something that nearly made him laugh: a man who had just been hired as a cook, wearing a white chef's hat and matching apron, ready to serve a midday meal for hungry firefighters. A chef's hat—up here!

On the Montana side of the Bitterroots, the biggest concern of Elers Koch was the string of upstart towns inside the forest—Taft, DeBorgia, Saltese. These settlements along the rail line needed evacuation plans, just like Wallace and Avery. Taft was clearly in harm's way, and as fire moved toward town, Koch dispatched nearly 150 men to the rescue. They were worn and disgusted by now, as soldiers are late in a losing campaign, "moving in to the front line, and listening to the artillery and shell bursts ahead," as Koch recalled. "Fire fighting is perhaps the nearest thing there is to war, and always requires extreme physical exertion, long hours, lack of sleep, and constant nervous attention."

For guidance, Koch turned to Frank Haun, the older ranger who had helped him from his first days as a forest supervisor. A man of clear vision and no sentimentality, Haun came up with a novel strategy to get the attention of people in Taft. Instead of starting a typical backfire that burned outward and cleared ground away from town, he considered lighting one that would burn inward, *toward* town. It sounded like madness. But with Taft as besotted as ever, in self-indulgent lethargy as fire closed in, the rangers needed some way to jolt townsfolk into awareness of the peril they faced. It was a joke at first, but the foresters gave it serious consideration when they arrived at Taft on Saturday, August 20. Ranger Haun went from saloon to saloon, house to house, trying to find some-one — anyone — from this town to volunteer. He also had to goad his own men, the flotsam from Front Street in Missoula, who were instantly drawn to Taft's seedy diversions.

"You hired out to be a tough man, didn't you?" said Haun, taunting his crew. "Who the hell wants to be a quitter?"

Most of the town, as it turned out. Haun was furious. Burn it down, he groused to fellow rangers — *screw 'em.* Truly, that was the only way to get their attention. Instead of readying for retreat or defense, instead of digging fire lines or packing clothes and belongings, instead of watering down roofs or gathering shovels and picks, the people of Taft went to work hoarding and then consuming their entire whiskey supply. As Supervisor Koch reported to his superiors, the Taft denizens decided that if they were going to be burned to death in an inferno that engulfed the Bitterroots, they would go down drunk.

10

Blowup

A WIND OUT OF the American West that tumbles in roller-coaster fashion is known as a Palouser, a Sahaptin Indian word that sounds poetic, named for the lilt of hills at the far eastern edge of Washington State, one of the most productive wheat-growing regions in the world. The skin of that land is lovely, stroked by easy breezes and nourished by soft rains in the spring. But the Palouse is one of those curious places in the West where a weather system can form benign and transform into something ferocious long after it has left the cradle of its creation. On one side is a desert, a high plateau that gets less rain than Phoenix in some years. On the other side are the well-watered forests of Idaho and Montana, with cooler air and steady moisture. When caught between the two extremes, the air over the Palouse can be volatile, or violent. So it was on the Saturday afternoon of August 20, when atmospheric conditions gave birth to a Palouser that lifted the red dirt of the hills and slammed into the forests—not as a gust or an episodic blow, but as a battering ram of forced air.

Stirring to life in midday, the wind rustled the tawny heads of wheat and tall grass before jumping over the Snake River into Idaho and barreling north into the Nez Perce National Forest, the longtime home of Indians who had saved Lewis and Clark from starvation. The Nez Perce country was open and park-like, with birches, cottonwoods, and big pines, room enough for the wind to bounce around, fresh spring in its step after every impact. In the canyons of the Clearwater National Forest, the air climbed swiftly through the mountains. The big river that gave the forest its name, flat and glassy in the lazy part of the day, became white-capped and shaggy as the Palouser raked over it. When it ran into walls of ancient rock, the wind compacted and accelerated. Forcing its way upward, following the contours of the land, the racing wind hit the first fires in a mix of pines at lower elevations. These fires had been ignored by the Forest Service, left to burn out once the underbrush was consumed. The wind took the hot floor of the simmering forest and threw it into the air, where it lit the boughs of bigger ponderosas and white pines, which snapped off and also rode the force of upward acceleration. Pine sap heated quickly and hissed as it reached a boiling point. Every headwall, every dead end of a canyon, every narrow valley served as a chimney, compressing the fire-laden air into funnels of flame.

The chain reaction of a wildfire had begun. Heated plant matter released hydrogen and carbon while drawing in oxygen, and the whole of it was on the run, a weather system of its own. Thus, three small blazes in grass met six bigger ones in the lower forest and then merged with a dozen others before joining twenty or thirty more, until the mass was bundled into a single wall of yellow and orange moving upward at fifty miles an hour into the crowded zone of Douglas fir, spruce, and larch, into groves of wizened hardwoods and withered cedars next to dried-up streams, moving faster than a horse could run. All at once, it burned at the scrub and limbs of the lower tier of the forest, it burned at thick midheight, it burned large boughs, which broke away in the storm, huge cones popping in fireballs, and it burned at the crowns, the highest tips of the trees exploding into the air, flying off to light the crowns of other tall trees. The densest part of the forest, between three and five thousand feet above sea level, was ready-to-burn fiber when the flames moved through it. In pops and cracks and snaps and gulps, in gasps and whistles, the fire metastasized—more clamorous with every fresh intake, charging ahead. Any leftover little fire that might have smoldered and smoked in a last gasp was given new life by the wind, yanked from the ground, pitched into the river of flame, into the current of the now unrecognizable Palouser.

Midway through the Clearwater, the wall of flame took over the forest, hundreds of feet high, at least thirty miles wide in some parts, and still gaining strength, still fanning out, consuming oxygen in heaves, and picking up intensity as its core temperature rose. The fire was a classic convection engine now: heat rising, pulling the hottest elements upward, a gyro of spark and flame. After racing through the Clearwater and Nez Perce forests, leveling nearly all living things in the Kelly Creek region, the fire swept up trees at the highest elevations. At this altitude, along the spine of the Bitterroots, the wind moved without obstruction, and the fire itself threw brands ten miles or more ahead of the flame front. The storm found the Montana border and spit flames down into the heavily settled Bitterroot Valley. It found the Lolo forest and crossed over the pass and along the summits, jumping ridgeline to ridgeline. At the peak of its power, it found the Coeur d'Alene forest, leading with a punch of wind that knocked down thousands of trees before the flames took out the rest of the woods. By now, the conscripted air was no longer a Palouser but a firestorm of hurricane-force winds, in excess of eighty miles an hour. What had been nearly three thousand small fires throughout a three-state region of the northern Rockies had grown to a single large burn.

The advance force of the firestorm, just ahead of the flame wall, was so strong it uprooted bark-armored trees that had held to a piece of ground for three centuries or more. Entire sections of the forest were mowed down as if they were blades of grass. Deer were trapped by falling timbers; some were crushed, others suffocated. Smaller animals emerged from shelter in the hollows of trees, driven out by heat and smoke, only to die in the collapsing forest.

Funnels, columns, and whirlwinds formed within the storm, each breaking out in a separate dance of gas and flames. Explosions and the charge of the wind brought a sound that shook any leaf or limb not consumed by flame.

Through the Coeur d'Alene that night, the burn picked up every fire along the ridge separating Wallace from Avery, every fire in the upper reaches of the St. Joe, and every fire downriver. Its only imperative was to find more fuel. It moved west, downstream, toward the towns of St. Maries and Coeur d'Alene and close to Spokane, and it moved east, up the Bitterroots, toward Grand Forks and Taft, over the divide, toward Missoula. It moved northeast, into the Cabinet and Pend Oreille forests, across the Canadian border into British Columbia, and farther still to Glacier Park and the Blackfeet and Flathead forests. Firebrands were tossed ten miles or more, torching the ground ahead of the incendiary waves. As the storm approached a piece of untouched ground, it announced itself with a roar and a light on the horizon and finished with a sea of flames, suffocating the woods. If there was a river in the way, the fire leapt over water. If there was a lake in the way, it rode its own wind to the other side and alighted on fresh timber. If there was a town in the way, it engulfed it without blinking, exploding a barrel of kerosene or a tank of oil, taking tents and timber, taking shellacked houses and plank sidewalks and cedar-shake churches, all ready for the burn.

11

The Lost Day

I N T H E T W O Y E A R S that Bill Weigle had been in charge of
the Coeur d'Alene National Forest, a time when he had been
snubbed by mine owners, scorned by timber thieves, and nearly
killed by rebellious saloonkeepers, nobody ever needed him as
much they did on the evening of August 20. He was, after all, only
four years removed from that Yale graduating class when he was
given oversight of the 1.8 million acres of the Coeur d'Alene. Ed Pulaski was different, of course, because he was one of *them.* Weigle
had the stamp of Gifford Pinchot on him, which he tried to down-
play — suspect until he could prove his worth in the woods. But on
Saturday, as winds clocked at sixty miles an hour and flaming embers rained down on the town of Wallace, as voices were raised to be
heard above the whirring and whistling of firebrands, people called
the name of Bill Weigle in desperation. They could not find him.

In town, horses chafed at the hot breath of the advancing fire,
coughing and spitting to keep it out of their system. By dusk, everyone who was not eligible for evacuation was supposed to fall in line
under the command of Mayor Hanson and Forest Supervisor Weigle, working in an orderly fashion to protect Wallace from the fire
at its doorstep. They knew nothing of its size or power, nothing of
where it had come from or where it was headed. They had no ad-

vance notice, no intelligence. All they knew was that the winds had picked up suddenly in late afternoon. Even small children understood what that meant: it was the great fear of the summer-long fire siege. Just two days earlier, Weigle had reassured people that the lines up on the ridge were holding, that Pulaski's firefighters—a collection of global castoffs on the St. Joe side of the divide, and a disorganized and dispirited crew above Wallace—had things under control. His one caveat was that they could contain the blazes only if the wind did not start to blow. If, if, if. And now it was here, a Palouser of such power that it seemed there was nothing that 1,000 men or 10,000 men or 100,000 men could do to hold it back.

The exact timing of the evacuation was Weigle's call. Seeking firsthand information to aid him in his decision, Weigle had gone up Placer Creek Saturday afternoon on horseback. He was alone. About three miles in, he was stopped by an obstruction: heavy timber blown across the way. It was an ominous sign. If the wind was strong enough to uproot big trees that had held to the ground for ages, what would it do with fire in its embrace? He tried to get around the downed trees, but the canyon was too steep, so he tied his horse and continued uphill on foot. Five miles in, he saw flames coming down the ridge, much larger and closer than anything to date. And this was a type of fire he had never seen, a stampede. Looking up, he saw towering columns of black smoke above the treeline, and then—the strangest of things—the columns themselves would explode into flame, sending off fire hundreds of feet above the treetops, like the towering spigot of a refinery. What he saw—known as fire whirls—can reach temperatures of 2,000 degrees, with a downdraft in the center and violent updrafts on the outer rings. Weigle knew then that Wallace was doomed, and he had to get back to sound the evacuation alarm.

He raced down the dirt roadway, running two miles through the heat and thick smoke. Halfway to town, he met a man stumbling uphill in the other direction, breathless, in a hurry to get to his family. Weigle recognized him as Speedy Swift, his first name an ironic reference to his slow movement, who had a homestead a few miles in, next to Placer Creek. Swift had been sick, and had gone into Wallace to see a doctor. He had started up the road with a two-horse carriage, but his ride was blocked by the same timber across the way that had stalled Weigle. His illness made it hard for him to walk, he explained.

"Can you help me?"

"What can I do?"

"My wife and baby are up there."

But Weigle had that other task, to get back to Wallace, where the town awaited his word. When he asked the man for specific directions, Swift pointed up beyond the smoke, where it looked as if fire was already on top of the forest. His family may have burned to death an hour or so ago. Weigle had his doubts. Swift begged the forest supervisor to save his family. Begged him.

Weigle told him to sit. He turned back to where he had seen flames shooting above black columns. If he could do the rescue quickly, get in and help the homestead family and get out, he would still have time to make it back to Wallace and order the evacuation, or so he thought. He made a dash for Swift's ranch. There he found the charred and smoldering skeleton of the homesteader's barn. He heard voices of men. Through the haze, he followed the voices to the Swift family farmhouse. Firefighters—nearly a dozen, hired by Weigle just a few days earlier—were carrying water in buckets from a well, talking in the clipped, elliptical cadence of people in chaos.

What were they doing here? They were supposed to be up on the ridge with Pulaski, or with the Italians, trying to hold the fire line. When the bad winds started up, with horrid howls and explosions, when the columns of smoke appeared, that's when they feared for their lives and decided to go downhill, the men told Weigle. Could he blame them? They had run down the trail and found the primitive road along Placer Creek, the road to Wallace. But as the smoke thickened and the fire gained on them, they took shelter at the

Swift homestead. But see here: the family's barn had burned to the ground. Now they were trying to protect the little house, pouring water on the exterior, as much to save themselves as the structure. The space around the house was cleared. And what about the family, Weigle asked, a woman and child? They were safe for now, after being taken down to a creek and covered with wet blankets.

With that news, Weigle turned and ran again, back down the road to where he had left the homesteader, and beyond to his horse. It was dark now, but it would not have mattered if there had been residual daylight; the smoke was too thick to see more than few feet ahead. Weigle felt disoriented, dizzy, moving through the indecipherable muddle of the atmosphere. He took deep, steady breaths and tried to remain calm, to find his way. He called out for the homesteader, but his voice was a faint cry amid the screaming wind and the percussive pops of superheated trees exploding.

Swift was nowhere. The heat burned against Weigle's eyes and up his nostrils. Flames all around. The back of his hand caught fire for an instant, the skin stinging, as if a dozen hornets had poked him. When his mop of red hair started to burn with a sickly smell, he reached for a handful of gravel from the road and rubbed it on his head. But now the fire was in front of him, big downed timbers engulfed by tongues of flame across the dirt road. He could descend no more. He had no choice but to go back uphill yet again. He remembered a tunnel he had passed, a mining hole. Trudging onward in the black of a burning night, Weigle found the mine about a half mile along the way. If he was to survive, he had to crawl inside and wait out the firestorm.

In Wallace, the boy mayor, Walter Hanson, was pressed to make a decision. He had spent the afternoon organizing the exodus. Meanwhile, he hurried back to his family's frame house—his mother had already been evacuated—and hosed it down with water. Late in the day, with Forest Supervisor Weigle missing, Mayor Hanson went up Placer Creek himself for a quick look. He was turned back by heat and flames lunging from the mountains. The roar of the firestorm, more than anything, shook him. No matter Weigle's fate, the mayor now decided to act on his own. Back in town, he sounded the alarm, ordered the troops to start the evacuation, and reiterated his previous command that all able-bodied men had to assist under threat of jail or death.

Nobody had ever heard the Bitterroot Mountains bellow as they did that Saturday night. People were chased from their homes by the screaming wind as much as by the alarm. One shopkeeper called it "a continuous staccato or rumbling crash, with cracking sounds and no let-up whatsoever." Another said it was like "heavy horse carriages crossing a wooden bridge." In the darkness, the streets were packed with people, some fleeing for the river, intending to wait out the fire in the shallows, others riding horses and carriages straight out of town, unsure of whether they were heading into the fire or not.

They had just moments, everyone in town, to decide what was worth saving. Some put their furniture in a pile in the backyard, in the hope it would be around should the house burn. A small girl grabbed her father's Masonic dress hat. A neighbor asked for help in moving a piano to the street. A few people filled their bathtubs, creating their own water reservoirs. Nellie Stockbridge, a refined woman from Chicago who had devoted her life to photographing Wallace as it came of age, took a pair of prized glass plates from her studio and fled, leaving the rest of a life's work behind. Most people milled around the train depot, wading through rumors and cries of panic, the young women holding babies, the elderly sitting on benches, all jittery, primed to flee. They could see fire on the ridgetops that bordered town, a rippling trim of purple and yellow gases moving ever closer.

About 9 P.M., a thick flaming ember landed just outside the *Wallace Times*. Buckets of oil, solvents, and grease—press lubricants—were lying about in open-lidded containers. It took just minutes for the newspaper building to catch, as the oil exploded and the wooden structures quickly fell to flame. Nearby, an old furniture store burned and collapsed, its main support timbers crumbling with a loaded thud. A new store, next to it, had just opened, filled with the latest in upholstered lounges and chairs. It soon fell. Firemen waited a few blocks away, hoses in hand, ready for battle, but the wind knocked them back and they realized whatever water they could bring forth would scatter and spray, useless. A twenty-mile-an-hour wind, blowing steadily, will toss a cowboy hat off a head. A wind of forty miles an hour hurts the eyes and makes it hard to walk without faltering. At sixty miles an hour, the air is strong enough to throw a person to the ground. That's the power of wind only. Add fire and debris to it, add thick, flaming branches or chunks of bark in an airborne stream, and it becomes a brute force.

"The wind was blowing so strongly that more than once I grabbed onto a telephone line to keep from being blown down," said Leo Worstell, a merchant, describing how he secured himself with insulated lines strung at eye level. Word came that the bridge separating the main town from the hospital run by the Sisters of Providence was aflame. The fire department relied on horses and bicycles to get from one place to another. But before any effort could be made to rescue the nuns, the span burned, and the splintered remains crashed to the river. This meant that the hospital, with about two dozen patients, was cut off from the evacuation effort.

"Words cannot depict the horror of that night," said a witness, Carl C. Getz. "The train whistles were screaming, the heavy boom of falling trees and buildings, the crackle of the fire, the buildings were swaying and steaming from the heat."

Ed Pulaski found his crews scattered along either side of the ridge separating Wallace from Avery, in varying stages of panic and retreat. Any effort at organized firefighting had vanished with the approach of the storm. Moving upward, Pulaski faced wind so strong it was a struggle to stay in his saddle. Worse, his packers turned on him. They were bringing fresh supplies to the lines—vital for any

effort to keep the crews in place. But now the packers dropped their
loads well before they reached the fire camps, dumping blankets,
food, and other supplies. Pulaski had ordered them to press on—it
did him no good to drop the loads this far from the destination—but
his words had no effect. The packers retreated in the direction they
had come, toward Wallace.

One fire crew was scattered all over the ridge, some of the men
lost and crying for their lives, others full of adrenaline and primed
to make a dash. "Out of the smoke would come Pulaski, waving
his arms, hollering, 'Come on! Come on! Follow me,'" a firefighter,
William Chance, recalled. Pulaski rounded up about fifty men. One
idea, suggested by several crew members, was to take refuge in a
nearby alpine lake. Pulaski knew the lake well; he had named it for
his only child. Elsie Lake was deep, holding runoff at the basin of
steep slopes, but it was not a good option, Pulaski said—they would
drown or break limbs trying to find the lake in the darkness. He
had a better plan. One by one, the remaining men, stricken by fear,
muttering incoherently, were collected in the dark. If they could
hold together, Pulaski explained, they could make a dash for Wallace, down the West Fork of Placer Creek. After the desertion of
his packers, Pulaski needed to show more strength to back his authority. Strapped to his side was that .44 revolver. Thereafter, when
confronted with mutinous or confused men who spurned his orders,
the forest ranger put one hand on his pistol and said he intended to
use it if pressed. His word was law in the burning woods.

When he had gathered his men, Pulaski told them the plan—a
brisk hump downhill. Follow him, was the order, though some
wanted to stay put. They were surrounded by a wind that tossed
flames from crown to crown. Big trees fell at random, and horses
whinnied and bucked.

"Try to make Wallace," Pulaski said. "That's our chance."

They started down through the maze of fire, the ground shaking with the sound of falling trees and hissing flame. One of the
men, S. W. Stockton, middle-aged and overweight, had consider-

able trouble keeping up. He was known as Dad because of his age; he'd talked his way onto the crew because he'd been a Texas Ranger once. But he was in no shape to be chasing fires or running from a wall of flame in the heat of August. After stumbling, he pleaded with Pulaski to stop. To stay behind was to burn to death. Pulaski dismounted. Dad said he could walk no farther. This was it.

"Take my horse," Pulaski said.

Stockton was stunned. "Get up," Pulaski said. "I'll help you."

Another straggler at the rear of the column was not so lucky. He had fallen behind, unable to walk, or perhaps paralyzed by fear. Motionless, he called out for other crew members to sit with him. They would have none of it. When he started to burn, his hair and clothes aflame, his voice turned into a murderous cant, the sound of life at its end, and it only pushed the men farther from him. "They were running like scared rabbits," the Forest Service later reported. And when, days later, the man's body was found, it was mistaken for a burned-out log.

After a few more switchbacks on the downward trail, Pulaski's crew ran headlong into the maw of the firestorm. Now they were trapped. Pulaski froze for an instant, seeking an exit. He guided his men out of the creekbed and through unburned forest, trying to dodge the front line of the fire. But the storm moved in random rages, flames looking for fuel in all directions. The heat intensified, and the flames closed in. Trees fell behind them and ahead of them. Pulaski realized that it was impossible to reach Wallace; they would have to walk through the firestorm to go in the direction of town.

They had but a few moments to live, perhaps, and what a way to leave the earth: skin curled up in flame, face burning, lungs scorching inside with every breath. Men fell to their knees, covered their heads, and wailed. A horse jumped and screamed, its tail on fire. Pulaski had an idea: a mine tunnel less than a mile away, a hole he remembered from his prospecting days.

"Why not stay here?" a man shouted. "Here's safety!" He had found a hole in the side of the mountain, clearly a mine tunnel,

but not the one Pulaski had in mind. Several men packed themselves inside, but there was little room for the rest of the fleeing
firefighters.

"This won't work," Pulaski said.

He stumbled around the steep, smoking ravine, looking for his
mine. The ground burned nearly as much as the trees overhead. The
forest was smothering them, its gases, its heat, its searing convection
winds fanning the flames upward. Next to the desiccated creekbed,
Pulaski ran his hands over the timbers of an open hole—the mine
he was looking for. He draped a wet gunnysack over his head and
went inside, sniffing at the air, probing the ceiling, trying to deter-
mine if it was large enough to hold them all.

"In here!" he ordered. "Everyone inside the tunnel." Even then,
some men were hesitant to crawl into a darkened hole of a mountain on fire. Pulaski put his hand on his revolver, repeating the
order.

"Everyone inside. Now!"

Other options were foreclosed by the fire. The path where the
men had trod a minute earlier was now covered by flames. With
this last nudge of fire, men shoved and leaned to get to the mine.
Inside the tunnel, voices clashed, men pushed and struggled, tears
poured forth. Two horses made it inside with them. Stockton had
dismounted and found a little pocket of darkness near the horse
that had carried him, Pulaski's mount. The air had been cold, but
it quickly warmed, and then just as quickly went stale and hot. The
outside heat was sucking all the cold air from the tunnel. How long
till the oxygen was gone?

At the mine entrance, the timbers caught fire, drawing more air
from the tunnel, taking it from the men who needed it to stay alive.
Pulaski wetted his shirt in the puddles of water on the ground and
tried to smother the flames at the entrance. He also used his hat as
a bucket, scooping water and throwing it on the flaming timbers
at the mouth of the mine. He thought that by shielding the entrance with wet cloth, he could keep the fire from drawing clean

air out. His filter worked at first, before the cloth heated enough to catch fire. Now their porthole to the outside world was open, and what they saw, from the last part of the forest that was not burning, prompted panic.

Pulaski ordered everyone back, as far into the tunnel as they could press themselves. "Nobody goes anywhere. I want everyone down, face on the ground. If you sit up, you'll suffocate."

One man fought with another for space. In the fight, he started to strangle the man. Another felt himself next to the second horse, the body warm but no longer moving. The horse was dead, lying in a puddle. Face-down in the muck of the tunnel, men started to choke and gag. The smell of burning flesh was thick in the cave, the air heavy with death. Bodies twitched and convulsed, people spitting back the mud from the ground. One man fainted, falling face-first to the floor of the tunnel, and then another did the same thing. They would die here—it was obvious in the way that one sees death in all its certainty—not in the sea of burning flame outside. This death in the darkest reaches of hell was better, perhaps, than death by suffocation, better than getting engulfed by flame. The realization was too much for one man; he reared up out of a crouch, taking quick steps toward the light, stepping over men lying face-down. He headed for the flaming forest, an outside world where everything appeared to be burning. Pulaski planted himself at the entrance and drew his gun for the first time. Nobody doubted he would kill the man—justifiable homicide by the logic of this moment.

"The next man who tries to leave the tunnel," said Pulaski, "I will shoot."

By Pulaski's thinking, the only chance of surviving was to stay put in the mine. The fire was *out there*, taking everything. The man retreated, cursing Pulaski. He would soon get another chance to flee. Fighting to douse the flames on the timbers supporting the mine, Pulaski wobbled, his head light, his breath labored. He fell to his knees, feeling weak. Fresh wet blankets that he had wrapped around the timbers now caught fire. When Pulaski rose and tried to knock them away, his hands burned. A few seconds later, his face was aflame: the fire was in his eyes. He scooped up a hatful of water and poured it over his head. He replaced the burning blankets with the last available damp cloths. But this effort pushed him over; it was too much. His skin had burned. Same with his eyes, his hair. He could not see, not just to the entrance, but anywhere. He was blind. The flames had taken his sight. Pulaski fell back to the floor of this coffin of crying men and dying horses, fell to the ground, unconscious.

On the other side of the ridge, the sprint to cover started as soon as the winds fanned through the forest Saturday evening. Unlike Pulaski's crew, the Italians, Greeks, and homesteaders on the terrain that sloped toward the town of Avery and the St. Joe River had agreed on an exit plan, should they be surrounded by flames: flee for Beauchamp's two acres. Their ranger, John Bell, had gone to town earlier in the day to get fresh provisions, just as his boss Pulaski had done. There were fifty people in this crew, broken off from the original two hundred working under Pulaski. When they heard and then felt the hard, violent front of wind, they fled for the homesteader's clearing, but by the time they got there, the fire had caught up with them. The men jumped into the shallow creek and fell to their backs, half submerged, their heads covered with dampened clothes, their noses just above the water line for breathing.

They could see the fire, smell the fire, and hear the fire, moving over the clearing with a roar and a thump. Now they could feel the fire. Fingers, exposed by holding wet clothes around their heads, were singed, and it felt as if needles pricked their skin. One giant fir crashed atop the creek, crushing to death a man who lay in the water. Another tree landed across the legs of a firefighter, breaking both limbs and pinning him to the ground. For the other men, to stay in the water seemed like certain death, held by falling timbers. But to move could also prove fatal. "There was no damn horse fast enough in the country to keep ahead of that fire," wrote one survivor.

Beauchamp had dug a little open cellar for storing things, a primitive hole in the ground, about three feet deep, five feet long, a few feet across, and not yet finished. At one end of the cellar he had started to carve a cave of sorts. The pit could hold three men at most; seven rose from the creek and tried to find shelter there. Beauchamp was the first to run for his hole, followed by six others, including Giacomo Viettone and Domenico Bruno. Two weeks earlier, they had left the tight, perilous air of the pits in Arizona Territory for the woods of the northern Rockies, thinking it would be more like Rivara. Now they squeezed themselves into the small hole, their faces pressed down, scrunching man-into-man in hopes of avoiding the flaming tree trunks that crashed to the ground. They pushed forward, squishing each other to get into the cave opening, crammed so tight that some could no longer breathe.

In his cave outside Wallace, Bill Weigle too struggled for breath. So much air was being sucked out of the dark hole and into the firestorm that soon his oxygen would be gone. Like Pulaski, Weigle went through the same mental calculus. Did he have a better chance of survival outside or inside? The forest supervisor decided to take his chances with the fire rather than suffocate in the mine tunnel. He soaked his clothing in the puddle at the base of the hole, held a wet hat over his face, and took his first steps away from the tunnel. All the world was on fire—flames overhead, flames to the left, flames to the right, the ground alive. Weigle fell to his knees, scratched a depression in the sand, and planted his face down in the dirt. This kept his nose, eyes, and mouth from catching fire, but not the rest of his body. The flames found the back of his neck, his hair, and when he put his hands over his head, his already burned fingers were singed again. The pain was unrelenting.

By midnight, the flames had passed over him, leaving a smoldering wreck of a forest, smoking and burning at the ends of roots and tree trunks. He walked several miles to the place where he had left his horse and the homesteader Speedy Swift. He called out for Swift, looking around the hot, dead trees for any sign of him. A few feet away, Weigle found his horse—on its side, dead. Whether the horse had been suffocated by smoke or burned to death, Weigle could not tell. By all indications, his horse had broken loose from his lash, then fell to its death not far away. It was a blackened corpse.

An hour later, Weigle arrived at the outskirts of Wallace. Bridges to town were burned. There were no lights on, nothing to indicate that Wallace had lived through the hurricane of heat and flame. He saw flames coming from the east end of town, smoke over everything else, and still the wind rained fiery flotsam, blowing overhead and at eye level. If anything, the wind speeds had picked up as the air was pulled along to higher, hotter ground. Weigle stumbled over to the city reservoir, at town's edge. Debris burned next to the main water line, and the wood stave pipe was on fire. It looked as if it might break, depriving Wallace of any remaining water. Using his hat, Weigle scooped water from the reservoir until the wood stave fire was out.

Weigle reached town at 2 A.M. The city was coming apart, the fire still raging. He heard screams and hysterical voices. He saw people running through the streets, sobbing and shouting. He saw a flurry of suitcases and satchels clutched by people on horseback, fleeing in the dark, west toward Spokane. He saw soldiers trying to get people from one part of town to the other. He found neighbors in their backyards, still digging holes in which to bury their possessions. He looked for the mayor, for some guidance. He looked for the fire captain. His face was badly burned, as was his neck, his hand, his fingers, but Weigle made his way to Forest Service headquarters. There he tried to get updates. A few rangers were working one of the few telegraph lines still open, tapping in frantic code, planning to flee themselves in just a few minutes. Weigle wanted basic information.

Where was Joe Halm? The rookie ranger had been sent deeper into the forest than anyone, sixty-five miles from the nearest road.

He had a big crew with him. Missing was the best answer Weigle could get.

Where was John Bell and his band of immigrants in the St. Joe drainage? Bell's crew was supposed to keep the fire from dropping down on Avery. Anyone heard from Bell? No reports. Nothing. No messages. Missing.

What about Avery, over the divide? The town was supposed to evacuate, but the way out may have been cut off by fire that burned the railroad trestles. There were soldiers in place. But for now it looked as if nobody was going to get out of Avery.

And where was Ed Pulaski, last seen on his horse making his way up Placer Creek with packers and fresh supplies? Pulaski was his best man, the human firewall. *Where's Pulaski?* He asked again. Not a word had come in. No signal or scrap of information had arrived. Missing.

Weigle sent one message to headquarters in Missoula and spoke briefly to reporters before leaving the building for the town's fire line, where volunteers were trying to save what was left of Wallace.

"All crews are hopelessly lost," Weigle said in his dispatch to Greeley. "We are badly in need of more men."

He was in no shape to help, the burns on his face and hands raw, with blackened, opened skin. The mayor ordered him to the hospital, the one in town. Just then, Weigle met up with a man who had made a long trudge down Placer Creek by himself. The story he told was a nightmare: firefighters crammed into a mining tunnel, lying in the mud with their dying horses as the forest all around burned and collapsed. He had crawled over bodies and found his way down the ravine to town, the man said. Everyone who was left in the tunnel was dead, he reported. And that included Ed Pulaski.

12

The Lost Night

THE REPORTS COMING into the Forest Service headquarters in Missoula and passed on to the Army's high command and President Taft defied credulity: about three million acres, an area 50 percent larger than Yellowstone National Park, was burning — "the fiercest forest fire in the history of the country," as *Collier's* reported later. The numerous smaller blazes that had raged throughout August were now a single all-consuming storm. The Big Burn, some in the press called it, a fire that had run from central Idaho, east into Montana, west into Washington, north into British Columbia, and was still on the move. Smoke drifted hundreds of miles from the blowup, into the Dakotas and Colorado and Alberta and Wyoming. It was as if a volcanic blast had disgorged the airborne remains of the forested northern Rockies into disparate parts of the United States.

"It was frightening, as what seemed to be great flakes of white snow were swirling to the ground in the heat and darkness of high noon," wrote Norman Maclean, who as a boy of seven was camping with his family in the Bitterroot Valley of Montana, downslope from the firestorm.

The rangers who had watched the small blazes build all summer, who had assembled a force of firefighters bigger than any group ever put together to face flame in the country, found them-selves at a loss for words. Most often, they described the firestorm as a hurricane. Other terms came from all parts of the district. A once-in-a-century event. A catastrophe that might well wipe out the fin-est white-pine forest standing, half a dozen towns, and a generation of young men who had gone to the woods at the call of conser-vation.

"All hell broke loose," Bill Greeley reported. For the minister's son this was as emphatic as he got. His rangers—those still in con-tact—were sending dispatches that made it sound as though vir-tually all of the forested domain of the United States government was under attack. They wrote of giant blowtorches flaming from treetop to treetop, of house-size fireballs rolling through canyons, pushed by winds of seventy miles an hour. They told of trees swell-ing, sweating hot sap, and then exploding; of horses dying in sec-onds; of small creeks boiling, full of dead trout, their white bellies up; of bear cubs clinging to flaming trees, wailing like children.

"Never had any of us seen such a sight," wrote Will Morris, a young ranger who had cleared a patch of ground a few miles above Wallace late Saturday afternoon, hoping the storm would hopscotch over him. "In the direction of the city of Wallace great masses of smoke were blowing wildly up the valley of the South Fork. South-ward toward the St. Joe stood a great white cloud pillar, apparently still, looking like a great thunderclap or the steam cloud that at-tends the eruption of volcano." Even taking a breath, he said, was a taste of a boiler room— "as if the very air was afire."

By late Saturday night, more than five hundred firefight-ers were missing, many presumed to be dead. There was Weigle's haunting message—"All crews hopelessly lost"—but others were just as grim. It was the "hopelessly" part that sank many hearts. The brightest lights of Gifford Pinchot's agency were somewhere behind an unknowable wall of flames and black smoke. The word in Missoula was that Wallace had fallen. In a dispatch from 3 A.M., *The Missoulian* reported: "Wallace is believed to be destroyed; there

has been no communication directly with the city since 11 o'clock."
Then a later report was appended. "Wallace has fallen at last," the
front-page story reported. "This morning, unless an act of Providence intervened, only the ashes and smoldering embers mark the
place where yesterday morning stood the most beautiful city in the
Coeur d'Alenes."

From the inside, Wallace was a prison of heat and betrayal.
"Flames were eating up the residences on the east side, and everywhere was a confusion of women and children rushing to and fro,
shouting and screaming, little hope being entertained of saving
any of the city," Charles D. Roth told the *Seattle Times*. What had
started in a combustible alley next to the newspaper building, then
jumped to the city's biggest furniture store and a planing mill, had
fanned out to torch nearly a hundred structures. After the evacuation signal had been sounded, some people refused to leave, afraid
to go into the hive of fear and chaos in the streets. Out of habit,
some men fled to the Oasis Room, one of five brothels in town. Others crawled inside holes dug in their backyards. The Coeur d'Alene
Hotel, a three-story rooming house that stood by the river, was fully
enflamed, black smoke pouring from open windows and the roof.
As the fire coursed through the hotel, it killed a man who lay frozen on his bed. Within minutes, the walls collapsed. When the Sunset Brewery started to burn, more than two thousand wood barrels
of beer broke open, spilling suds into the street. Downtown, people
tried to send out messages from the telegraph and telephone switch-
boards, manned by seven operators.

Now the mayor declared full martial law. Hanson's concern in
taking the extraordinary measure was looting. It was one thing to
lose the city to flame, but another to its own residents. There were
sights to make a mayor proud: volunteers, young and old, hosing
down buildings, working shoulder to shoulder with the fire department to keep Wallace from collapsing. Rail workers for the Northern Pacific used a tank car drawing water from the river to control hot spots all over town. Women with babies and small children,

cooling their heads with wet towels, mouthed a mother's primal re-
assurance as they made their way to the trains under a shower of
firebrands. And the soldiers from the 25th Infantry were perform-
ing well while people all around them were losing their heads. The
troopers' job was to make sure the evacuation trains were boarded
by the elderly, the sick, women, and children. This task the soldiers
had done, showing no fear or favor, the mayor said later, even if
some had to nudge men with the tips of their bayonets.

But there were also things to make a mayor lose faith in people
—folks he had known since he was a kid now betraying him,
going back on their promise to stay and fight for their homes.
One man had pushed aside a pregnant woman, taking her seat on
the coach. He was pummeled by a fireman. All these prominent
men—bankers and business owners, insurance brokers and builders, families who had names on the sides of buildings, and people
who had made a fortune draining the mountainsides of their precious metals—they were disgusting, men without honor. They el-
bowed, shoved, and bullied their way onto the exit trains, ignoring the mayor, almost taunting him to do something. At one point,
windows in the train shattered and a door broke down. Under martial law, the mayor could arrest people on the spot. But realistically,
there was nowhere to put them. The jail had been emptied of prisoners, and it was likely to burn. Felons were working the fire lines.
In the end, Mayor Hanson had taken the advice of his fire chief:
"Let the bastards go."

As winds shoved the fire east, it took buildings, bridges, commercial signs, standing poles, and ornamental trees. It took a cigar factory, a lumberyard, a bank. And it burned property owned by Weldon Heyburn. The Idaho senator had been in town earlier in the
month, working to advance his lucrative law trade. He briefly made
news when he shut down a visiting small orchestra that tried to play
a song during a public performance that was not to his liking, showing the flash of temper that earlier led him to fulminate against a
national commission on the arts. He had kept up his law practice

long after he was named to the Senate and had become a wealthy man, helping mining syndicates that dealt in public-land speculation. Along the way, he was handed pieces of the action. While other senators spent the summer months working on behalf of constituents, Heyburn serviced his mining clients, using the power of his name on official stationery, his public duties nicely dovetailing with his private interests. Through every vote in the Senate, through hearings in which he belittled rangers of Gifford Pinchot's service and questioned them about expenditures for the smallest of things, through scoldings where he insinuated that rangers were un-American, he had done his best to kill the Forest Service. But some of his penurious pruning now came back to haunt him. As the men who were supposed to protect Wallace were trapped in tunnels and holes, without enough shovels to dig the trenches that might save their lives, a mass of flame washed over Wallace and burned the ledgers and notations, and up higher, one of the mine-processing operations of Weldon Heyburn, senator and speculator.

A few doors away from Heyburn's office, the evacuation trains were packed, one ready to go east, one west. Each direction was uncertain, for there was fire up and down the valley. It seemed that the best gamble was to move. The coaches had no room for another dog or child or suitcase. Even the coal and supply cars had been put to use. Away the trains went at last, away from Wallace, screaming into the night. People wept at the thought that they would never see their homes again, never see husbands or sons, those men holding hoses, dashing from one flareup to another. Goodbye, Wallace.

The biggest concern now was Providence Hospital, the pride of Wallace, looking like a European spa set against the Alps. It was cut off from the rest of town by the river. Earlier, the nuns had summoned carriages to evacuate. But when the bridge went down, livery stables said they had no way to get to the hospital. Crews went to work placing I-beams across the South Fork of the Coeur d'Alene, trying to fashion a rickety span. Inside the hospital were patients, nuns, nurses, doctors, and assorted workers. Also, as the night wore on, people who said they were homeless, and feared death by fire, had asked for refuge in the hospital. The nuns could not turn them away. Trees close to the hospital went up like rockets as the nuns moved to evacuate the sick. There was still a train on the hospital's side of the river, a small branch line with coal cars and a caboose. This would have to be their rescue.

But the train engineer had a problem: the tracks nearest to the hospital went only one way, east, toward Montana. The latest word from other stations was that the big wooden trestles that held track on this route had caught fire. So, a choice: flee into the heart of the burning forest at night, on a line that might well plunge into ravines of flame, or stay and cook inside the hospital. The nuns decided to make a run for it on the train. They gathered their sick — those just a day or so removed from primitive operations and the chronically ill whom they cared for as part of their service — hauled them onto coal cars and caboose, and fled. Space was at a premium, as it had been on the evacuation trains, forcing several nuns to straddle a pile of ore.

"Wait!" came a cry as the train pulled out. "The basement. There are three patients still behind."

The tiniest of the nuns at Providence, Sister Antioch, ran from the train toward the hospital. She found her way to a basement thick with smoke. Three elderly patients were moaning in the dark. The nun helped them up one by one and led them outside. But by the time Sister Antioch had rescued them, the train had gone. The nun and her wards were left to fend for themselves.

Emma Pulaski and her daughter held tight to each other in the berm of crushed silt at the edge of a reservoir as the air around them heated. Neighbors had pleaded with her to get on one of the trains; if she didn't go, surely she would never live to see Sunday morning. But Emma had made her plan, a pact with her husband. In the stifling air of Saturday night and into Sunday morning, she watched from her refuge as fire transformed all that she knew as home. "Wallace was a mass of flames," she wrote, and above her, "the flames leaped from one mountain to another until it seemed as though the whole world was afire." That world included her husband, of course, who was somewhere in the middle of the firestorm. From the relative safety of her redoubt, she tried to suppress thoughts of his horrid death.

"Ask God to save daddy and his men," Emma told her daughter.

After five hours inside the tunnel, the men who had followed Ed Pulaski started to stir. The air was thick with smoke and carbon monoxide; men gasped for breath, fearing suffocation or poisoning. Their bodies convulsed in darkness, flopping inside the tight corridor of the mine. An hour or so before dawn, a couple of the men moved toward the entrance, crawling over Pulaski's lifeless body.

"Come on outside, boys—the boss is dead."

"Like hell he is."

The last words spoken came from Pulaski himself, snapped to life perhaps by a small stream of noticeably cooler air. Pulaski tried to stand, but his legs were numb; he wobbled, bracing himself, struggling to get his footing. He could see out of one eye, and what he saw was a greyish white thicket of smoke, but no flaming orange. He dragged himself to the entrance, stepped outside. His body buckled in the first step, a drop, for the tunnel was dug into the side of a steep ravine with no level ground. His lips, throat, and mouth were parched, but when he bent over to drink from the creek, he gagged and spit it back. The water was warm, full of ashes.

A barely discernible light allowed the fire crew to look around and assess the damage. What had been all-encompassing green a day before was a horizontal forest of smoldering trees in grey, brown, and black. The woods had been leveled, trees atop trees, their roots facing up. Pulaski could not see a standing fir, a live fern, a huckleberry bush, a flower, or a blade of grass. The earth had been transformed, all living things changed by fire.

They took a head count and came up with five men dead. *Are you sure?* Pulaski asked. They touched the bodies—one, two, three, four, five—slapped the faces, poured water over them. No pulse. No life. Yes, five men were gone, as were two horses inside the shaft. But forty-one men had made it alive, including the old Texas Ranger, Stockton, the man who had been given Pulaski's horse. When the horse fell, it backed up the water in the mine, creating a puddle about a foot deep. Stockton thought that two men had drowned in that puddle while they were unconscious. He stayed alive by planting his face in a pocket of air between the bodies.

"We have to move," Pulaski said. "We don't have any choice. We have to get down."

But how? Men pointed to their bare, blistered feet—the soles of their shoes had burned off. Some sat dazed, staring at a snag that crackled above them. Awake for some time, Pulaski still could not see at all out of one eye, and thought that the other eye would go as well. His boots were burned through at the bottom. His clothes were rags. The fire had seared his face, his hands, parts of his body.

"We have to move."

Domenico Bruno and Giacomo Viettone were huddled with five others in the little half-built root cellar on Joe Beauchamp's homestead when the wind knocked down nearly every tree in the surrounding area, carrying the fire with it. One big timber fell atop the hole, trapping the men and burning them at the same time. The firefighters who had chosen to stay put in the creek heard the screams of the men as flames roasted them in the pit. Just as sickening were the last cries of the man under the dead-weight clamp of a fallen tree. The big fir held him by his foot while the rest of his body burned. He clawed with his fingers, squirmed and kicked with his free leg, but could not break loose. About half a mile away, a lone timber worker, Arthur Hogue, watched the forest fall.

"Looking down the valley, one could see the fire coming on with a rush and roar," he wrote in a letter to his mother. "Flames would leap across from one summit to the other in one continuous stream of fire . . . It would have been a most beautiful sight had one not realized that in the next moment you might be caught in its fiery folds."

Precisely what killed the Italians is unknown—smoke inhalation, carbon monoxide poisoning, or trauma from flames. Their bodies were so burned and blackened they could not be identified, and their hands, with the skin gone, were clenched into fists.

The men in the root cellar "were cooked alive," said David Bailey, who had thrown himself into the creek nearby. "All of them tried to get at the very end of the small hole and they were piled up in an awful heap. It was impossible to take out their bodies, for they would fall to pieces."

Later, the Forest Service summarized their deaths this way: "Killed by falling trees and burned beyond recognition in Beauchamp's clearing." The newspapers did not name the two men from Rivara Canavese. A story headlined "Seven Victims Buried in Hole" mentioned by name each of the other men who died, and said something about them—their hometowns, their backgrounds, a good word from a friend or family member. Domenico Bruno and Giacomo Viettone, who had traveled more than six thousand miles to find work to help their peasant families in the Italian Piemonte, who had bounced from mining towns in Wyoming and Arizona only to find themselves as foot soldiers trying to save the dream of Teddy Roosevelt and Gifford Pinchot, ended their journey in anonymity.

"Two unidentified Italians," the papers said, and thereafter in news stories and some memorials, they remained as such.

But in one record the immigrants had names and notations: a crew chief's time book, with hours logged on behalf of the Forest Service. It showed that Bruno and Viettone had worked seventeen days without a break since being hired on August 4.

The Italians were killed on the east fork of a creek well up in the mountains. One mile away, on the west fork of the same creek, another crew made a sprint to save their lives. These men were work-

ing under one of the youngest Forest Service employees in the region, Lee Hollingshead. He was twenty-two, and listed as a mere
forest guard, not yet a ranger. In the rush to find men to lead into
the flaming woods, Hollingshead had been elevated above his lowly
status and given nearly half as many men as Pulaski. When the big
firestorm hit his crew, they were surrounded, the flames heaving
over them with no escape plan in place.

Hollingshead knew at least one thing about a wildfire, a retreat
strategy the Indians had used: it will never burn the same ground
twice. So the young forest guard led forty men at a run back through
the fire to get to a clearing that had just been overrun by flame. The
dash cost them — burns on hands, face, and feet, hair afire — but
they made it.

Nineteen other men in his crew took another route. They ran
for a tiny cabin, owned by a man named Dittman, a place where
they had tied up their horses and stocked some provisions. As the
Italians had done, these men crammed into a tiny space in a group
shove, pushed up against one another, a clump on the floor. Fire
followed them into the one-room cabin. The walls curled, the roof
was ablaze, humans caught fire. As the ceiling fell in on them, a
load of fast-burning shingles and dried crossbeams, the men tried to
run outside, but made it only a few feet. The next day, when Hollingshead arrived after spending the night in the clearing, he found
eighteen bodies burned beyond recognition and the charred corpses
of five horses and a black bear. One man was unaccounted for, a
firefighter named Peter Kinsley. While wandering in the flaming woods toward Wallace, Kinsley twisted his ankle and fell to the
ground. That close to the earth, he found a tier of breathable air. It
was enough to save his life.

While no one was sure whether it was heart attack, flames, or suffocation by smoke that killed Patrick Grogan, his time of death was
reasonably certain. Grogan's watch stopped at 7:27 P.M., Saturday.
Since being hired as a cook in the first week of August, Grogan had

become a favorite of fellow Irishmen from Butte—copper miners, most of them, down on their luck or too old to work the pits of feudal Montana. He and his dog were a cheerful sight, Paddy full of stories and song, with a union-tough sense of loyalty and justice, always insisting on extra helpings of food for those who had been without. A picture shows Grogan with his greasy chef's apron, his cap pulled over his forehead, looking well fed for a man of 1910. He is making breakfast in Avery—flapjacks, bacon, and fried potatoes on outdoor stoves—in the photograph. On August 20, Grogan was dispatched to the steep mountains about six miles outside town, on Storm Creek. He was part of a crew of seventy men sent to dig a fire line around a blaze threatening Avery. His boss was the regional forester, Ralph Debitt, a quirky thirty-five-year-old with the requisite swagger and repertoire of ready bullshit needed to live among the railroad toughs of Avery.

On Saturday, Debitt left his firefighters to go into town for supplies. Avery was abuzz with troops and trains, homesteaders and merchants, and hundreds of firefighters awaiting instructions. As the ranger of the St. Joe district, Debitt was supposed to be in charge, and he seemed to be in this place or that, but never at the right time, and never when he was needed to make a decision. Debitt had no sooner arrived in town that evening than the wind came roaring up the St. Joe River. It was strong enough—it seemed to some—to lift the swift river from its ancient stone bed and toss it to the forest. At the same time, word reached town by telegraph downriver that the fire was sprinting toward them and would soon overtake Avery. Debitt sent a messenger back to his crew in the mountains with instructions for them to retreat immediately to town and evacuate. The messenger ran the distance uphill, and found the seventy men in panicky debate about what to do. A few miles away, another crew was having a similar argument, as flames rained from the sky and spit from the woods.

"I can't take it!" said a firefighter, Oscar Weigert, a twenty-three-year-old bricklayer from Montana. He looked possessed, saying he wasn't going to roast to death, wasn't going to die like a sausage on a grill, wasn't going down without a fight. He said this over and over, at times fingering his .32-caliber pistol, as he stuffed so much tobacco in his mouth it made it difficult to understand him. He carried the gun, he explained, because he wasn't going to take any crap from people. His gun was his insurance. The flames shot thousands of feet beyond their launches from the top of the burning forest, a sight that made Weigert all the more jittery. Again he swore this fire would not kill him. He would not stand by and burn. This was not the Army. The Forest Service could not force him to fight and die.

"They'll never catch me in this fire," he said. Just then, complete darkness fell over the forest, though it was hours before sunset. Weigert snapped. He ran for the woods. Seconds later came the sound of gunfire—two quick shots, heard by dozens of members of the crew. Weigert had killed himself.

The men in Grogan's camp thought they too would be killed in the most painful, horrific of ways. When the messenger arrived with the order from Debitt to make a run for Avery, Grogan would have none of it. He gave a short, passionate speech in the wind. He was not afraid of fire, he said. And at the age of fifty-nine, a grandfather of six—one of the oldest men fighting in the Bitterroots—he was not afraid to die. He thought the plan to flee would surely kill them. Who knew the way down? Look—it was nothing but columns of shooting flame and black smoke. Why not stay put on the fire line they had dug? At least they had a strip of ground to stand on that was free of fuel. Odds are, the fire will sniff the earth and move on, looking for something else to burn.

"I can't see no less danger here," Grogan said in his thick brogue.

His plea made sense to nearly half the crew, twenty-eight men in all. They stayed with Grogan and his dog, ready to face the fire in their clearing near Storm Creek. The other half fled for Avery around 6:30 P.M., a stumbling dash downhill, tripping often in the brush and snags. There was no proper trail back to town, just a bush-whack tread through the smoke. The fire caught up with them on the way, though it moved much slower going downhill than uphill. The ground burned, and trees overhead snapped and buzzed. Some of the men lost the soles of their shoes to hot ground and continued to run barefoot. But all of them made it the six miles to Avery—a remarkable retreat considering what they ran through. Avery now was an uncertain refuge, people fighting over whether to board an evacuation train or stay, just as had been done in Wallace. Two hours—at most—was all they had.

Back at Storm Creek, thousands of five-ton pines and centuries-old firs came crashing down. Great swaths fell all at once, entire flanks of flaming forest blown to the ground. Grogan and his dog were incinerated on the spot where they decided to stand their ground. Everyone else scattered. Some tried to run uphill, toward a canyon wall, and found themselves clawing and trapped. Others ran toward Avery, where the fleeing crew had gone. None of them had a chance; they had waited behind too long, and now they were a small part of what kept the Big Burn alive.

The fire was at its peak when it washed over Storm Creek, devouring hair, flesh, bone, skin, and cloth as one, killing all twenty-eight men who had stayed behind. While Grogan's silver timepiece showed 7:27, another watch was stopped at 7:34. It belonged to a man who had run the farthest distance from the clearing, buying himself seven minutes. The glass had melted in the watches, and coins found near blackened bodies were warped from the heat.

"Through a mistaken sense of bravery," the sheriff wrote in his report, "they refused to leave."

Grogan had worked 206 hours since his hiring on August 6, mostly twelve-to-sixteen-hour days, the logbook showed. On August 16, five days before his death, he had worked a twenty-four-hour day. His body was found next to that of his dog.

"A common laborer," the Forest Service noted in its record, just before dispersing Grogan's earnings to his children. Because he was

Irish, it added this about him: "Mr. Grogan was a man that drank but not to excess."

The British Empire, at its height in 1910, lost not just Irishmen in American forests, but Englishmen as well. Louis Holmes was from Birmingham, and was well known and well liked in the Coeur d'Alene Valley, where he worked as a restaurant cook. He stood out because of his accent, which made everything he muttered sound slightly more intelligent than the talk of other cooks, and because he was brimming with grand plans. In 1909, he went home to England and opened an American-style restaurant—his big dream being to bring a taste of the American West to Edwardian Britain. But it proved to be a failure. Steak, beans, and other trail fare just didn't taste the same in damp old England. Destitute, his hopes shattered, Holmes returned to the northern Rockies in 1910 and resumed work as a chef.

In this valley, in a state larger than Britain, he found his place. Holmes was hired by the Forest Service to cook for a large crew fighting in the Coeur d'Alene National Forest. Caught in the firestorm, he rushed into a mine tunnel near the Idaho-Montana border. But as Pulaski and Weigle had discovered, these shafts drew deadly smoke and gases inside, as clean air was sucked outside. Next to Holmes was a boy of seventeen, Val Nicholson, who had defied his parents, volunteering for fire duty in the heat of August. He was a local kid who wanted work, and to do something with the Forest Service. Fighting fire, he had a certain confidence that belied his age. But inside the mine tunnel, as the life was snuffed out of him, Nicholson was a child again, his mates recalled. The teenager died in the lethal air of the cave, most likely from smoke inhalation. Holmes met a similar fate. The boy and the Brit were among eight people who lost their lives in the Bullion Mine tunnel. In its one-line death notice about Holmes, the Forest Service said it could not find a next of kin to notify. But in Holmes's pocket watch was found a small photograph of his mother in England.

Another Birmingham native, Edward Hale, survived, as did a note he wrote to his mother:

"In Bullion Mine, August 21, 1910, 2:05 A.M. Mother dearest: this is my last. I am in charge of fifteen men in a drift. We are trying to hold out the smoke but chances are slim for us all. Forgive me if I have ever mistreated you, for I do love you. Goodbye. Ed."

13

Towns Afire

SKIPPING ALONG THE CREST of the Bitterroots midway through its two-day rampage, the fire took deep inhalations from either side of the summit ridge, consuming towns made of thin-cut timber and primitive planks in Montana and Idaho. The wickedest place in America, as a Chicago paper had described Taft, started to burn not long after midnight Saturday and fell in a few minutes.

The blowup took the saloons and gambling halls, the bunkhouses and chow joints, the stumps in the streets and the sex cribs in trees. Taft was kindling for a firestorm of this size, a tight bundle of shellacked wood, sun-dried boardwalks, and awnings of cloth and velvet. Though the Milwaukee Road had finished its transcontinental line through the Bitterroots a year earlier, there remained much work for crews of single men, with trestles to maintain, coal houses to stock, tracks to repair, tunnels to clear. The feat of engineering that had blasted through the spine of a mountain range drew on the same people who had constructed towns such as Grand Forks, in Idaho, and Taft, on the other side of the tunnel in Montana. These men stayed to keep the trains running; they left when fire chased them out of the woods.

It was in Taft, of course, that Forest Service officials had thought of trying to destroy the town before they let the fire do it for them. From the start of their uneasy presence there—like a colonial outpost in hostile territory—to this fiery end, the rangers' attitude toward the town was one of disgust. The caches of whiskey and rum, the slot machines, the hundreds of hookers, the killers and felons who mocked the rangers as Pinchot choirboys and fingered their guns to back up their liquid courage—that's what Taft represented to a forest ranger. After Koch's foresters were unable to muster even the smallest force to defend the town, they looked for a suitable place to start a most unusual backfire—toward Taft. They gave people fair warning, gave them a chance to leave on one of the small exit trains. Then they were going to burn the hellhole to the ground, saving only the Forest Service cabin. A backfire would clear enough ground near the station to give the rangers a fighting chance to save their small imprint inside Lolo National Forest.

Most people took the rangers at their word and left when the train came through, whistle blowing, the conductor warning of "last call" to get out of town. But a hard core of Taft denizens stayed behind and tried to drink themselves to death. For all their surface bluster and hard-shelled scorn for the Forest Service, the big men were helpless when it came time to fight for the life of their town. True to form, the men who made their money on this concentration of vice showed no interest in saving anything but the sources of their passion. They pried open their whiskey barrels and set to the task of chugging hard rye as the night wind tossed hot brands into town, as the air filled with screams of falling trees, as the wall of destruction moved on Taft. They drank and laughed and spat and drank some more.

As it turned out, Koch's men had no time to organize a precision backfire. The inferno galloped over the ridge all too quickly for any action.

"All hell has busted loose!"

Elers Koch was in Missoula, trying to keep track of the firestorm as it moved through the Lolo in the middle of the night, when that call came from a ranger in Taft. The foresters needed a rescue train to come back to get them. Throughout the day and into the evening, Koch had received hundreds of messages. Most were urgent requests for instructions, but some had a tone of deep fear, the minds of the senders focused by the very real possibility of burning to death.

"I've lost nearly all my crews." This was a call from another ranger down the divide in Avery. He had not been able to reach his boss, Bill Weigle, who was missing Saturday night, and so he called Missoula for the other Little G.P. in the region whom everyone looked to in a crisis.

"Mr. Koch," said a ranger from the Idaho side of the divide, "the fires have all gone wild . . . I don't know where my family is and my men and pack strings are all out in the path of the fire, and I am afraid many of them can't escape alive."

From Mullan, a town not far from Wallace, a man said it was like being "inside a deep bowl which is completely lined with seething flames, yourself a spectator in the center."

If Koch knew that his men had toyed with the idea of burning Taft, he never let on. His larger concern was a string of nearly a half-dozen towns, the rail settlements inside the Lolo. Not just Taft but Saltese, Haugan, DeBorgia, St. Regis. If the fire came that far downslope to the east, it might move on Missoula, less than a hundred miles from the ridge.

"This is the last call. Fire is breaking into Saltese. We'll do our best to hold it," said the ranger on the Montana side.

Just ahead of the fire, people heard a train whistle, an incessant get-out-of-the-way series of blasts. A crowd of dispirited firefighters gathered by the tracks, ready to abandon the settled valley and hop aboard. It was the main train from Wallace, carrying the women and children from that town. It was full, steaming east in a race to outrun the fire.

"The whole horizon to the west was aflame," Ranger Roy Phillips said. Then, a shock: the engine never slowed. "The train did not wait for us," he said.

Now the telephone lines went down, leaving Koch without a way to keep track of his men, the hundreds of firefighters spread throughout the Lolo and its necklace of towns. He had not slept, but then nobody who had been hired by Gifford Pinchot slept during the blowup. A few hours later, the sky still dark but for a throbbing light from inflamed mountainsides, Koch took a train up toward the fire to see how close he could get, to see if the towns could be saved.

"The sky turned first a ghastly, ominous yellow," Koch said. "It was completely terrifying."

The binge drinkers of Taft lolled in the street alongside a string of false-fronted saloons, hotels, and restaurants, trying to suck dry the last of their whiskey barrels, ever more oblivious to the collapse around them. One of the drunks caught fire and screamed for his life. Trying to snuff the flames that seared his skin and lit his hair, he rolled around in the dirt of the main street. A ranger picked him up, stomped the fire off him, and led him to a boxcar. Unable to start their backfire, Koch's men boarded the relief engine that had just arrived, the last chance to get out of Taft before it fell. They crowded in with the drunks, riding slowly downslope toward the other towns. Koch was headed toward them, coming from the opposite direction, from Missoula.

Taft had been named for the president, a man who was hearing reports of a catastrophe as first light came to his summer retreat on the Massachusetts shore. He was told that more than five hundred firefighters were missing, scores were dead, that three states were ablaze, that enough timber to build a city nearly the size of Chicago had been knocked to the ground or burned to cinders, that a half-dozen towns lay in the path of a hurricane of flame, and that he may have to send more troops. He was also informed that the Forest Service, which Pinchot had considered the finest agency of government servants, was being routed.

The town of Taft was home to "all races and colors, and to all appearances, John Barleycorn was the bosom friend of most of them," a doctor's wife, Edith Schussler, wrote of her time there, using an old term for a slave of grain alcohol. She was horrified by the place, as a refined woman from an eastern city might be. In truth, Taft had few blacks, but many drunks. What she saw as "all races and colors" were mainly Montenegrins, whom the locals snubbed with a phrase that often appeared in the papers too—"mountain niggers"—and Sicilians and other southern Italians. Hungarians, seldom identified by name, but called "bohunks," were also a big presence. And down in Avery, two-thirds of the residents were foreign-born, mainly from Greece, Bulgaria, and Japan. These people had built a thirteen-thousand-foot-long tunnel, the St. Paul Pass, blasting and chipping through rock at the center of the mountain range. It was the kind of job that prompted frenzied efforts to blot it out with strong drink.

Now the potent alchemy of fire had transformed what had been a rowdy eyesore into a geyser of sparks, shooting upward into the Montana night. And while Taft had not been saved, nor had the outpost of Gifford Pinchot, the rangers consoled themselves with the fact that not a soul had died in Taft during the chaos of the night. By threatening to burn the town just ahead of the blowup, Koch's men had managed to scare most of the residents into evacuating. However crazy the plan, it worked. Those who stayed behind to drink, and those who were hired by the government to fight fire, all had made it down to Saltese, about ten miles east of Taft. The freight cars pulled into Saltese with a soot-faced and sweating cargo of survivors.

Saltese was supposed to be a safe harbor, but Ranger Haun said the hills around town were alive with flames leaping from the tips of the tallest trees. Haun—the older man revered by Koch for his even temper and tough-nutted advice—had two hundred firefighters at his command. It was Haun who was the first man to back Koch when he had reached into his own meager savings account to find money to pay for firefighters, money that might save the forest. He set out now to protect Saltese. Why they let Taft crumble while making an effort to save Saltese was never explained, but virtue—or the lack of it—certainly had something to do with it.

Haun had only a few minutes to act, to lay down a protective backfire. He tried to enlist a group of refugees, including some section crews from the railroad. They refused. Fight for this town? Instead, they commandeered the train and headed east again, downhill, leaving everyone else behind. Their path to freedom was blocked a few miles out of town by downed bridges, which forced the train of rebels and mutineers back into Saltese. And there the Forest Service put them to work.

Half the men were ordered to turn hoses on the buildings of Saltese—high spray, full throttle. The other half worked the backfires. A self-started blaze was always tricky, because it could turn inward, on the fire-starters. The wind was variable, and thus Ranger Haun had to calculate his backfire so that the air would carry the flames away from town. On his order, the fires were lit. Small trees and brush caught immediately; flames rose to eye level and then went off in a great burst of speed and energy—as the rangers had desired—into the woods to meet the approaching fires. The ground was cleared quickly, leaving no fuel to give the fire energy to come into town. Saltese was saved.

But there was one casualty—left over, as it turned out, from the debacle of Taft. The severely injured man who had been burned while drinking howled in misery as Koch's men fought to keep Saltese from going to the sky. In Saltese, he was dressed in cotton gauze and oil for his burns, a remedy that was popular among lumberjacks and miners, and then told to lie quietly in an empty boxcar, protected from fire by the metal shell. A fellow drunk from Taft went to look in on his friend. In the dark, he lit a match to see; it fell to the floor and caught on the man's absorbent dressings. The oil-and-gauze combination swiftly burned, and the man jumped from the car screaming yet again. This fire covered his clothes, the fresh dressings, and most of his body. He burned to death—the lone loss of life from Taft, killed by a friend of the jug.

Coming from the other direction, Koch was still trying to get into Saltese, or close to Taft if he could, but his train was delayed by obstacles. More than once, the slow-moving locomotive put on its brakes as it climbed the Bitterroots, and Koch and his men jumped out to remove flaming branches or downed trees from the road that took them upward. He worried, as did everyone, about the deep ravines they had to cross on wood trestles that had been treated with oil as a preservative. They wouldn't know whether one of these bridges was afire or had been weakened or fractured until they were actually upon it. Nor did Koch know the fate of the towns ahead: that Taft had fallen, that the woods outside Saltese had caught fire, followed by Haugan, or that a fourth village, DeBorgia, was next.

By the time Koch made it to DeBorgia, about eight miles short of Saltese, less than twenty miles from Taft, fire was at the door. The Big Burn had jumped down the canyon that followed the St. Regis River on the Montana side of the divide. This town had a fine new schoolhouse, several bars, and a good hotel, and was set in a much broader clearing than the railroad towns that hugged narrow ground next to the tracks. In the dark, people milled around with their lanterns and hoses. The town constable jumped on his bicycle and rode to ranches in the vicinity of DeBorgia, warning people to flee on the train that had just arrived. When Koch got there, he had no Kipling verses in his head, as when he cruised the High Lonesome with his bride or alone on horseback. He was going on adrenaline, a kid trying to keep a tsunami of wildfire at bay, trying to save at least one town. Koch now fought the fire by hand, with help from rangers who had assembled buckets of water. It was a pathetic sight — Little G.P.s running around in the dark and swell of flames carrying buckets against the biggest wildfire anyone had seen in America, grains of sand compared to a mountain.

Throughout all the informal tutorials at Pinchot's Grey Towers and his family mansion on Rhode Island Avenue, fire had been described as a predictable foe — an enemy that could be conquered by orderly assaults. Man could win, as Pinchot had said many times. Based on the reports from his rangers farther up the mountains just before the lines went down, Koch knew something of the firestorm's strength and speed. But violent, unfathomable updrafts made the front line of flame stronger than anything in the textbooks. A town like DeBorgia could go in a whiff.

Koch dashed around the streets, desperate to make some dent, looking for a place to set the backfire as buildings burned. Some ditches, a primitive fire line, had been dug in advance. But Koch soon realized that all of it was futile; they could not rescue this town. The bucket brigade was helpless. A backfire was meaningless. The ditches were a joke. He called for everyone to get out, straining to be heard ahead of the galloping wind.

"I can't describe that wind," said a Northern Pacific section foreman, Fred Wence, who'd lived in DeBorgia for twenty years. "It reminded me more than anything of a Dakota blizzard. The dust and cinders and sand went through the air like snow and I couldn't keep my eyes open on the street. The wind didn't come from any one direction. It blew first this way and then that, whirling everything around and around. The fire jumped across the ditches almost before the men could get out of the way and came down toward the town with a roar." The firefighters and residents boarded Wence's Northern Pacific train, and the locomotive shifted into reverse, back down toward Missoula. The retreat was in some ways more harrowing than the ride uphill had been.

"The whole canyon was afire on both sides and the train had to run through it," Koch wrote. "The heat was so great that we couldn't stand in the open door of a box car." Peeking out of the boxcar, Koch caught a final glimpse of the town, the flames joining those of the others that danced all over the northern Rockies. In DeBorgia, sixty-eight buildings crumbled to ash. Only three structures withstood the fire. His beloved Lolo National Forest, put in his care, entrusted to pass on to future generations, looked to be in ruins.

To the west, on the Idaho side of the ridge, stood Grand Forks—for another few minutes at least. The honky-tonk dive where Bill Weigle had gone with a posse to arrest saloonkeepers had already burned once in 1910, because of an accident. Rebuilt, Grand Forks was a splintered-wood-and-canvas tent camp of unpainted fronts and split logs set on flat ground next to a creek, within a mile of the railroad that switchbacked up into the mountains. The Kelley brothers of Avery kept a store, the Bitterroot Mercantile, and a little off-plumb and leaky cabin held a sign of preposterous intention: ANHEUSER HOTEL. The one street through town was dirt, and the sidewalks were uneven boards, covered with oak barrels emptied of their liquor, serving as outdoor furniture of sorts.

The fire took Grand Forks in a sniff. Nature did what the Forest Service never could, clearing the ground of all attachments that weren't there when Teddy Roosevelt decided that this piece of ground would be set aside for the ages. People fled to the creek, and then to the railroad tracks and a small stop, hoping the Milwaukee Road, which always kept a locomotive in the woods on one of the side tracks, would rescue them. Just then, a railroad operator sent a message to his supervisors: "A big fire is sweeping down on us. What shall we do?" A second message, this an SOS, was tapped out, and then the line went down. The urgent plea had been received, though, and was passed on to Avery, the nearest town, where a much larger train was headed to evacuate everyone in the St. Joe Valley. The new instructions were for the engineer to back up about six miles and pick up the people who had run from the flames of Grand Forks. When the train arrived, the engineer was overwhelmed — "people clinging to wherever they could find a place to take hold," as a survivor wrote. Then the train inched down the valley, stopping at each of the trestles to see whether the spans would hold.

In the high reaches of the Bitterroots, a homesteader heard a bang on her door. This was a few days before the blowup, when the woods were a tangle of hungry and disorganized firefighters. Ione "Pinkie" Adair was twenty-six years old, with a shock of red hair that stood out, making it hard for anyone who had met her to for-

get her. You could see Pinkie in a fog, it was said, because of that
highlight of hair. She had been trying like other speculators to get
full legal title to her patch of ground so she could sell it to one of the
shadow companies buying timber homesteads. It was getting late to
make her fortune, and now the fire threatened to end it all. Smoke
had thickened over the days of August, like a swarm of insects. She
was as isolated as any person living in the United States of 1910;
the nearest town, Avery, was twenty-eight miles away by unmain-
tained path, basically a deer trail to the west. When she came to the
door that morning, a forest ranger named Ashley Roche, his face
smeared in ashen sweat, had some questions.

"Are there trails out of here — to the east?"

Though she lived alone in this forested hideaway, Pinkie was
used to strangers showing up in the summer with questions. She
gave the ranger the lay of the land. He then made a request that
sounded like an order.

"We have a crew of fourteen men and they haven't eaten,"
Roche said. "Will you get something for these men to eat?"

"Fourteen men?"

"We can pay you for your time."

"How much?"

"Dollar a day."

"For how long?"

"Couple of days. Couple of weeks. Nobody knows for sure."

"Dollar a day?"

"Yep."

On the forester's word, she agreed. Before leaving, she went inside and strapped her pistol around her waist, a .38 revolver. Pinkie
never left home without the gun, though her father had advised her
not to walk with the cartridge full, to prevent an accident. She was
the son that her father, a doctor who'd moved to the mountainous
wilds of Idaho from the level ground of Iowa, never had, learning
at an early age to shoot, ride horses, fish, and tame wild animals. On
horseback, Pinkie was a bit of a showoff. It was shocking then for a

young woman to ride a horse as a man did, full straddle, but her father was insistent. "If you're going to ride horses with me and go to the places I go," he told her, "you're going to ride horses like men." She did, but with her own flourish—Pinkie rode a white horse.

Following the ranger, pistol on her hip, she walked a few miles to the camp. She rustled up a couple of pots, and went to work on a mountain of potatoes, to be seasoned by a few onions. She made bread in a makeshift oven. The next day, Pinkie and the fourteen men walked three miles down a trail and across a creek to a larger camp, and were introduced to another woman, her fellow cook. To see a woman in these woods, at peak fire season, was rare. To see two was an even more unlikely sight.

"Can you cook for these men?" Roche asked, motioning to the crowd.

"Who are they?"

She looked around at dozens of hard-faced and hollow-eyed men. There were sixty of them, prisoners released from Missoula's jails on Koch's insistence.

"You want me to cook for seventy-four people?"

"Yes, ma'am."

She boiled buckets of potatoes, fired up pans of gravy and bacon grease, and slopped it all together. The eyes of the men were on Pinkie, watching her every move. She felt uncomfortable, to say the least, but had a certain confidence from her years in the woods. A prisoner, staring at Pinkie's piece, asked if she carried the gun all the time.

"It's with me night and day," she said.

"That a fact."

She told the prisoner to set an empty can on a stump, some distance from where she stood. She took aim and fired, hitting the can squarely with a single shot.

"What do you think of that?" Pinkie said.

The men were in terrible shape—dehydrated, hungry, many with diarrhea. They seemed to be defeated, waiting for something to happen rather than taking on the fires. That first night in the camp, Pinkie told Roche she didn't want to sleep near the prisoners.

"They'll be all right. Nobody's gonna touch you."

Pinkie resisted. Roche rounded up two Englishmen who had drifted into the Coeur d'Alenes after seeing a sign in Spokane: FIREFIGHTERS WANTED. IMMEDIATE WORK. What if the limeys were to keep her company? She grew to like them. What's more, they could sing, and one of them, named Eustas Collins, had a good voice; songs took the edge off the fire camp.

Pinkie cooked kettles of vegetables, tomatoes and potatoes, occasionally spiced with rations of bacon or ham, and in the morning she made sourdough hotcakes. After a while, as food ran low, it was just potatoes, and Pinkie could not stand the sight of them. One day as she labored over a brew of boiled spuds, hoping to coax something edible from them, she saw a deer off in the meadow, its ears twitching. Deer—all Pinkie could think of was fresh venison and how good that meat would taste in the pot. She walked slowly toward the animal, withdrew her pistol, and took aim. The deer stared back at her, not far away, unblinking. It would take just one good shot; Pinkie knew she had it in her. But she could not pull the trigger. As she held both arms out clutching the gun, her hands began to tremble—not from strain but from something inside her, she said later. It was a well-known condition among some shooters—the yips, the shakes, it went by various names. No matter how badly she wanted deer for firefighter food, she could not kill the animal. Back to the potatoes.

She slept on a bed of dried grass and wore the same clothes day in and day out. Smoke settled on the land like giant spider webs, and followed her to sleep, at its heaviest at day's end. She longed for clean underwear, a clear sky, and her little house in the mountains—alone, without potatoes. By the third week of August, even the tubers were just about gone. As the wind gathered speed in the upper reaches of the St. Joe, Pinkie noticed an awful look of dread in the faces of the men. The most hardened prisoners, who had teased and flirted with her, looked like little boys. It was in their eyes: she could see that they were afraid of dying. Friday night, she bedded down on her grass mattress next to horses tied to logs. The animals never calmed, never slept, and neither did Pinkie. Like a lot of people who grew up close to nature, she thought horses knew something she didn't know, that they could sense a larger disaster before she could.

On Saturday, August 20, nobody wanted to move, to fight fire, to take orders. They were paralyzed by collective fear, wondering where to go, what to do as the windborne smoke circled in on them, ready for the kill. Ranger Roche gave instructions: "Take your blankets and go down to the stream, and if the fire comes close, get in the water and cover your head with a blanket, leaving an air space."

Pinkie grabbed a blanket and went to the river with the sixty prisoners from Missoula, her two English escorts, and a dozen other men. The wind hollered something terrible, showing its heft as it fanned through the opening in the forest. *This is it,* the prisoners muttered. *We're going to die here!* Everyone moved to the river and waited. They could see only ten feet or so, but they could hear the fire all around—those deafening claps, explosions, trees falling on the ground. Pinkie could not lie still, nothing but a wet blanket to save her life. She had been raised to be stubborn and strong-willed, character traits that only hardened the longer she lived alone in the woods. She crawled up out of the river on her own, clothes drenched.

"Where you going?"

"I can't stay here," she said, arranging the wet blanket as a protective cover for her shoulders and neck.

Everyone else remained in the creek, half covered with water, waiting for the wave of flame to crest over them. The homesteader gal with the pistol on her hip was staggering away.

"What's that? You're crazy, lady."

"I won't die here in this creek."

"What're you doing?"

"Getting outta here."

She took off on foot through the smoke, wind, and flame, lurching into uncertainty. She planned to hoof it to Avery—almost thirty miles from the shallow stream.

"I won't die here."

14

To Save a Town

To AVERY THEY CAME, rushing in from homesteads and ranches and flame-ravaged villages, to Avery for the last train out of the northern Rockies, to Avery which stood untouched after Wallace had burned, after Grand Forks and Taft had been wiped off the map, after millions of trees were uprooted or charred in place, to Avery the town named for a Rockefeller at the height of the family's reach into the Far West. In all, about a thousand people remained in the path of the Big Burn. And once in Avery, in the stew of smoke and misdirection, they looked for the two faces of the American government, the Forest Service and the Army.

The rangers were in disarray, most of them up in the mountains with their dying crews. One exception was Ralph Debitt, who was in Avery after returning for supplies. The retreat saved his life, for the twenty-eight men who had not come to town fell to the flames, barely three miles away. Debitt looked stricken by the accelerating calamity, his authority weakened by loss of life and misinformation, by a chain of events he was helpless to stop. He mumbled. He ordered one thing, then reversed himself. He sent repeated messages to Koch and Weigle, contradicting earlier messages, looking for guidance. With Debitt paralyzed by doubt, it was up to the soldiers of the 25th Infantry, Company G, to take charge—a platoon of fifty-three enlisted men, all black, nearly all from the South, commanded by a single white officer, Second Lieutenant Edson E. Lewis. They had been in Avery since August 17, split from other soldiers still camped on the baseball field in Wallace.

"The papers said these men were a bad lot," recalled one prospector who was working with the fire crews. They were said to be "dope fiends," in his words, said to be gamblers and drunks, not to be trusted. The uniformed members of the 25th — pants tucked neatly into ankle-high gaiters, brass buttons polished on their heavy, four-pocketed jackets, rifles at the ready — may have been the first blacks the prospector had ever seen, just as they were for some of the immigrants. Not far from town, a black man known as Brown-Gravy Sam had operated a roadhouse restaurant, and did well by some accounts. But east of Wallace was a place called "Nigger Prairie," named for a man who had staked a claim with his Indian wife. He was found dead in the cabin. The murder was never investigated, though a slab was placed near the cabin with the words "Here lies a coon."

In Avery, the soldiers had set up their tents in a clearing just above the St. Joe River within shouting distance of the biggest house in the valley, the mansion of Spike Kelley and his bride. The steep slope behind their camp was denuded of trees, logged during the town's transition from Forest Service outpost to Milwaukee Road company town. By Saturday evening, the troops had lost contact with the others in Wallace. As refugees streamed into town, Ranger Debitt got on a train and disappeared; he said he was going to get a look at how close the fires were to charging up the length of the St. Joe. "Twenty miles of solid fire line was approaching Avery," Lieutenant Lewis wrote in his report to his commanders. Debitt may have disappeared out of fear, simply losing his nerve; the timing certainly was odd. "Keep order" were his last instructions. Vague as those words were, they were backed now by the same authority as was instituted in Wallace a few hours earlier; Avery was put under martial law. Early Sunday morning, Debitt sent another message back to the troops from a train stop:

"Get all the women and children out and notify all the rest of the people to be ready to get out at a minute's notice."

The soldiers went door-to-door. The Japanese, the Montenegrins, and other recent arrivals had little trouble understanding them; even with their weak grasp of English, they got the message. One boy wanted to take his teddy bear but was told by his father to leave it—*just get on the train!* The soldiers loaded water cans on the cars and secured seats for every woman and child in town. They went from coach to coach, shutting the windows so that the heat and fire would be kept outside. If the twenty-mile-wide wall of flame were to come upon them before the trains left, the orders were to lead everyone to the river and cover them with wet blankets, just as Ranger Roche had directed his crew with Pinkie Adair to do.

Less than an hour after receiving Debitt's instructions, the men of the 25th had the women and children on the train and ready to go. The Avery exodus was much more orderly than the evacuation in Wallace. In Avery, soldiers emptied the town of its most vulnerable citizens while keeping defiant men from nudging them out. In at least one instance, they had to decide whether a boy was man enough to stay behind. Harry Theriault, who was thirteen, had come racing out of the burning mountains, where he was working as a messenger and timekeeper. He had spent part of the night in a creek. When he reached Avery and skip-stepped to catch the train, a soldier stopped him.

"Women and children only!"

After Harry explained that he was only thirteen and should be allowed to board with the other children, the soldier consented. The doors were closed, the last of the windows shut, and the engine with its hundred or so refugees prepared to pull out of Avery.

Pinkie Adair hiked through the Bitterroots with just a damp blanket, following the thin, barely visible trail toward Avery, walking in her hobnailed boots, the spikes worn down. It was a long march even by Pinkie's standards, and her stomach growled, and she sweated in the hot air. She stopped to drink from the dirty creek and wipe her hair. On a good day, she could make three miles an hour with little rest. The farther along she got, the better she felt about her decision to leave the creek with the sixty prisoners, the two Englishmen, and the dozen firefighters. If she lost the trail, she would use the code practiced by homesteaders in a fire: four shots from a gun, one minute apart. Now such a signal would be worthless, of course, as no one would hear the sound; a gunshot was a whisper against this roar of the mountains.

In the predawn dark of early Sunday, Pinkie found herself walking on level ground, close to the St. Joe River, and heard voices. She also thought she heard a train whistle. And then the questions: What if everyone was just now leaving? What if she had missed the train? As she approached the outskirts of Avery, she was dizzy and faint with dehydration, her face smeared black, her hair a knot of greasy strands. She knew she was near town because she recognized a couple of the cabins. Also she saw the log palace, the two-story manse of Skip Kelley and his bride. She had only to cross the bridge over the St. Joe and she would be in town. At river's edge, she was stopped by a ranger.

"You can't go into town," he said. "Everyone's getting out. Train's full and leaving."

"I just walked . . . twenty-eight, thirty miles!"

"Sorry."

Pinkie pushed past the ranger, sensing that he wouldn't stop her, and if he did, she would fight him. She crossed the bridge, her hobnails clicking on the planks, and rushed toward the slow-moving train; it was packed, not a spare square foot of space available on the few cars. She shouted to the engineer, begging to be let on. The engineer looked at Pinkie.

"What's your name?"

"Adair. Ione Adair." She was a sight—eyebrows burned, revolver on her side, clothes ripped and dirtied.

"Where you from?"

"Forty-nine Meadows country."

"I know your folks."

"Yeah?"

"I think we can do you pretty well."

"How so?"

"On the caboose. We'll put you on top of the caboose here, on the back of the train. Hop on. Quickly now."

Pinkie jumped aboard, crawled up on top of the caboose, and found a handhold as the train chugged out of Avery to the west.

Only black soldiers and men forced to fight for their homes remained in town. The residents were machinists and boilermakers, laborers and track fixers, barkeeps and icemen who hauled loads into cars, the way to keep cargo cold on a transcontinental ride. On the surface, they were hard-edged men, known for brawn and quick fists; they had to be in the Bitterroots of 1910. But in the face of this fire they were lost. Though martial law had been declared, a democracy of sorts prevailed in the depot at Avery. Word came that a final train would be coming through the town, and that gave the men a choice: to battle the windborne flames for their town or leave.

With Ralph Debitt in tow, the train pulled into the depot. The ranger's report was bleak: to the west, trestles were aflame, burning trees were thrown over tracks, no part of the mountains was not burning. As the fire approached Avery in two waves, the soldiers and townsfolk got into a tense exchange. Lieutenant Lewis said he didn't know anything of the country or of forest fires. His men were soldiers; they were trained in warfare, trained to fight, and that was their initial impulse — stay, dig in, do battle.

"What about the tunnel?" a rail worker asked. "We could hide in there."

Less than half a mile from Avery, to the east, was one of the shafts dug into the mountains for the Milwaukee Road. It had been stocked with supplies — water, some food, blankets — in anticipation of the retreat. One faction wanted to retreat to the tunnel. Ranger Debitt disagreed. People died in those manmade caves during fires, the small, tight space filled with lethal gas. Debitt suggested a walk just upriver, to a bend in the stream, open enough that it might be safe from falling trees. A gun was drawn at one point in the debate. But despite this threat, no consensus was reached.

Later, at nightfall, most of those who had been arguing on the platform took blankets and went to the river, sloshing upstream — a decision of sorts, made by default after other options had been exhausted.

"All hope of saving anything was given up," Lieutenant Lewis wrote of the collective sense of defeat. They might save their lives, but nothing in town.

The bedraggled survivors walked perhaps half a mile, the way slow in the knee-deep water of the St. Joe. But it became clear that this plan was not going to work, Lewis wrote. For one thing, the water was too shallow, not enough of a protective cover. And, more important, the valley cut by the river was far too narrow. If big cedars came down, they would slam into the river and dam its course. Death by drowning, death by a fatal body blow from a tree that weighed as much as a train car — those were likely outcomes. The lieutenant, in accord with the rangers, reversed course — everyone back to town and the waiting train.

The men climbed into three units: an engine, a flatcar, and a boxcar. This train could only follow the tracks east, a route rumored to lead to certain death. Various reports had it that a tunnel had caved in, that a trestle and several bridges had burned to the ground, that the tracks stopped dead in midair over a ravine several hundred feet deep. For good reason, the Milwaukee Road was the most costly stretch of rail line ever built in the United States to that point. It had required Herculean feats of engineering and construction to overcome the Bitterroots' swales and hard rock, its high rises and deep forests. The plan that prevailed was to take the train a few miles out of town, to an area cleared by a burn years earlier. They could try to creep along the tracks, to come just short of a flaming edge or downed bridge, feeling their way to the clearing — a task for nimble feet, not iron wheels. Fire was directly ahead, though, which meant that to reach the clearing would require them to go through flames.

"We succeeded in breaking through the first fire wave, but we could not get through the second and we were caught between the two fires," Lieutenant Lewis wrote. "The scenes of the fires, the dense, stifling smoke, the intense, blinding heat and the roaring and crackling of the flames were indescribable. The flames seemed to be over a mile and a half high." The heat was so intense it burned the paint off the cars and blistered the varnish. That was on the outside; inside, with the windows sealed, the men felt as if they were broiling. The Buffalo Soldiers, their honor won on battlefields in the Civil War, in the high plateaus of West Texas, and in the Philippine jungles, now faced death in the wilderness West, not even heroic.

"We travelled back and forth attempting to get through at one end or another, but it was impossible," Lieutenant Lewis wrote. "Progress was constantly impeded by landslides or rocks, burned logs, etc. One fireman was killed while picking rocks off the track."

The men on board this train did not know it, but the other locomotive, the one that hauled out of Grand Forks to go to Avery, was also engaged in a stop-and-go dodge of the Big Burn. The engineer had finally taken refuge in a tunnel, parking his train to wait out the fire—a successful move, as it turned out.

For the infantrymen, the hesitancy on the track lasted through Sunday night, the soldiers frustrated by their inability to do anything. Passivity in the grip of a force that defies engagement may be the worst condition for a warrior. The men of the 25th tasted breath stale and hot; they felt their throats tighten with thirst and their leg muscles knot and cramp. They put up with the moans and whines of the men on the train whose town they were charged with saving, and some of them resigned themselves to dying with this group. When they looked out the window, they saw fire on either side of the St. Joe.

For a long time, the little train didn't move, was stopped in time, just like the men inside it. Then, in reverse, the engineer guided the two cars and his locomotive the other way, a retreat toward Avery. He stopped two miles from town, waiting for the fire to play itself out. First light came around 5 A.M., when it looked as if the winds had calmed, a reprieve before another roar. Avery remained standing, though it was empty of people.

Lieutenant Lewis picked up the narrative, the 25th Infantry against the blowup: "As it was seen that there was no escape through both the fires, preparations were made for a last stand at Avery. As day came on, the wind came up and the fires again started full." It was better, perhaps, to be free of the iron oven. At least in Avery the men could make a stand. On wobbly legs in the dawn of Monday morning, the men disembarked from the train and got to work on a new plan — the final strategy, they agreed.

Backfire, which had failed to get anywhere in Taft, was all they had. To the riverbank they went, just across the St. Joe from Avery, and started a fire. With the river at one side, the intentionally set fire had nowhere to go but uphill, into the scrub brush and downed trees, moving to greet the onset of the main blaze, so close to Avery they could see it a few hundred yards away. Other men were dispatched in front of houses and shops with buckets again, told to toss water at the first sign of firebrands from the big blaze. They lit the ground, waited, and watched. Their backfire took off up the hill, orderly at first, then scampering to one side, toward Spike Kelley's empty manse. It pawed at the place for an instant, like a newly awakened bear examining fresh prey, and then took the big house and its enormous living room full of antiques from Europe and China, the Gilded Age ornaments that Kelley had brought to this forest in the Bitterroots as a way to show what it meant to have a man of his standing in Gifford Pinchot's frontier. The two-story home, so large some people mistook it for a hotel when they stepped off the train in Avery, was destroyed in a great crackling burst, its combustibles reduced to snuff. And after taking Spike Kelley's log palace, the set fire moved upward ever more quickly, wind-aided now, to join the greater fire.

Lewis: "Both fires seemed to unite as they struck the back fire. About the same time the wind suddenly died out, and if it had not died out about that time, and if there had been no back fire, nothing could have saved the town or people. The flames sank rapidly and in about an hour it was evident that the danger was over and all that remained to do was to watch the fires which were burning out."

After successfully evacuating the town, after enduring a harrowing night inside a hot train, after hauling water buckets and setting backfires, the Buffalo Soldiers had saved Avery. Over the ridge, their comrades had helped get the women and children of Wallace out of town. Two towns, two missions accomplished. Whatever else people in the Coeur d'Alenes thought of the soldiers when they first arrived, by Sunday evening of the Big Burn, some minds had been changed.

"They stuck to their posts like men," said Debitt, who had strayed from his own post during crucial moments.

"There were no better firefighters picked up anywhere than the negroes," said a civilian crew leader, Con Faircloth. "They worked willingly during the day and at night they made the mountain echo with their songs. I never heard such singing in all my life."

"The negro soldiers of the 25th Regiment," one paper reported in a dispatch carried across the country, "have done heroic service and saved many lives and much property."

It was said by fair-minded people that their swift action had redeemed the 25th from the humiliating dismissal after Brownsville and their earlier role as enforcers for mining bosses during the martial law repression in the Coeur d'Alenes. "When the negro troops were last in the Coeur d'Alenes, they were cursed, reviled and sneered at," *Collier's* reported. "Early laws on the books in Idaho even excluded blacks from prospecting. Now they are hailed as an-

gels of mercy, rather dusky, perspiring angels, but angels at that."
In the northern Rockies, people came around to the conclusion, the
magazine noted, that "they were white clear through, even if their
skins were dark."

And the Seattle papers seemed equally stunned that the Buffalo Soldiers could perform so heroically. "I want to say something
about those negroes now," they quoted a man from Avery who
helped organize the exodus and backfire. "They were black, but I
never knew a whiter set of men to breathe. Not a man in the lot
knew what a yellow streak was . . . They never complained. They
were never afraid. They worked, worked, worked, like Trojans, and
they worked every minute. I can't say too much about them, but
I will say that my attitude toward the black race has undergone a
wonderful change since I knew those twelve heroes."

Although the 25th Infantry had not lost a man, four soldiers
were still missing among their ranks, soldiers who had strayed near
Placer Creek when the fires moved on Wallace. The troops pressed
the rangers to organize a search party for their lost comrades over
the divide, four among hundreds of people as yet unaccounted for.
Ranger Joe Halm and his crew at the headwaters of the St. Joe had
not been heard from since winds kicked up on Saturday afternoon.
Nor had some of the rescue trains reached their destinations. Many
train cars had gone into tunnels to wait out the storm, but had they
made it? The Milwaukee Road estimated that at least a dozen of its
bridges had burned, including one that was 725 feet long. On Sunday and Monday, crews were sent out to find the missing, including
the soldiers. At the same time, the 25th was given another assign-
ment: hike up the creek to the place where twenty-eight men had
been crushed and burned, and over to the hole in the ground where
Domenico Bruno, Giacomo Viettone, and five others had died in
a half-dug root cellar. These bodies were so badly disfigured that
only a soldier, it was explained, would be able to pry them from
the places where they had taken their final breaths and give them
proper burials.

15

The Missing

ARLY SUNDAY MORNING, with the firestorm yet to ebb and
communication down throughout much of the northern
Rockies, Bill Weigle had tried to put together a party to search for
Ed Pulaski and his crew. The Big Burn had swept over the Coeur
d'Alene and Lolo forests, the Nez Perce and the Clearwater, and
now moved north toward Canada and east into the forested half of
Montana.

In Wallace, volunteers were hard to come by. Those who had
stayed in town and battled the blaze through the night with hoses,
buckets, and shovels were battered and worn, retreating to the remains of their own homes in a town reduced to a heap. Having lived
through Saturday night, they feared the still-flaming forest. "This
was the hardest task of all," said Weigle. "The men were afraid to
go into the woods." What Weigle knew from a messenger at dawn
on Sunday was that Pulaski and about fifty men were inside a tunnel up in the Place Creek drainage. Later that morning, two other
stragglers arrived in Wallace with an update: five men were dead in
the mineshaft. Another had burned to death in the race for shelter.
But almost everyone else was alive. And the dead — did that include
Pulaski? No. He was alive, but might not make it down. He was in
terrible shape.

Up in the mountains, in what had been a fresh-scented crowd of cedars, pines, and larches shading the cool waters of Placer Creek, Pulaski was indeed having trouble finding his way downhill. The forest was gone, but more than that, the heap of the woods continued to smoke and burn in places, which meant that every footstep might land on a hot coal or sink into a pit of ashes. The bottoms of Pulaski's shoes were burned through, as was the case for most of his men. The path along the creek, which he knew so well, was hard to find, covered by downed timber or knocked out by the crush of the storm. It was an obstacle course. As the sun's rays pierced the smoke, Pulaski shielded his face. The only eye that worked was light sensitive to the point of pain. He thought on this Sunday morning that he would have preferred to burn to death rather than go blind. His men were in equally bad shape. What had been described a few days earlier as an army of firefighters marching briskly off to war was now a pathetic ragtag collection of humans thrown against the mountains—men broken, lost, wailing.

Holding her daughter, Emma Pulaski had spent the night in the bunker of mine waste, the impoundment where she had fled rather than get on a train. Emma and Elsie had watched the flames come down the mountains and burn through Wallace. They saw smoke columns and spires of fire rising from the town, heard whistles as the trains moved women and children away, the not-so-distant cacophony of fleeing residents, and all the while held their position in the crushed rock. Around 5 A.M., Sunday, mother and daughter rose and started to walk back to town.

The Pulaski house, to Emma's surprise, was still standing. News of her husband came in a progression of rumors and half-truths, from worst case to better, throughout the morning. First a neighbor greeted her with a hug and sad face: Ed Pulaski had died, she said, killed with all his men. Just after 9 A.M., another story: her husband was alive, but horribly disfigured by flame—"his eyes burned out and that he probably would not live," as she recalled. Less than an hour later, on the road to her house, she saw a tall man, a swirl of smudged cloth around his face, hands wrapped, walking slowly, guided by other men. Ed Pulaski looked crumbled and spent. "He was staggering," she wrote, "his eyes bandaged, he was blind and terribly burned, his hands and hair were burned and he was suffering from the fire gas." Pulaski and his men had been greeted with coffee and whiskey at the trailhead of Placer Creek by a party of women who had volunteered to do what Weigle could not find men to do—walk up the smoke-clouded, tree-cluttered road in search of the men who had tried to keep the fire from town.

"The world was black to my eyes," Pulaski said, but it lightened enough to find the arms of his wife and daughter.

What he could not see of Wallace was this: chimneys, sticks, open-faced basements, roofless buildings, and entire streets devoid of their houses and stores. One of two train depots was completely gutted. The Pacific Hotel was burned to a shell. The main bridge across the river was gone. The Coeur d'Alene Hardware Store was a pile of rubbish. The brewery was destroyed, as was the newspaper office. Trees at street level and on the first couple of terraces above the valley floor were gone, though a few black poles stood against grey carpet.

Hundreds of other men were still missing, and perhaps an equal number dead. Weigle had not heard from several of his crew chiefs, and he doubted that they had survived the blowup. He knew from his own struggle to get out of a collapsing mine tunnel, from his crawl along the hot forest floor, from the way the fire caught his hands and head, that the storm had a power that could take the strongest of rangers.

300 FIRE FIGHTERS DEAD

So read the headline in the *Seattle Times* two days after the week-end blowup. The casualty figure may have been high, the number a rough estimate, at a time when it was difficult for the Forest Service to get reliable information on its crews. The rangers and firefighters were, with one exception, only a day or two's hike from towns and roads, but in their isolation they could have been in the far, roadless Alaska wilderness. The paper reported other losses as well, and these they could name, for the most part. Among them were a mother and a year-old baby, said to have drowned in a well where they jumped to avoid the flames; the Wallace fire captain's father, who had gone back to his smoking house to save his parrot; a "well-dressed Finn," found with a gold pocket watch; the suicide, Oscar Weigert; the man whose friend accidentally set him afire in the boxcar; the twenty-eight men who decided, along with the Irish cook Patrick Grogan, to stay put in the creek above Avery rather than retreat; the ten who packed into the small cabin only to have its roof collapse on them; the Italians, Viettone and Bruno, and five others jammed into the cellar in Beauchamp's clearing; the homesteader himself, and another; a boy of seventeen caught in the Bullion Mine along with several Englishmen; a man from Persia; six of Pulaski's men, all but one in the tunnel; a prospector on the St. Joe River; homesteaders in northeastern Washington; assorted firefighters in remote pockets of Montana. Those were the known dead in the count taken just two days after the blowup. Many bodies could not be identified; what was at first taken for a charred log was found to be a firefighter, for example.

"Never in my life have I seen conditions so appalling," Weigle told a few of the reporters who had stayed behind. Since grown men refused to help, he enlisted teenagers, some as young as thirteen, to run up into the smoking woods in search of survivors. With Pulaski in the hospital in Wallace, his main concern was the kid who'd been hired out of Washington State College to learn the ways of the woods under Pulaski—Joe Halm, the ex–football player. Of all the crews fighting fire in Weigle's Coeur d'Alene, none were deeper in the woods than the men under Halm's direction. They were seventy-five miles up the St. Joe River from Avery, near the headwaters and high in subalpine timber. Greeley sent in help from the Montana side to look for Halm's men, but found nothing. News spread quickly.

JOE HALM AND CREW FEARED LOST

ST. JOE FIRE HEMS IN 180 MEN WHO
MAY NEVER ESCAPE

That last headline, from the *Spokane Spokesman-Review,* was accurate in that it conveyed the concern of Weigle, Koch, Greeley, and other Little G.P.s for a missing ranger, but it overstated the number of men in Halm's crew. Weigle sent out his young search party. They made it farther up the St. Joe than the scouts who had gone earlier, but came back with the same report: no hint of Joe Halm and his crew. A day later, this headline appeared in the *Idaho Press:*

NO CHANCE FOR HALM AND CREW
IN ST. JOE WILDERNESS

Three days after the firestorm erupted, about three hundred men were missing, including Halm's crew. The fire had gone north to British Columbia and east to the far reaches of the Rockies and then to the plains. In the wilderness of the narrowest part of the Idaho panhandle and some of the most rugged sections of northwestern Montana, the fire chased men to high ground and watery shelters. A crew of twenty-five working in the Cabinet National Forest raced up a creek, trying to outrun the storm. The fire was swifter and caught the men on a hill of loose, sliding rock. Those who stayed in the talus, clutching rock, lived. But four others took off in a downhill sprint and were burned to death. In a neighboring forest, the Pend Orcillo, a similar drama came to a similar end. Two members of a crew who'd been told to take shelter under wet blankets threw off their flimsy shields to make an escape attempt. They had gone only a few strides before flames lit them up, killing both men. And over in the northeastern part of Washington State, in the green country defined by the big Pend Oreille River, three homesteaders burned to death, caught in the fire while trying to save all that they had labored on.

The warmer air on the eastern side of the Montana Rockies,

where temperatures near 100 degrees were common in August, pulled the Big Burn to the high plains and lightly timbered brush country—an arid land, baked brown and red in this drought. Blackfeet Indians, who'd lived in this area for centuries, described smoke coming over the mountains like waterfalls, cascading to new ground. From there, flames moved east in the stampeding fashion of a prairie fire, taking dry grass and occasional pines before finding islands of fresh timber, cottonwood, aspen, and fir in the subranges of the eastern Rockies. The biggest cities in Montana—Bozeman, Billings, and Great Falls—now saw flames not far from their towns and tasted the smoke that had choked settlements to the west for nearly a month. The ashen layer crept into the Dakotas, Wyoming, Colorado, and as far as parts of Minnesota. In Yellowstone, nearly five hundred miles from the St. Joe River, tourists complained about the coarse blanket of fine-particled fog that settled over the world's first national park. They wondered: Was the park on fire? It was not. The smoke in Yellowstone, even smoke in Denver, was from the two-day storm in the Bitterroots. The airborne fallout of the Big Burn rode the brisk winds of the Midwest, north of Chicago, dropped soot over parts of New England, finally dissipating above Greenland.

Left behind in the northern Rockies were logs piled on other logs; millions of trees fire-stripped of bark and branches, stacked and tossed in the gullies and valleys; and hot spots, hundreds of them, burning coals and hard timber. The Spokane paper quoted a ranger as saying there were "no forests left to burn—the country has been wiped clean." The St. Joe country that Pulaski had found so restorative; the Bitterroot glens that Halm had found so enticing; the high alpine meadows where young Elers Koch and his Danish bride had pitched their tent; the ancient river-bottom cedars that Pinchot himself had touched and catalogued as he rushed to find suitable land for Roosevelt's pen to protect—all looked as if they had been mowed down by a reaper's swipe of fire.

Debitt sent a dispatch on August 23 to Weigle, an indication of how confused and dazed he remained. "The entire country has been burned over," he reported from Avery. "An indefinite number of men reported lost in the fire. Arrangements will be made to bury unidentified bodies . . . Food supply is short . . ."

And, to the press, Debitt added this conclusion, summarized by a headline:

HEAD RANGER DEBITT CONCEDES THE DEATH OF
RANGER HALM AND HIS PARTY OF 70

Joe Halm was twenty-five, well liked, one of the most celebrated athletes in the Pacific Northwest, the son of German immigrants who settled in the orchard country of the Yakima Valley. Halm's nickname was Joe Bunch, and in his college yearbook there were references to how Joe Bunch was always there in a pinch. His service for Gifford Pinchot had been brief: hired just before the Chief was fired, Halm had learned all about him from the mythology passed on by other rangers. Halm had put in barely a year in the service, but he loved it. "Strong, active, full of enthusiasm, broke but happy" was how he described himself after being hired by Weigle. The other rangers laughed at him for the silk shirt he wore the first day on the job, but he soon became a favorite. He joked at his own expense, never turned down a task, and his energy was boundless. Halm's loss was mentioned in a dispatch in the *New York Times,* in which he was lauded as "the best football and baseball player at Washington State College at Pullman" for four years. In fact, Halm was an average baseball player, but he had the shot put record, and his football skills were legendary, especially the drop kick that beat the University of Washington in Seattle.

He had entered the woods with seventy men. It had taken them the better part of a week to slash and hack their way up the wilderness to a fire in timber against the big western flank of the Bitterroots on the Montana line. They had their fire contained by August 18, and Halm assembled the men and gear for the march out. Job well done, Halm told them; they could be proud. Paychecks and a big meal awaited them in Avery, a three-to-four-day hike if they really hoofed it. Halm led his packers down to a supply camp, then returned to his core group of eighteen late Saturday.

The crew he had left and the wild-eyed men who greeted him now were not the same people. Fire, they said, was everywhere, encircling them. Yes, the smoke was much thicker, Halm said, the air was stifling and grey, but flames were not evident. No, no, they protested, the fire was closing in, they could smell it, feel it. In the time Halm tried to persuade them otherwise, the smoke turned a darker pitch, like resin; it was thick and gooey and free-floating. Then sparks began coasting into camp. The crew foreman, waving his big steel ax overhead, tried to calm the men, helping the younger Joe Halm. But it was like talking to horses intent on a dash.

To run would mean suicide, Halm insisted. They had to stay put, stay low, and hope the storm would skip over them. The cook was ordered to make dinner. Supper? Now? Yes, he was ordered, get started on a meal. And before the potatoes began to boil, the sky turned another color and the sound invaded camp. Some thought it was like falling water, though it had little resemblance to the sweet music of nature. Others described it simply as a roar, the advance notice of something beyond their darkest fears. What rode the wind took on another form, from fractured flashes of light to flame, and then jumped into the trees, all in a few heartbeats' time. The great front wall of the firestorm had reached them. Men dropped their shovels before Halm had finished his pleas, ignoring the foreman with his ax, and ran — downhill, uphill, scattering through the brush.

"We're not going to stay here and be roasted alive," one man shouted.

Like his mentor Pulaski, Halm had one fallback, something rangers trained in the chaos of the open West were not afraid to do. He hoisted aloft his gun and let the remaining firefighters know that he would shoot them if he had to.

"She's jumped a mile across the canyon," said the foreman. There was an order, a pattern, to afternoon thunder boomers, even to wildfires, even to freak events. But the speed of this fire was beyond the comprehension of any wrangler, miner, timberman, or ranger who thought he knew how nature worked. Halm tried to sound tough, though some men sensed that what followed was a hollow threat from a college kid.

"Not a man leaves this camp," he said again. "We'll stay by this creek and live to tell about it." The doubt was as thick as the smoke, judging by what a few men said later. But Halm had seen them through this week in the high alpine fire; he had been steady. "Every man hold out some grub, a blanket and a tool. Chuck the rest in that tent, drop the poles and bury it."

It seemed a futile idea, but the men followed Halm's order, shoving food and bedrolls into the tent, then collapsing it, placing poles atop it, and burying the cache with dirt. Not everyone followed his instructions. Several men grabbed canned goods and made a run for the creek. It seemed a logical place to hunker down, and Halm did not object. To the creek they would all go, a shallow trickle, barely a foot deep, just the faintest stirrings of the St. Joe in the driest year in a generation's time.

Brands showered down on them as they retreated toward the water. Trees, aflame and scowling, fell in the near distance. One man screamed and ran. He was a giant of a man, as the crew recalled him, a big Swede. Halm raced after him, losing his gun in the sprint. He caught up with the Swede and tried to coax him back. The big man was crying like a child, crying because he said he could not face death. Halm led him to the creek. They tried to lie calmly in the water, blankets overhead, but trees splashed down onto the little sandbar where they burrowed. One man was hit and went under. He was pulled up and set on the side. Soon all of them rose, because to stay in the water meant being crushed by burning snags weighing five times more than the big weeping Swede. Reaching for buckets, they threw water on other snags closest to the stream, an attempt to create a wet buffer.

• • •

The rangers in charge of the national forests on either side of the Bitterroot divide would not give up on Halm. After three separate search parties had come back without finding a trace of the men, one last rescue effort was mounted. Roscoe Haines, a deputy supervisor under Weigle, volunteered to go to the St. Joe headwaters. At a time when newspapers were printing lengthy obituaries of Halm, Haines was confident he could navigate the fire lines to find a fellow ranger. He said he knew the territory better than anyone.

Nearly a full five days after the winds lifted flames throughout the northern Rockies, Haines and his two rangers started hacking their way east. They had traveled by horse along a grey creek, then left their mounts with packers and started up on foot, following the Joe — they vowed — until it ran out of water, until they were up against the wall of the Bitterroots. Along the way, every few miles or so, Haines fired his pistol into the air. His signal shots rang through the still-burning woods, upward along the ash-choked Joe, and with every press of the trigger, he waited for a boomerang of hope.

At night, the fire passed over the sandbar, and trees no longer fell in the clearing. When the flames died down, temperatures plunged. Men shivered in their wet clothes, shaking as they nursed burned skin and coughed on smoke from the backed-up and slow-burning timber just upstream from them. They stumbled from the creek and found little clearings where they tried to sleep under damp blankets. Some slumped in a haunch, chewing on tobacco retrieved from watery pockets. In the morning, Halm did a head count: he had not lost a man. He could not account for others who had broken away the night before. But from his immediate crew, all were alive. The big Swede who had run into the woods presented a gun to Halm.

"It yours. You lost her in the creek last night," he said.

Over the next few days, Halm guided his men through the ruin of the forest, downhill, the only direction he could follow. For a forester, a man trained in the intricacy of arboreal life, it was a walk through a graveyard. "The virgin trees, as far as the eye could see, were broken or down—devoid of a single sprig of green," Halm recalled. "Miles of trees, sturdy, forest giants were laid prone. Only the smaller trees stood stripped and broken." When they reached the supply camp where they had left their packers, they tried to decipher the scene. A mass of cans littered the seared ground. Farther away, they saw what looked like a pack saddle, the leather burned, and then another saddle, melted. Close by, Halm was sickened by a big black carcass—a horse, burned to a crisp. "We hastened on," Halm wrote, finding "more horses and more saddles." And now, of all things, the wind picked up again, just enough to stoke coals that had died down in the hollows of trees. Halm guided his men to a cave in a rock face, an area already burned by the storm of Saturday night.

In the predawn darkness of the following day, with the wind back at ease, Halm's men set out again. "Torn and bleeding we hurried on," he said, "lighted only by the myriads of fires, I picking the way, the foreman watching for falling trees." They passed more evidence of the packers, more horse carcasses. But no humans. While they descended a steep slope, a large tree creaked and moaned as it fell, then rolled toward the men. "We ran for our lives, but the whirling trunk broke and lodged a few feet above." They paused to rest and regain their senses. Parched and hungry, they talked obliquely of the missing packers, wondering what it must have been like for men to die as those horses had died—skin burned off the bones. Still, since they had yet to find a human body, there was hope.

In daylight, Halm's men continued their search for the packers, but the going was slow, walking a few gingerly steps, dodging obstructions. They had to saw and chop through downed timber, much of it still hot to the touch. Halm parked his men and broke away at a level spot, which he recognized as a junction to some homestead claims. He wanted to check on a prospector a mile from the trail, a man he knew as "a cripple," as he said, panning for his one shot at making a buck in the high country. The cripple's cabin was an earth-covered dugout; it had survived the fire. Halm went inside, expecting to find a body. He found no clues of whether the prospector had stayed or fled.

Back with his men, Halm made camp along the creek and tried to put together a meal from the wet remains of their cache. As they sat grim-faced around a campfire, they spotted two more large animal carcasses—one looked to be an elk, the other a deer. A live grouse, its feathers burned off and missing a foot, hopped around their camp, "a pitiful sight," Halm said. Death was everywhere, the smell of it in the air, the look of it on the ground, the feel of it in the surreal mood of the woods. It was hard to be Joe Bunch, upbeat by nature and reputation, hard to see renewal or nature at work in the blown-down, burned-out remains of the Coeur d'Alene National Forest, especially here where the forest was at its greenest and richest. Halm's men were dehydrated, yet they could not drink from the little stream. "The clear, pure water running through miles of ashes had become a strong alkaline solution, polluted by dead fish," Halm said.

The next morning, hungry and exhausted, the fire crew followed Halm's exhortation to continue on rather than sit and wait for help. This was the sixth day of their wanderings, the sixth day since the big storm had flashed through on Saturday night, sending them into the creek in a fight for their lives. Late in the day, they met up with another animal—a white horse, alive. This they recognized by the brand as one of the packers' animals, and it gave them some hope, though the horse had been badly lashed by flame, its snow-white coat grey with smudge and dirt.

Downslope, separated by miles of blowdown and a ridge fire-shorn of all its trees, Ranger Haines shot a grouse for food. It was Friday, and his supplies were low. This shot was heard by a man named Frank Mills, one of the lost packers. He met up with Haines and told him other packers were not far away. They had been wandering all week, lost, scared, hungry, burned. But where, the ranger asked immediately, was Joe Halm? And where was the rest of the crew, the firefighters? This question Frank Mills could not answer. But Haines surmised a rough idea of their whereabouts, based on conversations with the surviving packers, and sent a messenger uphill.

Late in the afternoon, the messenger met Halm and his crew along the creek. Halm's men were overjoyed. Now they needed only to keep going a small way, a zigzag through a graveyard of big trees, to find the ranger who had never given up on them. By early evening, Rangers Haines and Halm met face-to-face, brothers of the woods. Sure, Haines said, he never lost faith that Joe Halm was alive because the kid was something special. Haines let him know that his death notice had been written up in Missoula and Spokane and even in some of the big papers. Joe Halm, star athlete, had died a hero in the Big Burn. Probably President Taft himself had heard about him and Pulaski.

Halm was starved for information. What happened to Grand Forks? Burned to the ground. What about Taft? Gone, also burned to the ground. Avery? Saved by the colored troops. Other fire crews? Terrible, terrible. At least a hundred dead, he was told, and many more still missing. Bill Weigle? Burned on his hands, neck, parts of his head, hair flamed off. Weigle had been trapped above Wallace just as the city caught fire, Halm was told, took refuge in a mine tunnel that collapsed when the supporting timbers caught fire. Weigle had at first kept this detail to himself. He was nearly buried alive. And Ed Pulaski? Perhaps the sorriest of the rangers, Pulaski took a faceful of flame on Saturday night, burned over many parts of his body, the skin so raw and festered, blind in one eye, unable to see very well in the other, now in the hospital in Wallace. Pulaski had saved all but six of his men. They would have died had he not forced them at gunpoint to lie face-down in the mineshaft,

the ranger said. And what about Wallace, Halm asked; what happened to the town he now called home? It was evacuated, and after a long night, the trains arrived safely in Missoula and Spokane.
Most people in town got out alive. But the city itself had suffered
a frightful blow, more than a hundred buildings reduced to ashes,
homes gone, streets full of rubble.

From Haines, Joe Halm also heard about the packers they had
been looking for all week. Turned out, they bolted on Saturday
night, scattered with fourteen horses. Hours later, they panicked,
fearing the horses would keep them from ever getting out alive,
and so they cut their animals loose. But they held on to one horse,
hoping it would lead them out, as if by a superior instinct. With
one man holding the tail of the mare, the packers followed it uphill. On the ridgetop, the line of the Montana-Idaho border, they
ran out of ground, but also found a place that was indeed free of fire.
From there, over the next week, they crossed down and back several times — once making forty miles in a single day, they said, until they heard the single shot when Ranger Haines fired at a grouse.
Every packer lived, as did the lone horse that guided them.

While the packers' story was encouraging, Joe Halm remembered the prospector who lived in the earthen dugout. Before going
home, Halm insisted they make one last effort to find him. For the
next three days, Halm looked for the old man, returning to smoking
mountains and creeks full of belly-up, rotting trout. On the afternoon of the third day, Halm found a lump of what appeared to be
burned flesh — "ghastly remains, burned beyond recognition." He
was not sure about the corpse until he found the prospector's glasses
and a cane. "In a blanket, we bore the shapeless thing out to the relief crew," Halm said.

While Halm was searching for the prospector, Roscoe Haines
led the other men toward Avery, sawing through downed timber
to find their way. In town, when he reached a working telephone,
with some of the lines restored by rail crews, he placed a call to Weigle in Wallace. Joe Halm was alive, he said. After days of walking,
the kid had made it out with his men. Alive. All of them.

For Weigle, it was the first good news in the week since they had found Ed Pulaski. The forest supervisor had been visiting Pulaski in the hospital and was concerned about his lack of progress. His burns were not surface injuries, and the pain made it difficult to get any rest. More than a hundred people were hospitalized alongside him, undergoing treatment for everything from smoke inhalation to burns that covered large portions of their bodies. A few beds down from Pulaski was a young Irishman, Patrick Sullivan, perhaps the last person to be hired by the Forest Service before the blowup. A miner between jobs, Sullivan was put on the payroll Saturday, August 20. He worked not even a full day. Sullivan was on Stevens Peak, about ten miles east of Wallace, with a crew of eighteen. They raced up to the timberline, burned an opening in the beargrass, and fell to the ground, hoping that by the time fire ascended the mountains, there would be no fuel for it in their refuge. The roar and hot blast came quickly, carrying a wall of flame up and over the mountains, never subsiding as it hit the bald opening on the peak.

One man died on the spot, his lungs seared; nearly everyone else was burned. The skin had melted off Sullivan's hands and arms, and he needed extensive care. He cried for something to ease the pain—whiskey, opium, anything to give a few moments' relief. After surface-dressing Sullivan's wounds, though, doctors and nurses would no longer treat him. They did not have authorization, they said; there was no contingency money for the injured. When word of this reached Pulaski, he was infuriated. Couldn't they see the man had nearly died for his country? How was this different from a soldier wounded on the battlefield? Hell, he would pay the man's doctor bills out of his own pocket, Pulaski said, if it came to that.

So once again the rangers felt obligated to cover the cost of what had been placed in their stewardship, the human and the natural world. A hollowed-out Forest Service had lived with daily humiliations, but this was a new low. Hospital bills mounted, upward of $5,000 for the injured in Wallace alone. The Red Cross raised $1,000, leaving the rest of the debt to the Little G.P.s. Just as congressmen had shortchanged the rangers of shovels, axes, and trail-building funds, charging them for the cost of horses and mules, and, in the case of Lolo National Forest, essentially forcing them to pay firefighters out of their own pockets, they stiffed the rangers again on medical costs. All these men, their fingernails melted off, skin raised and infected, lungs permanently compromised by smoke, joints strained and bones broken, muscles torn and hair lost, were left to fend for themselves. Give the enemies of the Forest Service credit, a few rangers noted—their antipathy was consistent.

16

The Living and the Dead

A T DAY'S END, there on the horizon, a surprise: puffy clouds without the smear of smoke, fresh formations all, crowding tighter as they moved. Clouds of dreams and serenity. Clouds of security and hope, familiar. As with most weather systems in that part of the world, this column of clouds came from the west, birthed in the cold Pacific in the last days of August, hurdling the Olympic Mountains and the Cascades in Washington before regrouping in the Bitterroots. Water, the master architect of the Pacific Northwest, was here again from the sky, here to the rescue of people who thought their world was at an end. Rising over the blackened, still-burning Rockies, the clouds bunched, cooled, and opened up, the bottoms shredded. It was what people had wished for all summer, what artillery from ships at sea and cannons from the ground had tried to induce — rain.

People had endured a summer without moisture, the driest in a generation, and a firestorm that produced winds like those along the Gulf Coast at the height of the hurricane season. For forty-eight hours, no one knew whether they would see another day or recognize their homes again. Now the most ordinary of occurrences, a steady downpour, arrived on angels' wings. It was enough to pockmark the land with water bubbles, enough to start trickles that found gullies that carried ash and debris and the flaky crusts of a once mighty forest downhill, rivulets of black, scouring the ground.

Dawn, first day of September, the rain broke off some to showers, the clouds opening and closing, and in between the gaps, a peak or a ridge could been seen from below, in bright sunlight. Mostly the air was clean, breathable, the killing smoke gone after a month-long siege, pushed to the east. Up high, the miracle was white and early—the first snow of the year, not a dusting but several inches or more in the alpine reaches. What ten thousand men from more than three dozen countries could not do, an early-season gully-washer had done. In Denver, on a day when sixty-four-year-old Buffalo Bill Cody took out an advertisement announcing his "absolutely last" show, a layer of smoke three thousand feet thick settled over the city, the caboose of the Big Burn, nearly a thousand miles from where it started.

On the ground in the northern Rockies, there were bodies to bury and bodies still to find. How many had died? The reports were inconsistent. At the low end, a hundred people, most of them firefighters. At the high end, twice that amount. The problem was discerning a human in a heap of crisp carbon. "The dead bodies where fire has swept directly over them seem to be turned to charcoal. Fingers, ears and even arms drop off when the bodies are touched," a reporter from Seattle wrote. Several men had been crushed in the way that George Cameron from Nova Scotia was. He was hit by a falling tree on Big Creek. It was only by deduction that rangers figured out that the half-melted boots protruding from beneath the massive hulk of a tree belonged to the young man from the east of Canada.

The soldiers of the 25th Infantry put other bodies in canvas and hauled them down the mountain. But then what to do? The body bags were placed in the shade by the railroad depots of Avery and Wallace. For a time, a half-built apartment was converted to a morgue. These bodies awaited funds to ship them to loved ones—a disgrace, as many families said, and an insult from the government.

Complicating the kind of casualty count that field commanders do after a battle was the number of missing. The fog of truth was no less opaque in this wildfire than it was in combat. After Joe Halm had been found and all his men accounted for, the tally came down somewhat. But looking out over all of Region One, and fielding a stack of telegrams and phone messages from families searching for certainty, Bill Greeley could not tell how many people remained missing. His best estimate, he said, was about 125.

Pinkie Adair had not been seen for some time. Her father, the doctor and homesteader who taught her how to ride, shoot, and think smartly for herself, had not given up on her, though it had been a month since he had heard from her. When the fires broke out in early August, before the blowup, he had tried to get into the St. Joe country to rescue his daughter. But he had been refused entry; the trail was blocked. After the blowup, he went to Avery, following rumors, and interviewed countless firefighters. They had stories to tell about the radish-haired young woman with the pistol strapped to her hip, "that gal" who had announced in the middle of the firestorm that she was going to leave, and walked right out of the creek and into the flames. Gutsy. And in town, some remembered seeing her, or someone like her, smudged and exhausted, limping. Had she not got on the train out of Avery? The doctor had checked, and there was no record of her boarding on the night when Avery looked sure to fall. Nor could anyone in the 25th Infantry remember seeing her.

Back in Moscow, Idaho, where the Adairs lived in a big house, came the sound of hobnailed boots on wooden sidewalks, an uneven gait, *clickety-clack, clickety-clack,* the boot spikes worn. This was how she announced herself, the signature walk, still with a bit of pride. She looked frightful, hair burned, eyebrows nipped away and patchy, skin boiled in places and red. For all of that, there was no mistaking that Pinkie Adair had found her way home, and another name was removed from the list of the missing.

• • •

Though suffering from his burns, Supervisor Weigle tried to get out and have a look at the scope of the destruction. Coeur d'Alene National Forest was hit harder than any other. Had this firestorm been an earthquake, his turf would have been the epicenter. The earthquake that knocked down San Francisco in 1906 and led to the city's immolation by fire came to mind for one survivor of the Big Burn. Elbert Dow had been on the scene for both disasters; the wildfire was worse, he said.

Nothing in Weigle's training — pictures, histories, or case studies — prepared him for what he now saw in the forest he was charged with protecting. He told reporters to imagine that an entire eastern state — New Jersey came to mind, or Connecticut — had burned, border to border, every acre. There was at least one fire on record of nearly equal size, the Miramichi blaze in Maine and New Brunswick in 1825. But no fire had consumed so much timber and brush in so little time. The bare facts were that the blowup covered 2.6 million acres of national forest land, and another 521,184 acres of private or state timber, for a total of just under 3.2 million acres. Greeley estimated, at first blush, that a billion dollars of timber was caught by flame.

"The United States has just ended its latest war, the fiercest forest fire in the history of the country," declared *Collier's.* The woods were a graveyard, random clumps of fried and half-burned trunks, a forest no more. The blowdown, millions of trees stripped of limbs and needles and tossed to the ground, made it difficult for horse or man to find a way up a mountainside. Trees stacked crosswise, a weave of horizontal timber, confronted Weigle as he poked his way amid the damage. He was astonished that even the greenest of trees, cedars with their moisture-resistant resin and thick bark, had burned through. Along Big Creek, just up the hill from Wallace, he found thousands of dead trout in a shallow, dirty creek. They died, he surmised, from suffocation, unable to find enough oxygen in water clogged by ashes and the fallout of burning trees.

The strain, the lack of sleep, and his own painful burns were taking a toll on Weigle. He was distressed by the caliber of men hired to help his rangers; many were worthless, didn't know a thing about the woods, and did not have to die. And he was mad at his government, feeling betrayed. If his national forest had been given just enough money to build a decent trail or two, the blowup may have been contained, for it would have been much easier to put people on a line, he said. He had always believed, like Pinchot, that fire could be overcome. If the Big Burn changed his mind, he did not let on.

Back in town, as Weigle stewed, one of the men who had survived the disaster at Big Creek, where eighteen firefighters were incinerated inside a small cabin after the roof fell in, showed up at the forest supervisor's two-story office in Wallace. He was roaring drunk, screaming at the rangers. This man was already hated because he had helped himself to food supplies that he was supposed to take to the injured. When he was found, drunk, after having stolen the precious food, a cry went up to lynch him. Now, face-to-face with Weigle, he challenged the forest supervisor to a fight. Weigle wasn't man enough, the drifter said. Weigle listened for a few minutes, then decided he had heard enough. He reached for the man's chest, pulled him in tight, then tossed him down a flight of stairs. Other rangers applauded and whistled; many of them had wanted to do the same thing.

For every blithering drunk, someone else rose to the occasion. To Weigle's surprise, Joe Halm was eager for fresh duty. He took a bath, had himself a big meal, got a good night's sleep, and informed Weigle that he was ready to go to work. Weigle told him to fetch his glass-plate camera, the one Halm had used to record homestead fraud, and sent him off to some of the places he had just seen. People would not believe this—not in Washington, not the president or the Congress, not the newspapers—without pictures. Halm returned to the woods where he had nearly died and did his job.

He shot pictures of the caves and pits where men had fallen, of streams where people had saved their own lives, buried in water but for their beaks. His camera captured the tunnel where Pulaski and his fifty or so men made their last stand, an unreal photograph. A few scarred sticks poked up from the rubble of downed timber, in a sea of grey and brown, the denuded hills already starting to slide around that tiny entrance where the wood frames burned, where Pulaski ordered a panicked crew to stay put or he would shoot them. Another day, following the rail line, he recorded those great trestles built by armies of shiftless men, now burned, broken, collapsed in colorless ravines. And here and there temporary graves, simple rock cairns marking places where bodies that looked nothing like human beings had been hastily shoved under a few scoops of still-warm dirt. From these scenes came pictures also of the few personal items left behind by the dead — glass melted inside timepieces, coins warped, a picture or two of a mother or a girlfriend, curled, burned at the edge, pressed behind the face of a watch fob, and on its other side, the clock stopped on the evening of Saturday, August 20.

Most of those who had lived through it did not spring back as well as Joe Halm. In Missoula, and up in the mountains that held the Clearwater and Lochsa rivers of Idaho, rangers told the story of a young firefighter, a small German immigrant named Heinrich, but known now as the Lullaby Boy. When waves of flame rolled into their camp in the rugged upper reaches of the Bitterroots, the boy started to sing and dance. He sang while in the creek, even after two rangers covered his head with a wet blanket and tried to hold him down. He sang in the midst of the firestorm. And he sang as stiff-limbed men crawled out of the stream. His eyes would not make contact, and he did not answer simple questions. The singing was a way to deny what he had seen, what he had feared. Days later, in Missoula, he continued to sing. "The Lullaby Boy was still crazy," Ranger Ed Thenon recalled around a campfire years later. "When they finally got him out to the Bitterroot Valley they sent him to the asylum in Deer Lodge."

• • •

As snow and rain muffled what was left of the fire, a partial list of those who were injured fighting the blaze appeared:

Danielson — Totally blind.

Varish — Totally blind, body badly burned.

Rickey — Hands, face and feet badly burned.

Blitten — Right arm burned, will have to be amputated.

Gayers — Face terribly burned.

Christianson — Mass of burns around the face and neck. Will probably die.

Darrick — Totally blind, burned about face and neck. Will probably die.

Carrigan — Feet burned; will be crippled for life.

Hickman — Face terribly burned and nose completely burned off.

Sullivan — Will probably lose both hands.

The last entry, Patrick Sullivan, was the man who moaned in agony just a few beds from Pulaski in the hospital in Wallace, denied further medical care because there was no way to pay for it. Making good on his promise, Pulaski agreed to cover the young man's hospital expenses — for a few more days. Sullivan could not move his hands; the skin was gone, the burns deep. He coughed constantly, trying to shake the mountain smoke embedded in his lungs. Sullivan had worked only that single day, which would do nothing for his financial situation at home. His mother had been abandoned by her husband seven years earlier, and had two girls in the house. She lived off her boy's meager earnings as a miner, $3.50 a day during good times. After getting his wounds cleaned and freshly dressed, Sullivan was checked out of the hospital, Pulaski's help having expired. What about the cough? He complained that it would not go away. Probably from cigarettes, a doctor told him. Most likely it will disappear in a few weeks. At home with his mother and two sisters, Sullivan was never the same. He could not split wood or swing a hammer or retrieve water. He was useless, because working with his hands was all Sullivan knew how to do. When he tried to curl his fingers around an ax handle, blood and pus oozed out. Sleep was impossible without excessive drink. The cough never left him. On Christmas Eve he died—twenty-nine years old. His death was never listed in the formal tally of those killed in the Big Burn.

Pulaski remained much longer in the hospital than did Sullivan, his care paid for in part by the Red Cross and in part by donations from other rangers. Early on, he took a turn for the worse, coming down with pneumonia. It was a persistent killer in 1910, the dread of so many families. His breathing was labored, his cough ragged. It hurt to walk, and sleep was inconsistent. Nurses put new bandages over his badly burned eye every day and gave him steam for his ravaged lungs. The eyeball itself had been seared by flame, and Pulaski was told he might never see again from that side. The other eye remained sensitive to light. Smoke inhalation had damaged his lungs, and the burns on his skin were infected. He received visitors, including many reporters, and his story soon became the most heroic note of this epic disaster. He was called, erroneously and repeatedly, a descendant of the Pulaski family of the Revolutionary War, but his story needed no varnish.

Those whose lives he had saved in the tunnel—the Texas Ranger given Pulaski's horse, the men he forced at gunpoint to lie in fetid water, others who considered mutiny—were treated and drifted away, after collecting a few days' pay. Pulaski had not just lost his energy; his very life force seemed to have ebbed. If he was ever to regain sight in one eye, the doctors said, he would need surgery. But it would be expensive, and Pulaski had no extra money after helping Sullivan with his doctor bills. The Forest Service could not cover him. The rangers took up a collection among themselves, again, and passed the hat around Wallace. They were indignant, to say the least, that the government "has even refused to pay their hospital fees," as Ranger Will Morris noted in his diary. "So we are going to each subscribe something ourselves." But among them, they failed to come up with enough money for Pulaski to get the surgery he needed. He went home to Emma and Elsie. "I take care of him," his wife wrote. "The experience cost him a weak throat, lungs and eyes, but that is better than being blind always."

Months passed before news arrived in the foothills of the Italian Alps that Rivara Canavese had lost two of its native sons to a big American wildfire. Domenico Bruno was twenty-four. Giacomo Viettone was twenty-seven. At first no one was able to identify them, burned in that heap of other bodies in the half-built cellar at the homestead of Joe Beauchamp. Simple deduction, a reconstruction of the eyewitness accounts, and time books found at the site eventually determined the names. Their families were owed back pay from the U.S. government. Each man had labored nearly three weeks, days of twelve to sixteen hours. Cables passed between the American consulate in Italy and the mayor of Rivara Canavese. The families were interviewed. "I was formerly a farm laborer," Domenico's father said. "And on account of our age, neither I nor my wife have been able to earn a living by labor for some years. I was wholly dependent upon him for support." The other Italian came from a family of seven children—all girls but for Giacomo. The father was old, broken by physical labor, unable to work; the mother was blind. They pleaded with the American investigators for compensation, a little sum for the loss of their boy.

During a lengthy inquiry, the American consul, Albert Michelson, found that the two immigrants had been supporting their families for at least five years, sending money home from the mines in Wyoming and Arizona, regular income. "The letters of the two deceased men demonstrate a willingness and desire to keep their parents from want," Michelson wrote his superiors in Washington. "That is admirable and convincing."

Yet nothing came from the United States. The families checked regularly with the mayor, who checked with the consul, who checked with his government, and all of them were given half-promises and uncertainty, but no money. "The family is in great want," Michelson wrote after one of the visits from the mayor of Rivara. By now Michelson was angry, sharing some of the indignation that forest ranger families felt in the northern Rockies. These grieving parents were "peasants," he wrote in one cable, living hand to mouth, and the least his government could do was to give them some small compensation for what the boys had done on behalf of the United States. "In ten years of service, there has not been a case more deserving," Michelson wrote. At last, two years after the fire, Domenico Bruno's parents were paid $200 for the loss of their son's life. There is no record of the Viettone settlement.

Families of the Americans who died were not treated much better. A few days after the seventeen-year-old boy Val Nicholson fell in the Bullion Mine, his father hiked up through the smoking debris and retrieved the boy's body. Young Val was dragged down to Wallace and buried. The grief overwhelmed his father, though—two weeks later, he died of a heart attack. That left the widow Nicholson, a mother with young children underfoot, and no money. She pleaded with the Forest Service for compensation after losing the two men in her life, but the government turned her down. There was nothing in reserve, no funds for the fallen American warriors in the Bitterroots. She then asked for something simpler: a stone slab for her son's grave. Government officials said they would look into it.

PART III

What They Saved

17

Fallout

As the sustaining cause of his life and the men who shep-herded that cause were engulfed in flame, nobody in the public arena was angrier than Gifford Pinchot. He had joined Roosevelt on the road, getting daily fire updates during the last week of August. For him, the dispatches were like hearing, blow by blow, of his hometown burning to the ground. He knew the Bitterroots better than most of the transient firefighters. By horseback or on foot, with rod and rifle, with surveyors' tools and primitive maps, he had been all over the land that had just collapsed. The news reports left him hollow, furious, and stunned. He and Roosevelt had all but written off fire, and now this: at least a hundred dead, the fate of some rangers still unknown, the destruction of an area big enough to hold their most outsized ambitions. His knights had never faced such a test. And yet, in the crucible of a wildfire of unseen magnitude, in the face of great loss, they performed as true heroes, he felt.

Anger and indignation in his voice, Pinchot went on the attack before the rains had yet put out the fire, seizing this calamity as a rallying cry in the same way that a band of Texans used the disastrous defeat of the Alamo. He blamed enemies of the Forest Service for leaving the agency so vulnerable. He had preached that forests must be preserved, in part to prevent a coming timber "famine." And by the early estimates of the rangers, the fire had burned enough wood to provide timber for the whole nation for fifteen years—an inexcusable waste, in Pinchot's telling. It could all be laid at the feet of people who had gone after the Forest Service since its infancy and were taking advantage of Taft's feeble presidency to kill it. On August 26, papers around the country carried on their front pages an Associated Press dispatch that had originated in the *New York Times.*

PINCHOT PLACES BLAME FOR FIRES

The immediate causes of the fire were drought, lightning, and locomotives—and of course a wind for the ages, that Palouser. But the Big Burn did not have to happen as it did. The fire was not inevitable, not a pure force of nature. It was "the ironbound reactionaries," led by Senator Heyburn of Idaho, who had left the people's forests without adequate stewardship, Pinchot said. They had blood on their hands. "The men in Congress like Heyburn," Pinchot said, "who have made light of the efforts of the Forest Service to prepare itself to prevent such a calamity as this, have in effect been fighting on the side of the fires against the general welfare. If even a small fraction of the loss from the present fires had been expended in additional patrol and preventive equipment some or perhaps all of the loss could have been avoided."

Pinchot's conclusion was a reach, to say the least. If ten times the manpower had been on the fire lines, if the entire nation's standing Army of roughly eighty thousand men had been in place in the forest, it's doubtful they could have done anything when the northern Rockies blew up in the face of those winds, with the woods so dry. But even if Pinchot knew it was absurd to claim that "some or perhaps all of the loss could have been avoided," he had another motive for going on the attack. Schooled in heroic mythology and his years with Roosevelt, Pinchot knew that public policy revolutions needed more than outrage—they needed a master narrative. With the Big Burn, Pinchot sketched the blueprint of a coming-of-age myth for an agency just five years old. If the Forest Service had lost the battle, it would now try to win the war behind the ousted Chief, using the martyrdom of his wounded Little G.P.s as a call to arms.

"The Forest Service has done wonders with its handful of men," he said. "Many of them have given their lives to protect the homes of settlers and the forests on which the prosperity of the Western people depend. To my mind their conduct is beyond all praise." Give them tools, money for trails and telephones, and funds to build lookouts, and the Big Burn would never happen again.

"Forest fires are preventable," he said. "It is a good thing for us to remember at this time that nearly all or quite all of the loss, suffering and death the fires have caused was wholly unnecessary."

Pinchot spread the word through extensive interviews. "For the want of a nail," he told the popular *Everybody's Magazine,* "the shoe was cast, the rider thrown, the battle lost. For the want of a trail, the finest white pine forests in the United States were laid waste and scores of lives lost. It is all loss, dead loss, due to the pique, the bias, the bullheadedness of a knot of men who have sulked and planted their hulks in the way of appropriation and protection of these national forests." Three other national magazines, *Collier's, Harper's,* and *American Forestry,* also took up the theme, lashing out at Congress. "This national calamity is blamable to the petulance and vindictiveness of certain men," *Everybody's* declared.

Roosevelt, whose every utterance was being recorded as he toured a country curious about whether he might take on President Taft, reinforced Pinchot's cause. He saw in these green-uniformed men out west something of what he had seen in the Rough Riders who stormed into a hail of bullets with him in Cuba. Few remembered the cause of that war, already an asterisk barely ten years after it ended. What they remembered were those brave souls who charged up San Juan Hill. In similar fashion, Roosevelt saw courage, selflessness, and strength in battle in the men who faced movable mountains of fire in August 1910. Teddy sent a telegram to Greeley, lavish in praise for the Forest Service, which was forwarded to every employee of the agency. What the rangers had done was enough to "make an American proud of having such a body of public servants," Roosevelt said. They had acted with valor and competence, he added, despite being undermined by Congress.

Senator Heyburn was taken aback. "Pinchot's charge is ridiculous," he said. "I won't need two-hundred words to answer it." He groused about efforts to portray the Forest Service as heroic, and then decided, after double volleys from G.P. and Roosevelt, to make a claim of greater absurdity. He blamed the rangers for the fire.

It was not that they didn't know what they were doing, or lacked funds, tools, men, or support services. The problem, Heyburn believed, was the very existence of the Forest Service as a force of preservation—enabling nature to run wild, as it were. This fire would never have happened had the Forest Service not tried to hold back the controlling forces of civilization, he said. The great national forests of the West needed loggers, miners, city builders, farmers, and ranchers to cut them down, thus preempting any big fire, because the fuel would be gone. In setting aside these vast public reserves, Heyburn implied, Roosevelt had all but torched the trees himself.

He pronounced Teddy's national forests a monumental failure. Of course, Heyburn had long opposed the very idea of public forests, just as he had worked against child labor laws and direct election of U.S. senators. But see here, this conservation idea, in practice, was a disaster! Here, in the biggest wildfire in American history, was proof of a point he had long argued, he claimed. The rangers themselves, from Greeley to Pulaski, all these Little G.P.s with their leather-bound book of rules of the woods, handed down from the great Pinchot himself—they were a menace, an impediment, interested only in collecting their paychecks.

"The exclusion of responsible settlers and the substitution of irresponsible persons as rangers account in a large measure for the fires," Heyburn said. "The presence of thousands of men in the forest whose principal industry is to establish the necessity for their employment will always constitute a menace to the forest." And then Heyburn went one step further. The fires, he said, were God's will—an angry God, enraged by the Forest Service. In letting so much land burn, God was doing what the Forest Service would not let industry do, clearing the land of its tangle of wildness to prepare for cities, industry, farms, and settlers. Heyburn won few converts, with the West still smoking, with men still nursing wounds in hospitals, with stories appearing daily of heroic and selfless acts by the young rangers.

Paired again on the road, Roosevelt and Pinchot grew stronger in daily battle with the enemies of conservation, coasting on a full tank of outrage after the fire, a righteous wind at their backs. The highlight of their tour was an address in Osawatomie, Kansas, ten days after the Big Burn. Pinchot wrote the speech, once again finding the words that fit the oratorical style of the man he worshiped. It had been eleven years since they boxed and wrestled together on a winter night in the governor's mansion in Albany, eleven years since they shared a dream of persuading Americans to see their land as something worthy of holding on to for the ages, eleven years since they dared to think that the Gilded Age's powers who controlled natural resources at the cusp of the twentieth century could be brought to heel. Over that span, they had set aside more than 230 million acres, freed the Republican Party from the grip of a handful of big trusts, and created an agency that embodied the spirit of progressive government—young men in the service of country, some of whom were dying in hospitals in a part of the northern Rockies stripped of its forest cover.

A massive crowd stretched to the horizon on the prairie. Roosevelt climbed atop a table placed in the midst of the audience, barely high enough for most people to see him. He launched into a declaration of "new nationalism," a creed that stressed people power over corporations, and conservation over hands-off capitalism. If there was ever any doubt that Roosevelt stood with the burgeoning insurgents in his party, he removed it on August 31. First he went after Taft, essentially labeling him a man who broke his pact with the voters, though he never named him. Then he called for "a graduated income tax on big fortunes," and an inheritance tax as well. He stood up for his Square Deal, urged passage of child labor laws to curb abuse of young children working in mines and factories, and said there should be government protection for workers knocked out of the job market because of physical disabilities. He urged further prosecution of the trusts, and regulation of banks, insurance companies, and railroads. As for the big swath of land left over from America's western expansion — it was your land, he said.

"I believe that the natural resources must be used for the benefit of all the people, and not monopolized for the benefit of a few," he said. Here, in the midst of an hourlong speech, Roosevelt's voice rose, and he punctured the air with his fingers. Of "all the questions which can come before this nation," he thundered, "there is none which compares in importance with the central task of leaving this land even a better land for our descendants than it is for us." Such a notion, he said, was still counterintuitive to many Americans — "another case in which I am accused of taking a revolutionary attitude." But he saw this cause as something vital to the United States' remaining a land of equals.

"Conservation is a great moral issue!"

In its dispatch from Osawatomie, the Associated Press wrote that the crowd's enthusiasm made it hard for Roosevelt to get through the speech. Standing near the makeshift stage, Pinchot was mesmerized — after a lonely year, here were the forester's words brought to rousing life by Teddy, every sentence a cannon blast at the enemy. "I've never seen a crowd that affected me as much as that one did," Pinchot wrote. Roosevelt's friend the writer William Allen White also witnessed the spectacle in Kansas; it took several decades for him to fully understand its ramifications. "It is hard to bring back today the sense of excitement, almost of tumult, that was in the air over this land in the summer and autumn of 1910," White wrote. "It was revolutionary."

Roosevelt had not yet declared his intention to challenge Taft for the Republican presidential nomination. But Taft, plowing through a round of golf at his summer retreat, was said to be so angry upon hearing Roosevelt's words that he threw his club twenty-five yards—one of his better shots. Later, he told his brother the speech made it clear that he and his mentor no longer shared the same political beliefs. And in a rare show of defiance, Taft vowed not to be rolled by a fresh Teddy juggernaut. "I will not step out of the way of Mr. Roosevelt when he is advocating such wild ideas," Taft wrote his brother.

Two weeks later, building on the momentum of the New Nationalism speech, Pinchot and Roosevelt spoke at the second National Conservation Congress, in St. Paul, attended by governors, leading politicians, and members of Taft's inner circle. The president himself made an appearance. Taft's remarks were tepid, greeted by blank stares. "Whatever conservation may mean," he said, "there is one thing it should never mean, and that is the mere tying up of resources." In Taft's mind, the nation should pursue a sober, business-minded version of protecting the natural world. "The time has come for a halt in general rhapsodies over conservation," he said. Politically tone-deaf as always, Taft could not read the mood of the crowd or sense that the country had changed. The Big Burn had stirred the blood of many Americans, and for them conservation was no longer an abstract debate. Roosevelt and Pinchot had personalized it—boys out west had died for it.

So what the crowd got from Roosevelt and Pinchot, by contrast, was the most tumultuous of rhapsodies over conservation. The fires in the Rocky Mountains, Roosevelt said, should prompt a renewal of the idea of protecting public land with a corps of young foresters. He urged Americans to seize the moment: expand the Forest Service, enlarge its domain, set more land aside. Pinchot gave perhaps the most energetic expression of the principles he and Roosevelt had enshrined with the Forest Service, and at the end he struck a valedictory note. "There are but a few moments in a man's life like this," he said. "I have fought for many years for conservation, and conservation has won."

In November, in the off-year elections, Taft's Republican Party was wiped out at the polls. The Democrats took control of Congress, pleasing Pinchot; he felt that Taft deserved to be repudiated, even if it meant the party that had been Pinchot's home since he came of age was trounced. "An overwhelming rebuke to the reactionaries," Pinchot said. Taft was adrift as never before. "Roosevelt was my closest friend," he said, describing the "agony of my spirit." But no sitting president could let such abuse stand and still be respected as a man, or a leader. Taft had to return fire. Pushed by his aides, Taft criticized Roosevelt in public, something he had never done. But the words no sooner left the mouth of the big man, now pushing 360 pounds, than he felt a stab of guilt over betraying the person who had essentially made him president. After his broadside against Roosevelt, Taft retreated to his sleeping quarters in the White House, threw himself on the bed, and wept.

Not long after the election, Senator Heyburn took one more stab at the Forest Service. Despite the public's renewed sympathy with the agency, he plowed ahead, proposing that much of the land that had been burned in the fires of August be taken out of the national forest system and given to private owners. He did not precisely state that nearly three million acres would no longer be in public ownership, but his bill set up a system by which burned-over land would be removed from the reserves — effectively doing what he had long intended. In this latest campaign, at least, he was supported by one of his hometown newspapers, which added a suggestion that had been a favorite remedy of Heyburn's: to clear-cut healthy standing forests as a drastic form of fire prevention. "It would really be better to cut down all the trees than to incur the imminent risk of such vast destruction and mortality as has accompanied these fires," the *Idaho Press* editorialized. "For it is better to devastate forests than to devastate settlements."

Pinchot sprang into action yet again, giving a flurry of interviews, lobbying senators, prompting thousands of telegrams protesting the plan. Here was Heyburn, he said, "who for years has tried in every way he could to injure or destroy the national forests" with a proposal to take millions of acres away from the public. It was a robber barons' renaissance. Pinchot had long advocated "a little rioting" to move public opinion along; now he was back in his element. "It was effective, and great fun," he wrote in his diary. "Like old times."

Heyburn's bill was defeated. And now Pinchot went from defense to offense. With the new sentiment in the country, the time was ripe for one of the most significant changes in the law since the reserves were turned over to the Forest Service in 1905. The big conservation dream of Teddy and G.P. had included not just western public land, but eastern hardwood forests. In order to protect them, however, the government would have to buy land from private owners and make it part of the reserve system. Even at the height of Roosevelt's popularity, right after his landslide election in 1904, he could not win congressional approval for buying land for the public in the East. But after the fire of 1910, the winds shifted dramatically. It was well within the national interest, at a time when conservation had been hailed as the highest moral cause of the day, to include much of the forested East in the public-land system, Pinchot and his allies argued anew. This time, after years of rejection, a bill doing exactly that passed the new Congress and was signed into law by a dispirited and overwhelmed Taft.

Over time, more than twenty million acres in the East were acquired and made part of the national forest system — woods along the spine of the Appalachians, leafy hollows in the Smoky Mountains, crowds of trees with brilliant fall colors in New England, rocky pockets of wooded wilderness in southern Ohio. All of this eventually became public land, thanks to passage of the Weeks Act in early 1911. The Big Burn, taking with it nearly a hundred men, had made the difference. "Opposition in the Senate to federal purchase of eastern forests had gone up in the smoke of a 1910 holocaust in Idaho," wrote the historian Harold K. Steen. The fire, as it turned out, had remade the American landscape in a much larger way than Pinchot himself could have imagined.

Barely ten months after the fire, Congress doubled the money in the Forest Service budget for roads and trails, giving the rangers what they had begged for in previous years. The convincing story Pinchot had told of ragged young foresters fighting a sea of flame carried the day once more for a majority in the new Congress. The coming-of-age myth was in place and had become part of popular culture. Zane Grey made a forest ranger the hero of his next book, *The Young Forester*, the story of a well-educated Pinchot progressive who saves the day from timber thieves and flame in territorial Arizona.

The budget win for Pinchot followed another victory: the resignation of his nemesis in the Taft administration, Interior Secretary Ballinger. "Feeling cheerful," Pinchot wrote after the embattled secretary stepped down. There remained only Senator Heyburn, who continued his tirades against the Forest Service and its founder. But in the midst of a late-night speech to a near-empty Senate chamber — a filibuster against an investigation of corrupt campaign practices — Heyburn collapsed.

He had ruptured a blood vessel, which formed a clot in his brain. Felled by a stroke, blind in one eye, half his face sagging, Heyburn was never able to regain his form. He died a few months later, in the fall of 1912. He was sixty years old, "a stalwart who was widely known for his unyielding bitterness," his obituary in the *New York Times* said. The most positive thing his colleagues in the Senate could muster in a sheaf of written memories was that he was "an intense partisan." With his death, at long last, the United States Forest Service was safe.

18

One for the Boys

THE BITTERROOT MOUNTAINS were slow to heal. Deep, lasting scars could be seen throughout the three states where the Big Burn hit hardest—fire-branded tattoos on the land to match those on the skin that the first rangers would carry to their graves. The Forest Service tried different things, planting saplings from a Rocky Mountain nursery, shipping nearly two tons of seeds from walnuts, red oaks, and hickories in the East to see if these hardwoods would take root in the northern Rockies. But though the rangers put thousands of starts into the ground, the blaze-cleared earth was so bare—in places stripped of its already thin soil to bedrock—that heavy rains washed much of the new life downhill. The trees that had remained standing were so weakened that they fell prey to insect infestations. Broad swaths of rust-colored firs, the needles lifeless after the sap was drained by beetles or boiled by the fire, ran through the forest. It sickened many of the rangers. They knew well enough that a forest after a fire is not a cemetery, set with stones—just a change of worlds. Still, it was hard to see any tomorrow in the ashen landscape.

"A feeling of great sorrow," Ranger Will Morris recalled of how he felt during his first good look at the land in September. "The canyons and hillsides were covered with a twisted mass of broken, blackened trees, in some places five feet deep."

The standing, staggered trees died slowly, unlike some of the towns that had been wiped off the map in a few hours or less. Other towns, in valleys where people tried to stitch their lives back together, seemed vulnerable now to forces just beyond their front doors. People would never again look at the woods in the same way.

After spending weeks in the hospital with little improvement to show for it, Ed Pulaski came home a different man. His energy was gone, Emma could tell. He was angry, nagged by an ulcerating bitterness; it was a struggle to button up his frustration. Despite multiple, slow-healing burns, blindness in one eye, and badly damaged lungs, Pulaski returned to work. He had to: he was not entitled to sick pay, under Forest Service rules at the time, and the family had no other source of income. He was a sad sight around Wallace, the tall ranger with the unsteady gait who seemed to avoid eye contact.

The town, unlike others ravaged by the fire, was coming back with a flourish. The lure of good money for silver and other treasures from the mines was a draw for new capital and fresh energy. Wallace was rebuilding in iron and stone, a phoenix, while Pulaski was going in the other direction. To see him was to be reminded of two days in August when the land blew up, the walking, wounded face of the Forest Service. And to some — the men who had shoved women from the exit trains, or turned the other way when Weigle begged for help to rescue Pulaski from the mine — he was a reminder of their cowardice. Of course, he was a hero in the Coeur d'Alenes, as he was throughout the country. Everyone said so: Ranger Pulaski, such courage! But that meant little; in truth Pulaski was a broken man, best kept at a distance.

For two years following the burn, Pulaski's days were filled with painful indoor work: answering queries from the government about those who had gone into the tunnel with him. Prodded by Pinchot and higher-ups in the Forest Service, Congress was shamed into passing a measure that would compensate people who were unable to work because of injuries suffered in the line of duty. But it was a cumbrous process for the Forest Service, and forced Pulaski to relive that one horrific night over and over again. One firefighter, John Brandon, requested money for the horse he lost in the mine on August 20 — he valued the beast at $40. The government refused to pay more than $30, and asked Pulaski for verification.

"I was blind at the time and could not have attended to such things if I wanted to," Pulaski wrote back, clearly annoyed. Another man claimed that smoke from inside the tunnel had left him so ill he could no longer look for work — his lungs were permanently compromised, and his burns had not healed. The government had doubts about his case, asking Pulaski for more details almost two years after the fire. "Please write everything you know concerning Mr. Christensen's case," they demanded of Pulaski.

Dutifully, he inhabited that hot, gas-filled earthen space dozens of times for dozens of cases, always signing off as "The Assistant Ranger."

Humiliated and sick, with little money for his own medical care, Pulaski asked his supervisors for help with his case. They shared his outrage. Roscoe Haines, the ranger who had braved the still-flaming forests in the St. Joe country to find Joe Halm, took up Pulaski's cause as a claims supervisor for the region. He wrote up and down the chain of command, a vertical nag. Surely the government could not treat the hero of the Big Burn this way. Word came back from Washington via a regional forester who wrote to Haines:

"I regret exceedingly that it will not be possible to allow this claim of Mr. Pulaski, since he is certainly deserving of remuneration for the permanent injuries affecting his eyesight. The only method by which further compensation could be secured for Mr. Pulaski would be by special legislation through Congress. The only other suggestion which occurs to me at this time would be for Mr. Pulaski or some of his friends to place his case and the story of his saving 40 of the men at the mine tunnel before the Carnegie Commission for the allotting of medals and awards to persons of bravery."

In the end, Pulaski did not get a dime from the government for the ravages fire inflicted on his body. The reasoning seemed to be that since he went directly back to work after leaving the hospital, he was not disabled, and therefore was ineligible for compensation for lost work time. But of course the reason Pulaski had returned to his job, despite his serious medical troubles, was that he needed the paycheck just to stay alive. His only remaining recourse, as the regional forester had suggested, was to tell his story to the Carnegie Hero Fund in the hope that it would find him worthy of some small change from the fortune of a man who once embodied Gilded Age wealth. He had to beg from the rich.

But Pulaski would not grovel, as he showed when he scolded his neighbors for being careless with their public forests at that Chamber of Commerce luncheon. It was undignified, he felt, to try to win a hero's reward for what he had done. So Ranger Haines did it for him, collecting stories from the people who had been in the mine tunnel. When he solicited Pulaski for his own account, the wounded ranger refused to comply. Haines had to trick him; he told Pulaski he needed the narrative for Forest Service files, nothing else. Nobody would see his account. Pulaski sent along the most basic of details: the story of returning to the fire with the packers after leaving his family to certain doom, the rounding up of panicky firefighters, the retreat downhill, the offer of his horse to the obese former Texas Ranger, the dash into the tunnel, and the threat to shoot anyone who tried to leave the mineshaft.

"I hope you will regard this letter as confidential and send it back or destroy it when it serves its purpose," he wrote to Haines. Instead, the supervisor sent it on to the Carnegie commission.

When not doing paperwork, Pulaski tended to graves, alone, at great pain and some financial cost. It was an abomination that the dead were treated no better than the living, he thought. At the least, a memorial should be erected to those who lost their lives—eighty-five people, according to the Forest Service's official report, completed in 1911. The dead were scattered throughout the Bitterroots;

some remained where they had fallen, the bodies never retrieved, left to the elements under a few feet of fire-blackened earth. Others, in Wallace, were put in graves marked by wooden slabs. Pulaski pulled weeds and mowed the lawn around these tombstones, all the while reminding his supervisors that the dead were owed a proper memorial. He did this on his own time, using his own money, though he worried that the government might frown on such a thing.

"I would probably get called for mixing in," he wrote. "But I think the only way for me is to clear the weeds and grass off each year as I have on my own time."

He found refuge in his blacksmith shop, sometimes working late into the night, experimenting with a tool to help firefighters. He crafted an ax and a hoe-type blade on a single handle. One side could be used to cut wood, the other to dig and scrape a fire line. It was an ingenious idea, one of those inventions that look obvious in retrospect, and it was instantly duplicated across North America. Pulaski tried to patent the tool, as yet another way to get money for eye surgery, but when faced with a blizzard of forms, he said the hell with it.

The Carnegie commission returned the application to Ranger Haines — sorry, but no hero's reward for Ed Pulaski. "While Mr. Pulaski's act is commendable, from the facts you gave it does not appear that he did anything more than was necessary to save his own life, and for this reason his case, I regret to say, does not come within the scope of the Fund."

Haines was livid. Pulaski could have stayed in Wallace when the woods blew up, saved his own ass. He could have fled downhill, back to town with the other firefighters. He could have retreated with the frightened packers, who escaped as soon as they dropped their loads. There was "conclusive evidence to show beyond all doubt that Edward Pulaski did risk his own life voluntarily to save the lives of fellow human beings," Haines wrote. He fired up a fresh round of queries, trying to compile overwhelming evidence to win the Carnegie money for Pulaski. Among the crew members who wrote on his behalf, Fred Libby said, "I know that he could have saved himself on more than one occasion but would not forsake his men." The ex–Texas Ranger, "Dad" Stockton, credited Pulaski with saving his life, without doubt. Haines went back to Pulaski with questions, this time letting him in on the scope of his mission. Pulaski could not believe it—who were *these people* to challenge his honor?

"Do you think I would have stayed there when I knew my home and family was in more or less danger, if I did not realize that there were men being killed and that I might help them by staying at the same time staking my own life to help them?" The words were as stinging as any Pulaski ever put to paper in his years in the Forest Service. And he gave a hint, at last, at the depth of his bitterness. "I did think that U. Sam might have taken notice of me and sent me a leather medal. To show me that men put to the test are not forgotten."

Alas, there would be no medal, leather or bronze, and no money from the Carnegie Hero Fund, and no patent for the Pulaski tool.

By 1911, Gifford Pinchot was exhausted. The scraps of a year when he and Roosevelt were in the news nearly every day had clearly drained him. Sleep was uneasy. His stomach bothered him. His skin was splotchy; his brushy mustache was starting to grey. He stooped a bit. He looked gaunt, hollow-eyed, and had lost the glow of youth that had made him one of the most eligible single men in the capital. He still summoned his long-lost lover, though she was much harder to bring to life. And of course she was forever twenty-eight years old, an immortal beauty in the full blush of her life, while Pinchot was slipping well into middle age. Seeking restoration of body and soul, he checked himself into the Kellogg sanitarium in Battle Creek, Michigan, an institution founded by the breakfast cereal magnate and known for its naturopathic remedies. Pinchot was a celebrity there, and gave frequent talks to other clients. But he was lonely for Laura.

"Not a clear day," he wrote after his first night in the sanitarium.

"Not a clear day," the next day.

"Not a clear day," again, through his two-week stay in Battle Creek.

It continued like this for months, with only the occasional dream encounter, which he found unsatisfying. One note showed a hint of optimism that he could have further mystic encounters with Laura: "Not a clear day, but not blind."

Fully rested, Pinchot immediately sought to get the wings of Teddy Roosevelt aloft once more, building on the political triumphs that came in the wake of the Big Burn. Any day without a full schedule, as before, prompted much guilt and self-loathing. "Shamefully stayed in the house all day, loafing and catching up . . ."

Even with Heyburn gone, he had his enemies. A mob stormed the docks in Cordova, Alaska, and burned an effigy of Pinchot — cheering with gusto as the image of the founding forester fell into Prince William Sound. They were mad that coal in some national forests in Alaska was off-limits to mining. That protection was one of Roosevelt's final acts as president, three years earlier, but the mob blamed Pinchot because he was the easier target. Another man, Pinchot's old friend and camping mate John Muir, was the other face of this movement, in addition to Roosevelt. Muir, in failing health, had not spoken to Pinchot in some time, a breach dating to their opposing views on damming the river in the Hetch Hetchy Valley in Yosemite. But in a gesture that showed Muir was not blinded by this dispute to what Pinchot had done for the larger cause, three hundred of his Sierra Club followers ventured into a grove of coastal redwoods just north of San Francisco and selected what they considered the most perfect of the big trees in Muir Woods. There they placed a plaque on a rock with this inscription:

THIS TREE IS DEDICATED TO
GIFFORD PINCHOT
FRIEND OF THE FOREST
CONSERVER OF THE COMMON-WEALTH

As Pinchot focused his energy on the second coming of Roosevelt, he initially faced stiff opposition in his own party. Many Republican insurgents had planned to back Robert La Follette, the Wisconsin governor who had taken strong early stands against the sitting president. He was a friend of both Roosevelt and Pinchot and was a driving force behind some of the major progressive initiatives. But then La Follette gave a rambling, shockingly incoherent speech in New York before a group of donors, power players, and writers. It was two hours of gibberish, which an aide attributed to fatigue and alcohol. Afterward, the consensus was that this man could not be president.

All eyes turned to Teddy. And so in early 1912, he ended a two-year tease, declaring: "My hat is in the ring. The fight is on, and I am stripped to the buff." It sounded as if he were ready for another wrestling match with Pinchot. Using the key points of his New Nationalism speech as a platform, Roosevelt won all but one primary and one caucus—still not enough, by the undemocratic rules of the day, to become the nominee, but it demonstrated that his vote-drawing power had not diminished. He swept New England, the West Coast, and states in between.

At the convention in Chicago, Roosevelt should have carried the Republican banner. But Taft's men controlled the national committee, and the fix was in. "Those elements were mostly rich men," William Allen White wrote, "well placed, well housed, well fed, well clad, who hitherto for a generation had been able to control American politics." And they still controlled the party of Lincoln. Roosevelt thought his popularity alone would prevail. When he arrived in Chicago, he was mobbed in the streets as his car made its way along Michigan Avenue. In a speech before supporters, Roosevelt said he stood for the underdog, though as White noted, "It was a middle-class revolt."

The lightning that split the Republican Party came during five days in June. In the face of certain defeat in the fall, and despite Roosevelt's preeminence in the primaries and his superior popularity, Republican power brokers declared that the beleaguered and unpopular sitting president would be the nominee.

A riot seemed at hand. More than a thousand police officers rushed to control the convention. But rather than storm the stage, Roosevelt's forces walked out and marched over to a nearby auditorium, Orchestra Hall. There, they broke away from the Republican Party and declared a new group, the Progressive Party, with Teddy Roosevelt at the head of the ticket.

Roosevelt gave a speech that "tore the roof off," the press reported. And when asked how he felt, he responded, "I feel as strong as a bull moose!" Thereafter his Progressive Party was more commonly known by that favorite T.R. term. Pinchot wrote the party platform, which he described as "a contract with the people." It was also a contract with Roosevelt's will, which faced an extreme test when Teddy was shot in the chest while campaigning in Milwaukee. Blood dripping through his suit, he continued with the speech for ninety minutes before leaving to see a doctor. The bullet had missed his vital organs.

On Election Day, the country chose a liberal majority, but split its votes between three left-center candidates: a Democrat, Woodrow Wilson, who was president of Princeton University; the fiery Roosevelt, on the Progressive ticket; and the perennial socialist, Eugene Debs. Taft was routed, winning only two states, Utah and Vermont, the worst showing ever by an incumbent president. Roosevelt, with 27 percent of the vote, set a mark for third-party candidates that would not be surpassed through century's end. Debs peeled off 6 percent. Wilson won with 42 percent.

The Bull Moose Party faded away almost as quickly as it came to life, built as it was on Roosevelt's personality. But many of those self-described Progressives never went back to the Republican Party, a break that shaped the GOP for the next hundred years.

Taft returned home to Ohio, to practice law, to eat in peace, to putter around the golf course every now and then. In 1921, he was named to the Supreme Court, the job he had always wanted. At the same time, his weight fell to 259 pounds—down a hundred pounds from the peak of his presidency. Of the four years when he occupied the White House as the nation's most powerful man, he wrote: "I don't remember that I ever was President."

Teddy Roosevelt went off to South America to explore an uncharted waterway, the River of Doubt, in the center of the Amazon rain forest. The trip nearly killed him, an epic of illness, food shortages, disease, and danger on a river that swallowed boats and men. "I had to go," Roosevelt said. "It was my last chance to be a boy." He came home ill and underweight.

He retreated to Oyster Bay to be with his big family. His public career was over, though he was only in his mid-fifties. "I am having a horrid, unimportant time," he wrote to a friend, eight years out of office. He found solace in the profession that had sustained him before he entered politics—writing. His sight was nearly gone in one eye, after taking too many punches during White House boxing matches, but he was as prolific as ever, producing as much in a few years' time as some professionals do in a career. At the start of American involvement in the Great War, Roosevelt tried one last time to enter the arena—"to warm both hands before the fire of life," as he put it—requesting permission to lead an infantry division in France. He was turned down. Two years later, on January 6, 1919, this most vigorous of presidents died a relatively young man, at the age of sixty, from an embolism.

Pinchot took the loss hard. No man would ever inspire him so much, and no man's friendship would have greater value. With Roosevelt, every day was an adventure, part of a journey toward something finer, Pinchot felt—"life at its warmest, and fullest and freest, at its utmost in vigor, at its sanest in purpose." Without Roosevelt, the world was smaller, the causes less animating. In Roosevelt's autobiography, Pinchot was mentioned often, which gave the ever-needy forester the love in print that he required in regular doses from his old boxing mate and political partner. Pinchot would remind people that Roosevelt had once said it was G.P. himself who was the "true keeper of his conscience." And for the rest of his life, Pinchot took particular comfort in an additional compliment, this a single line about him from Roosevelt's auto-biography:

"Among the many, many public officials who under my admin-istration rendered literally invaluable service to the people of the United States, he on the whole stood first."

Six years after the fire, Pulaski still tended the graves, still strug-gled to get through the day without pain, still lobbied for a proper memorial for the dead. He wrote a memo to the government outlin-ing the costs of his proposal: Concrete, $200. Granite slabs engraved with the names of the dead, $215. Soil and grass, $20. But for this $435, the Forest Service would need an act of Congress, he was told.

Eleven years after the fire, in 1921, Congress appropriated $500 to the Coeur d'Alene National Forest "for the markings of the graves in Wallace, Idaho." Pulaski used the money to get the names of the dead etched in stone. But other bodies were still scattered, and it bothered him. Finally, in 1933—nearly a quarter century after the Big Burn—a central graveyard was established on a grassy slope in the dreamy little town of St. Maries, Idaho. Remains were dug up from different locations and moved to the burial ground, at rest in one place at last.

Pulaski didn't live to see the memorial. He retired from the For-est Service in 1929, full of scars, inside and outside, and no small amount of bile. His poor vision never improved, and it was perhaps responsible for a severe car accident. He died in 1931, from compli-cations related to the accident and from other troubles. His name lives on; to this day, there is hardly a firefighter among the millions of men and women who have fought flames in the woods who is un-familiar with the Pulaski—the favorite tool of the trade—and the story of the man who invented it. The Forest Service keeps more than ten thousand Pulaskis in ranger stations across the United

States. And many in the agency credit their very existence to a pair of men: Gifford Pinchot and Ed Pulaski.

"His personal story of heroism on August 20 became the saga on which the future of the United States Forest Service was built," wrote Rocky Barker, the western natural history writer.

Ione Adair moved back to Moscow, Idaho, her homestead lost to flames. She found a job teaching elementary school students, then got elected county treasurer and tax collector. Often, at Sunday dinners, she would regale people with stories of the walk to safety from the creek at the height of the Great Fire of 1910. It was odd to some that Pinkie always turned up her nose at one dish served at these big meals. It was something that stayed with her after the Big Burn, she explained: the commandeered cook of prisoners and roustabouts could not eat another potato.

"Do you have any idea how many potatoes men eat?" she said.

Bill Weigle left the Coeur d'Alene country one year after the fire. The forest supervisor needed to get far, far away, and the posting for a chief ranger up north, overseeing the fjords and rain forest of watery Alaska Territory, fit the bill. The Tongass National Forest may be the wettest place under the American flag, with ten times the rain of Idaho, home to moody islands of ancient spruce, 1,200-pound brown bears, and salmon runs so bounteous they allowed the native Haida to live well and refine a stylized art form, carvings on big cedar poles. It was a green refuge for Weigle, a place for a fresh dawning of the Great Crusade. In that part of Alaska, with more than ten thousand miles of coastline, Weigle became one of a new breed of forest rangers to travel exclusively by boat. The sixty-four-foot *Than*, with its well-stocked bookcase and well-used writing desk, was Weigle's home on water for a decade.

Over the years, Weigle was repeatedly asked to tell his story of the Big Burn. After he completed the official report in 1911, he turned his back on the fire—he'd had enough—until late in life, when he wrote a recollection for a journal run by Idaho forestry students. His third and final act with the agency was in Snoqualmie National Forest in Washington, outside Seattle, where he worked for the service until 1933. Afterward, as superintendent of Washington state parks, he helped to develop a public-land system, much used to this day, and a scenic alpine road—the Mountain Loop Highway—through the wet, thick-timbered lowlands of the Cascade Mountains. Like the Tongass, the west side of the Cascades is one of the rainiest places on earth, something Weigle was never heard to complain about.

The hapless ranger Ralph Debitt, Weigle's colleague in the Coeur d'Alene, ended his brief marriage to the Forest Service shortly after the fire. He was accused of taking funds for personal use, and a host of other misdeeds big and small. He was faulted for being indecisive during the two days in August, at best an errant commander, at worst a liability. A few months after the fire, Debitt left his ranger post and disappeared, leaving no trace in Forest Service records. People in Avery say he became a cult leader in a nudist camp.

His sometime neighbor in Avery, Spike Kelley, got a $10,000 insurance payment for the big log home that was burned down in the backfire to save the town. After getting his check, he also left, with his wife and servants.

Joe Halm flourished in the Forest Service. He kept his ranger job while studying at night, learning enough about engineering to pass a federal civil service test. For the next three decades, he won a Forest Service survey engineer, one of the best-paying jobs in the agency. Halm Creek, where he kept his men from dying, was named for the ranger, and later added to the National Register of Historic Places—a lonely dell in the reborn forest of the upper St. Joe country. Halm never tired of recalling how he survived the Big Burn. He especially loved all the obituaries printed about him, including that story in the *New York Times*. In his telling of the nation's largest

wildfire, written in 1944—one of the last exhaustive accounts written by a survivor—Pulaski was the only real hero.

For the new men moving into ranger shacks throughout the West,
there was one overriding lesson to come from the Big Burn, and it
would be applied in every district. Gifford Pinchot's name would be
honored by generations to come, and so would that of Ed Pulaski.
The Forest Service would summon these ghosts in green for a great
cause, a new, sustaining mission. But it was a cause that Ed Pulaski
might not join, and one that Pinchot, living out the later years of a
remarkable life, came to doubt.

19

Ashes

THE LIMBS WERE STIFF, the eyesight starting to fail, the back sore. Old age was not for a man who lived by the tenets of the strenuous life. Still, action was what Gifford Pinchot craved, as he said from the time he shed the insulation of Manhattan wealth to study forestry. So there he was in Missoula, 1937, ready to revisit the West he had tried to shape to his principles, ready to tramp through national forests whose boundaries he had drawn, ready to see what nature had done to bring back life snuffed by the fire of more than a quarter century ago.

Once again he would sleep on cold ground, wade through icy streams, try to find God in the earthly heavens — his second home. And so what if he was seventy-two years old and many of his friends were dead. The early leaders of the Forest Service were also gone, most of them, their names now attached to mountains and lakes, a type of immortality that would please a forester. The enemies, Joe Cannon and Weldon Heyburn, William Clark and Will Taft, were in the ground as well. Clark, the graft-peddling senator and life-time opponent of conservation, had died at the age of eighty-six in his mansion in New York City, leaving an estate worth $200 million and a city he helped to found, Las Vegas. The most populous county in Nevada is named for him.

With Teddy long gone, another Roosevelt, his distant cousin Franklin, was president and a Pinchot confidant—though not nearly on the level of intimacy that he had shared with T.R. Laura had disappeared, no communication from the spirit for more than twenty years. This freed Pinchot to fall in love with another woman. And a year before his fiftieth birthday, Pinchot had married Cornelia Bryce, a woman sixteen years younger than he, an heiress and a crusader, a suffragette and politician. No longer would Pinchot talk to Laura at an empty dinner table; with the effervescent Cornelia, politics was always on the menu—"the best of all indoor sports," as she said. They had a son in 1915, a year after their wedding.

The Gilded Age parties seemed so long ago now that one in four Americans were out of work, the soup lines a regular feature in the cities, life itself a slow-motion stumble to an early grave. Pinchot had seen America change its face and personality a half-dozen times since the Big Burn—from the Great War, all those men lost in a meaningless conflict, including Quentin Roosevelt, the youngest of Teddy's six children; to the frothy heights of the Jazz Age; to Prohibition and the Depression, eras defined by mood. And looming now was war in Europe, Nazi Germany on the prowl. But age was just a number, as the vigorous elderly always said. Pinchot read *Gone with the Wind*, not the kind of tome that usually found its way onto his tower of bedside books. He liked it quite a bit, particularly one line he found resonant: "What better way can an old man die than doing a young man's work?"

His plan was to spend the rest of the summer touring the mountains, from the Cabinets in Montana to the Cascades in Oregon to the High Sierra in California. Reacquaint himself. He had first been there after coming home from Europe in 1890, footloose and full of youthful gloom. Shortly afterward, he'd returned as a confidential forest agent, looking over the big land for a president with a plan. In his eighth decade, Pinchot wanted a long, last taste of the wild before knees became too arthritic to move uphill, before hip joints felt rusted cold, before he lay dying with regret that he had not made one final expedition to see what became of the Great Crusade. For this trip, Pinchot shipped his touring Buick out to Missoula by rail, and from there he would launch his adventure—free again in the High Lonesome.

They called him Governor now, after two terms as the executive of Pennsylvania. In the Keystone State, he had been somewhat of a pioneer, sending an army of young workers into the woods, overhauling Pennsylvania's forestry system by buying land and putting it into public trust. On a small scale, he tried to do for the commonwealth what he and Teddy Roosevelt had attempted to do for the entire nation. After the presidential election in 1932, FDR had asked Governor Pinchot to advise him on restoration in the natural world. The new president considered himself a tree grower, getting his hands dirty on the family estate in the Hudson River valley; it was one of his small hobbies. He was also a fan: a Pinchot lecture on deforestation "started me on the conservation road," Franklin Roosevelt said. The High Plains were just starting to blow, wracked by drought and poor farming, the grass stripped away. And big pieces of the national forests were cut over, as Roosevelt had seen on his own tours out west during the campaign. Perhaps there was a jobs program—taking young men from the cities and putting them to work planting trees and grass or building trails—along the lines of what the forester had done as governor.

Pinchot sent the president several reports, delighted to be of use. And in his first hundred days in office, Roosevelt launched the Civilian Conservation Corps, with a camp in the George Washington National Forest in Virginia. Within four months, 250,000 men were put to work in the woods. By 1935, the corps had grown to 600,000 nationwide. Forestry once again was in the headlines and at the center of public discussion. Restoration was seen as one way out of the Depression.

There was more. The meat of the progressive agenda that Teddy Roosevelt had spoken of in his years in office and campaigned on during the Bull Moose run of 1912 found its way into law through the younger Roosevelt. Social Security for the elderly. Workers' compensation for people knocked out of a job by injury or sickness. Regulation of the stock market and banks. A minimum wage. A graduated income tax. On these issues T.R. had been ahead of his time; it took his cousin, advised at times by Pinchot, to make them stick. And as the soil blew on the plains, another of Teddy's insights looked prophetic, something Pinchot pointed out. "When the soil is gone, men must go," T.R. had said, "and the process does not take long."

Pinchot's passion, his zealotry in battle, and of course in feuds, had not diminished. He had been an enthusiastic supporter of Prohibition, often chasing bootleggers himself alongside Pennsylvania cops. What fun! Though the dour Pinchot was a zesty Dry, his wife kept a stash of house whiskey for special guests at Grey Towers. The smart set laughed at him behind his back, as always. Still a bit odd, this gangly formal millionaire, the mustache as brushy as ever, but snow white, giving his face a somewhat ornithological look.

Since Teddy's death, he had nourished a dream of being president himself. Yes, why not run for the presidency? As he asked his brother Amos one winter night while sitting before a fire in the family castle: Who was better qualified for the highest office in the land? After eight years of Woodrow Wilson, would not the country desire a return to a Republican from the party's glory years? But party bosses wanted no part of Pinchot's progressive revival—no surprise to anyone but Pinchot. In order, Republicans turned to Warren Harding, a dreadful president who died in office; Calvin Coolidge, a presence so benign that when he passed away Dorothy Parker famously said, "How could they tell?"; and Herbert Hoover, who found a place deep in the cellar of failed presidents.

Pinchot's comeback was impressive nonetheless; he made the cover of *Time* magazine, the height of prestige at the peak of the print era. In 1929, the year of the Wall Street crash, he left the despair of the United States and sailed to the South Pacific on a three-masted schooner with his wife, son, and an old college mate. Once again he was following the advice John Muir had given him as a young man: "Radiate, radiate, radiate far and wide as the lines of latitude and longitude on a globe." In crossing oceans, he visited the Galápagos Islands, Darwin's living laboratory and inspiration for his great work. After returning home, Pinchot urged protective status for the Galápagos, fearing that this fragile, accidental refuge of biodiversity would not survive heavy human visitation.

Pinchot won a second term as governor in 1930. Six years later, he saw one last chance at the highest reaches of power, and tried to interest Alf Landon, the Republican presidential nominee in 1936, in considering the old forester for his running mate. Vice President Pinchot — it would be a bit of a comedown, but one had to make some concessions to age. Landon brushed him aside. Pinchot then wrote several speeches for him, but they too fell by the wayside. As Pinchot recorded: "Listened to Landon's speech to the young Republicans. Mostly wind & when he said anything it was wrong. He used not a word of the speech I sent him." Landon was crushed at the polls, losing by ten million votes. Pinchot did not shed a tear.

"I take it as a tremendous defeat for concentrated wealth," Pinchot wrote of the Democratic victory in 1936. "It means more and better national security legislation, conservation, labor and corporation control . . . a smashing defeat of the few by the many." After that election, Pinchot at last decided that he was done with elective office, and appears to have been done with the Republican Party too. His true family was the Forest Service. He had been the guiding hand and the hidden hand. When the agency was wayward, it kept him up at night. When it was in trouble, he was troubled. When it seemed to be healthy, he was soothed. Lobbying, lecturing, hectoring — he never missed a chance to speak up for the Forest Service. At a public event in Washington, when someone called him Governor, Pinchot corrected him.

"I have been a governor now and then," he said, "but I am a forester all the time — have been, and shall be, all my working life."

• • •

In Missoula in 1937, Pinchot was stirred by the long shadow of the Bitterroots, the ever-changing light on Lolo Peak, and the three big trout streams that converged in the valley. Those closest to Pinchot knew that if there was one thing to put in his casket, like the pharaohs with their afterlife icons, it would be his fly-fishing rod. In Montana, he fished the Clark Fork, which flowed out of the scarred land of the Big Burn. In the Lolo National Forest and the Coeur d'Alene, where the winds had turned demonic on that Saturday night in 1910, the trunks of big trees still stood blackened and weatherworn. In the twenty-seven years since the fire, thousands of burned trees had come down by lightning, wind, and gravity. Yet it was surprising how many of them remained—stripped and bare and mostly hollow inside. In other places, the forest floor was covered with uprooted giants, slowly decaying where they had fallen.

But it was not a still life. After many fits and starts, many experiments, the new forest was starting to take hold in early maturity. Deer and elk liked the young trees for winter browse, and bear gorged on huckleberries that took to the cleared land. Up higher, on the big peaks that afforded broad vistas, the Forest Service had erected a series of fire lookout posts. These were sturdy cabins of a sort, wood-framed and big-windowed, held to the ground by guy wires. From these aeries, an ever-vigilant force kept watch over the woods. Any hint of smoke was quickly reported. They had zero tolerance for this ancient agent of the natural world.

A few of the rangers who had led the charge of men into the flaming Bitterroots were still around. Pinchot looked up Elers Koch, wearing his Forest Service greens, the pants tucked into mid-ankle boots, based as before in his beloved Montana. Koch and his wife, Gerda, now had three strapping boys in their family—Stanley, Thomas, and Peter, the youngest seventeen years old. As Koch had made his way up the Forest Service ranks, he was consistently prodded to take a job in Washington, D.C. The Chief's title was within reach. But Koch preferred to stay in Montana, with his summers at Seeley Lake next to the family cabin of Norman Maclean, and a few steps from some of the best fly-fishing waters in the world.

Still full of spring, Koch was known among the small group of alpinists in the northern Rockies as the first person to climb Granite Peak, the highest mountain in Montana. He had the Kipling verses in his head whenever he roamed the High Lonesome — no change from his youth. And he had seen his share of forest fires. "A forester in the Northwest dates the events of his life by fire years," said Koch. Without doubt, none could match the blowup of 1910, not in size or ferocity or the way it captured the public imagination. Koch knew the fire was a once-in-a-century burn. He knew the Chief had elevated his knights to mythic status because of how they responded to the fire, knew that Pulaski's story helped save the agency, knew that generations of foresters were hearing vivid tales of hurricane-force winds and people who tried to live through a night "when the mountains roared," as Koch himself described the firestorm in his report. The story was sacred text to the still-young Forest Service, just as Pinchot had intended it to be.

But Koch took away a different conclusion. Though he revered Pinchot, he disagreed with him about the lessons of 1910. The men may have been heroic, but they were routed, and perhaps those who lost their lives never should have been forced into battle against a fire of that magnitude. Perhaps it would have been best just to get out of the way. In that sense, the dead were not martyrs or heroes so much as victims of a flawed policy. To Koch, the fire "was a complete defeat for the newly organized Forest Service," he wrote.

Complete defeat. That was not what young students heard around the bonfire on summer nights at Grey Towers. Bill Greeley, the regional forester, handpicked by Pinchot just like Koch, also felt that way, but he came away determined to change the central task of the Forest Service. In the view of the religious Greeley, fire had won — akin to Satan destroying God's garden. And with the full power and backing of the U.S. government behind him, Greeley vowed that fire would never win again. Never. One year after the blowup, Greeley was promoted to a high administrative job in Washington. He took with him the images of mountains stripped of their green cover, the desperate effort to round up hoboes and immigrants to beat back the flames, young men rotting in hospitals, their festering skin slow to heal. "I was spurred on by vivid memories of blazing canyons and smoking ruins in little settlements and rows of canvas-wrapped bodies," said Greeley. "This fire woke up everyone."

As he had once been an evangelist for the Progressive Era idea of forest protection under his mentor Pinchot, Greeley now became equally fervent in his belief that foresters had one overriding duty in the woods—to keep fire at bay. Of course, Pinchot also had considered fire prevention to be a job of the service, but not the overriding mission. He had sold the public on firefighting as an idea, not a raison d'être. Greeley was taking Pinchot's earlier claims, science in the service of mastering fire, to the extreme.

Worse for the progressives, Greeley wanted fire out of the woods not for preservation's sake, but to make sure there were plenty of trees for the giants of the timber industry to get at. Under Pinchot, loggers had limited access to public forests. What Greeley was calling for was a much bigger role, making the industry a comanager of sorts. He said logging in the national forests could increase dramatically. Much of this land was "ripe for the axe," he wrote.

Pinchot was appalled. In his mind, the timber industry was the enemy; to partner with it would be letting the wolf in the hen house. "These are men who have already destroyed this country and reduced to desert conditions an area larger than the forests of Europe," he said. "It puts the Forest Service in the position of throwing contempt upon its basic reason for existence."

While Pinchot attacked Greeley in the press, his former acolyte quietly worked the corridors of power. And in 1920, Greeley was elevated to Pinchot's old job, becoming the third Chief of the Forest Service. By then, Pinchot and Greeley were barely on speaking terms. Under the new Chief's reign, logging increased and fire prevention was elevated to job one—the lessons of the 1910 fire put to good use, Greeley preached. The Forest Service became the fire service, protecting trees so industry could cut them down later. And

what a turnaround now followed Greeley: the big timber companies *loved* the Forest Service under him. It was their ally, the source
of much profit, not some antagonist calling for limited tree cutting
and standing seed trees—the "Koch Specials" the forest supervisor
had insisted on, to much derision. Taxpayers would pay for building roads, scouting the big timber, and snuffing the fires, then offer
up trees more than two centuries old for a pittance to the industry.
Logging doubled, tripled, quadrupled, grew tenfold. This, in the
people's forests.

Where was the Little Man to whom Pinchot and Roosevelt had
promised the forests? At the least, Pinchot argued, public timber
should be sold only to small, family-run logging outfits, not the big
syndicates that Pinchot and Roosevelt had assailed. But Greeley
thought industry giants were best suited to maintain the kind of
fireproof national forests he envisioned, with the assistance of his
rangers. Nearly one hundred years after the Big Burn, the timber
industry was still sending out long accounts of the fire with Greeley's conversion as the central moral of the story — "his finest hour,"
as Idaho Forest Products put it. What's more, the legacy of the 1910
fire was written into the code that every ranger followed, or else.

To Pinchot, "Billy was a traitor," Greeley's wife recalled. As if to
prove Pinchot's point, Greeley left the top job in the Forest Service
in 1928 for a position in the timber industry, becoming an executive
with the West Coast Lumbermen's Association. Now the breach
with Pinchot was complete, the betrayal set in stone. The 1910 fire
had indeed saved much of the United States—in the sense that it
ensured the viability of the Forest Service, the stewards of this great
experiment. But those stewards were now engaged in a mission at
odds with Pinchot and Roosevelt's founding vision.

In Montana, Pinchot arranged for Koch and other rangers loyal
to the original ideals to show him around. Pinchot had always
preached of a "working forest" for working people—small-scale
logging at the edge, preservation at the core. But what he saw in

1937 was not pretty. With better machinery and government roads, industrial clear-cuts had come to the woods, entire mountainsides clipped of all trees in a single sweep, the land literally scalped, a scorched-earth force. Pinchot was horrified. A picture from 1937 shows him sitting on the stump of what had been a massive tree sheared by a big saw; he does not look happy.

On to Oregon Pinchot went, into the rich woods on the west side of the Cascades, part of what was once considered a temperate rain forest. And there he saw more destruction, mountain after mountain, clipped of its national forest trees. So this was what saving the forests was all about, as the old man saw with his own eyes.

"Absolute devastation," Pinchot wrote in his diary. "Mostly a clean sweep, taking everything . . . The men who did this are nothing less than public enemies." One week later, more of the same. Roads cut deep into the wild. Flanks cleared of the web of complex life. Slash burns. Slides. Mud and stumps. "The Forest Service should absolutely declare against clearcutting in Washington and Oregon as a defensive measure," Pinchot wrote.

Two years earlier, in 1935, Koch had also made clear his unhappiness with the drift of his employer when he wrote an essay for a leading forestry journal. In it, he said the agency he had given his life to had lost its way. "The Forest Service," he wrote, "opened up the wilderness with roads and telephone lines and airplane landing fields. It capped the mountain peaks with white-painted lookout houses, laced the ridges and streams with a network of trails and telephone lines, and poured in thousands of firefighters year after year in a vain attempt to control forest fires." He missed the land he had first explored with Pinchot, and wondered whether large portions of the national forests scorched by the Big Burn should simply have been left alone—wilderness for wilderness' sake, a home for fire along with everything else in the wild.

"Has all this effort and expenditure of millions of dollars added anything to human good? Is it possible that it was all a ghastly mistake, like plowing up the good buffalo grass sod of the dry prairies?"

• • •

Building on Greeley's edicts for fire prevention, the Forest Service launched an even more demanding new policy in 1935, the ten o'clock rule. Thereafter, any fire spotted in the course of a working day must be under control by ten o'clock the following morning.

It was a losing and futile idea; in practice it proved to be fatal. On August 5, 1949, a crew of fifteen smokejumpers leapt from a plane into a burning mountainside in Mann Gulch, Montana, acting on the ten o'clock rule. Less than two hours later, all but three of them were dead or fatally burned. They had lost their lives in the same horrid way that men in the Big Burn had gone to their deaths—trying to outrun galloping wildfire, trapped on all sides by an explosion of flames, choking on hot gas. Koch's Seeley Lake neighbor Norman Maclean spent the last fourteen years of his life trying to understand the 1949 fire and why those young men had to die. In large measure, it was because of a lesson that Greeley and others applied from the Big Burn—or as Maclean put it, "1910-on-the-brain." "Rangers for decades after were on the watch for fear that 1910 might start again and right in their woodpile," he wrote. "Some even lost their jobs because a fire got away from them."

The ten o'clock rule would stay in effect for most of the century, until rangers who realized that fires were critical to the health of a forest started to have a voice. Budgets escalated as the fire control mission became ever bigger and more intrusive. From the air and on the ground, with chemicals dropped like bombs and with bulldozers to scrape perimeter lines, the Forest Service attacked all fires, growing into a force of nature—or against nature, depending on the view.

"The Great Fires of 1910 shaped the American fire landscape more than any other fire in any year throughout the twentieth century," wrote Stephen Pyne, the fire historian.

By trying to stop all major wildfires, the Forest Service had only fed the beast. The woods were full of dry, dying, aging timber and underbrush—fuel. Big swaths were unhealthy, in need of a cleansing burn. Even with their armies, their aerial support, their billions in taxpayer money to hold back the flames, rangers became increasingly helpless. As firefighting took up nearly half the Forest Service budget, it was a mission at odds with the course of the natural world, and common sense. It was not what Roosevelt and Pinchot had in mind. The years brought bigger, hotter, longer, earlier wildfires. With a warmer climate, it all added up to something catastrophic on the horizon.

At last, a truce of sorts was declared in the final years of the century by Jack Ward Thomas, Chief of the Forest Service. Some fires would be fought, some would be allowed to burn.

"Fire is neither good nor bad," said Thomas. "It just is."

There is evidence that Pinchot had arrived at the same conclusion during his 1937 trip out west. In his Buick, he traveled more than five thousand miles, over single-lane roads of primitive gravel, chugging up to the Continental Divide, along roaring streams. Smoke was often in the air, despite the strongest efforts of the Forest Service. Pinchot chased trout in riffles and got up early for sunrises. When the legs felt strong, he hiked high for better views. With him was Henry Graves, one of Pinchot's oldest friends from Yale and the agency, and one of the original seven members of the Society of American Foresters, formed at Pinchot's house in 1900. When Pinchot was fired by Taft, it was Graves who took over, as second Chief of the Forest Service. They made for quite a couple in the summer of 1937, two elderly eastern gentlemen in tweed jackets and ties knotted around their necks touring the national forests they had once overseen. In Portland, Graves and Pinchot were invited to a Kiwanis lunch, but it turned into a humiliation. To Pinchot's surprise, "nobody seemed to know us."

Like Teddy Roosevelt, Pinchot intended to have his words outlive him. It would not matter if the man who mistook his life for forestry was a mere asterisk in the storytelling of the young nation; Pinchot would have his say in at least one sphere. In 1937, he was just getting started on his conservation memoir, a book that would take nearly a decade to finish. It was encyclopedic in detail, with much settling of ancient scores and with frequent praise for the saintly Roosevelt. He never mentioned Laura. John Muir had died years earlier, in 1914, and with Roosevelt gone for nearly two decades, the book would give Pinchot the last word on the conservation ideals this trio had presented to the world. He was out west in 1937 in part to test his beliefs as he began to summarize his life. He wanted not just to see how the legacy had held up, but to seek some of the old magic in the land. Pinchot's publisher also asked him to revive his 1914 book, *The Training of a Forester.* So it was really two books that he mulled while touring.

Going over the earlier book, the old man blushed at some of what the young man professed. Did he really believe—still—that forest fires are "wholly within the control of man," as he wrote? Could generations of college-trained foresters really hope to contain something as elemental as wildfire? Was fire indeed the biggest foe of the woods—"no other so terrible"? And could man himself shape nature to his design? It appears that the younger Pinchot had made a pact with his hubris: in promising in the early days to whip wildfire, he won enough public confidence to see the Forest Service through its birthing pains. But the price of that bargain was now clear in the idea that the timber industry had embraced while co-opting the Forest Service: yes, fire would be defeated, at all costs, to keep standing trees for industry. If universal suppression meant sick, overburdoned, ready-to-burn forests, that was another cost, one that would not become obvious until later in the century.

In the last years of his life, Pinchot showed a more humble side. A forest was "a complex community with a life of its own," he would write in the new memoir. And that complexity included fire. Also, he was appalled that the public forests had become mere commodities. He could force a reflexive statement of principle—"the national forests belong to the people," as he wrote in California—but the landscape told a different story, of logging, private concessions, lodges: "Most dangerous thing I've seen on national forests." Growing increasingly cranky, he sought solace. "Even in the wild places you can't get away from people."

Finally, near the end of the tour, he was back in the High Sierra, the Range of Light, John Muir's temple—"the only spot I have ever found that came up to the brag," as Ralph Waldo Emerson had said. It was there that Pinchot had undergone something like a religious experience when he stood under a huge waterfall in Yosemite, jumping in and out of the spray. Now Pinchot ditched his companion and the crowds in Yosemite to search for a touchstone of his youth—"went off by myself. I had to." His heart beat heavy and his breath was labored as he hiked over granite, much of his dexterity gone. The closer he got to the high points in this sanctuary, the more excited he got.

"Washburn Point—incredible."

He pushed himself farther, risking collapse, to find another landmark.

"Glacier Point left me all in. Went and stood on the overhanging rock where I threw my bed 41 years ago & looked down." He wheezed and gasped in the mountain air, sweating and somewhat parched. It did not matter. "If it cost me a year of my life," he wrote, "it would be worth it." Onward and upward he pushed until rock, ground, and forest came to an end, until there was nothing but a sharp edge of blunt earth protruding in the late light of the range, where he could see well beyond the park boundaries to national forest land that he had once scouted on foot and horseback. He remembered it then as roadless, the only trails being those hacked by Indians and prospectors. He had taken notes on the flora and fauna, commented on the age of the bristlecone pine trees at the highest elevations, the scrub oak in the valleys, the condors overhead, the trout in alpine tarns. He had lassoed that wild land in ink, returned to Washington, and sent the sketch to the president, who preserved it for posterity. What did Michelangelo feel at the end of his life, staring at a ceiling in the Vatican or a marble figure in Florence? Pinchot knew. And those who followed him, his great-great-grandchildren, Teddy's great-great-grandchildren, people living in a nation one day of five hundred million people, could find their niche as well. Pinchot felt God in his soul, and thanked him, and weariness in his bones. He sensed he had come full circle.

"One of the great days of my life," he wrote. "I think the greatest sight I ever saw." Of course he had seen it before, but to an old man it had more power. For a fleeting moment, after more than five thousand miles of driving around in pursuit of something lost, Gifford Pinchot found what he was looking for.

He lived another nine years, barely enough time to finish the book, and to feel that his life philosophy had been vindicated by the second of two Roosevelts to be president. Just before World War II ended, Pinchot and Cornelia went to see FDR at the White House. Much had changed since Pinchot roamed the halls with Teddy; the war atmosphere made it seem more like a command center. To many in Washington, Pinchot was an embarrassment—or worse, a bit of a joke. The reputations of Muir and Teddy Roosevelt had grown immensely since their deaths; they were the heroes in the fight for conservation, while Pinchot was an afterthought. The very fact that he was still around, still making speeches, still annoying his enemies, this gangly relic from the turn of the century, was a big part of the condescension. His life had spanned from the last year of the Civil War to World War II.

For Pinchot the meeting was all about a big idea that he had carried for some time. The war would soon be over, and he wanted Roosevelt to summon the nations of the world for a conference on conservation, to take stock of a planet shattered in midcentury by iron and atomic blows of nations against each other. What people had in common was this earth, which for the first time they could destroy with the press of a button. Such a gathering had been proposed by Teddy Roosevelt in the last days of his presidency in 1909. Nations had accepted, the meeting was set—but then President Taft killed the conference. Would Franklin consider reviving such a thing?

Indeed he would, and promised to bring it up at his Yalta meeting with Winston Churchill and Joseph Stalin, as postwar planning gained steam. The world was going to be reorganized after this dreadful war, and what better time to start thinking about it in different ways. In a letter to his secretary of state, Roosevelt wrote, "I repeat again that I am more and more convinced that Conservation is a basis for permanent peace. I think the time is ripe."

Roosevelt died before the global conservation conference could take place, and Pinchot fell ill with leukemia. The forester's last day was October 4, 1946. He died at the age of eighty-one. At his funeral at Grey Towers, his son Gifford Bryce Pinchot slipped a favorite fly rod into the casket.

Three years after his death, the Forest Service renamed the green-mantled land south of Mount Rainier as Gifford Pinchot National Forest. At the dedication ceremony Cornelia held back tears. When it came time to speak, she apologized to the foresters and dignitaries for being so emotional. Then she steadied herself and tried to give an account of her husband's legacy, a man who had already started to fade from history, a footnote. Cornelia wanted the rangers, politicians, and reporters gathered to know one thing about her dead husband: "Conservation to Gifford Pinchot was never a vague, fuzzy aspiration," she said in the forest given his name. "It was concrete, exact, dynamic." And then, summoning the voice of the old progressive and the spirit of the words Pinchot had written so many times in speeches for Teddy Roosevelt, she said Pinchot's idea of humans never taking more from the earth than they put back was simple, an American virtue. It was, she said, "the very stuff of which democracy is made."

Elers Koch retired from the Forest Service in 1944. He spent the next five years writing his life story and advocating for protection of wilderness in the Rocky Mountain West. His children were grown and his beloved Gerda was gone; she had died of cancer in 1942. The war brought another blow to Koch: he lost his oldest son, Stanley, in the Allied landing at Normandy. The fog of depression that followed the death of his wife and his boy would not lift; it was like smoke from the summer of 1910. At the same time, he found it increasingly hard to move around, his muscles aching from the daily little cruelties of sciatica, his hands knotted by arthritis. Nobody would publish his book. On a late November day in 1954, Koch killed himself. He was seventy-three. Forty-four years after his suicide, his book, *Forty Years a Forester,* was published and became an instant and influential classic among people who loved the outdoors. Koch Mountain, a 9,072-foot peak in the Bitterroots, is named for him.

Pinkie Adair outlived them all. In the late 1970s, she sat for several days with Sam Schrager, an oral historian, as part of a project of the Latah County Museum Society. Talking about her homestead in the wild Bitterroots, about foresters on horseback and stagecoach rides on moonlit nights in town, about the pet bear her father kept at the house in Moscow, she could have been recalling medieval days. She got the last living word on the Big Burn of 1910, at least among the major players in the drama. What was the fire like? She said it was chaos in the woods, martial law in town, so many people lost. Even so, a thrill.

"It was exciting," she said. "Very exciting."

The interviewer seemed taken aback at the words from the mouth of this old lady, with her thick glasses, curled fingers.

"You never knew when you got up in the morning whether the wind was bringing the fire your way or taking it some other way . . . very exciting."

Pinkie died at home not long afterward, on November 26, 1977. She was ninety-four years old.

On August 20, 2005, a day when the sun baked the Bitterroots with not much of a breeze to break the heat, top brass from the Forest Service assembled along Placer Creek, less than a mile from Wallace, Idaho. They came to the northern Rockies to remember that

other August 20 nearly a century before. An honor guard in crisp
green uniforms and white gloves marched in single file along the
road to the creek. They carried flags and blew bagpipes, the sound
filling the forest and the steep slopes of the mountains. They also
carried Pulaskis, shiny and chrome-plated, holding them across
their chests like riflemen clutching their weapons.

The faces of these foresters, from members of the high command, who had taken two days to travel from the capital, to first-
year rangers just learning the ropes, both men and women, were
solemn, as at a funeral. For a time, nobody said anything; the pip-
ers blew their mournful sound into the woods and tried to imagine what it must have been like for Ed Pulaski and those people in
the mine tunnel in 1910. When at last the bagpipes were stilled and
the speeches began, people spoke about a man who did not sound
like the one who had spent his last years feeling betrayed by this
agency. To the end, Pulaski loved the land, perhaps more than some
of the rangers stamped by the Yale School of Forestry. But he never
could understand why the government did not love men like himself back.

On this day, Pulaski was eulogized in mythic terms, a hero certainly, and the best kind, a selfless one. He was described as no-non-
sense, and not so much a forest ranger as an old-fashioned woodsman, born to the wild. The occasion was the dedication of a trail
and memorial to the man who could not get the government to do
the same thing for the fallen firefighters while he was alive.

Time had been good to Pulaski. This fire, with its force unleash-
ing energy greater than the atomic bomb dropped on Hiroshima,
had grown with the passing of the years and the telling of the story.
It was not just the largest wildfire in the history of the United States,
these forest dignitaries said; it was still known as the fire that gave
the agency its mission. One speaker said the fire of 1910 was like
the terrorist attack of September 11, 2001. "The 1910 fires gave the
new agency a defining purpose," said this speaker, Mark Rey, "to
demonstrate that destructive wildfire could be controlled and pre-

vented." Rey was an odd choice to preside over this ceremony in the woods. He had been a powerful advocate for the logging industry, a lobbyist and partisan, arguing fiercely against protection for dying species and wild land in the public forests. When President George W. Bush came into office, he put Rey in charge of the very agency that he had long fought.

There was no mention of conservation on this August day in 2005. No mention of the Great Crusade, the fight to keep forests in public hands, of Roosevelt's cry to "leave it as it is," or Pinchot's progressive passion. What Pinchot fought for his entire adult life, facing ridicule and much resistance, what Pinchot tried to institutionalize with the Forest Service, was taken for granted.

This day was about a dead man named Pulaski, who wore a uniform, and the people who followed in his footsteps. From here on out, Placer Creek as it flowed from a thousand feet above the valley, right near the mine where Pulaski had taken refuge, would be one of the nation's sacred places — in the National Register of Historic Places.

The people who lived in the Coeur d'Alene country never forgot Pulaski. They spent years nagging the government. And now at last there was something — a descriptive trail along the stations of the cross where Pulaski fought to keep his men alive. A hiker could set out in the chill of the morning, well before the sun reached Placer Creek, starting where Pulaski and his wife said goodbye, and move upward in the narrow canyon, reading the signs along the way, trying to fathom that Saturday night in August 1910. Some evidence of the Big Burn remained. Here at the ceremony site was a big cedar stump, charred and black. And up the trail, visible among stands of thick pine and fir, were the last remnants of standing burned timbers, midnight-black skeletons. Beyond the mineshaft and up on the ridge, a hiker could roam in peace not far from where the Italians died in that horrible pit, flaming timbers crushing them.

The woods were quiet and largely left alone on this day, as they had been for some time. In the years after World War II, the na-

tional forests were industrialized, logged at a frenzied pace. What
Pinchot the old man had seen in 1937 — green hillsides reduced to
rubble, mud, and slash — had been repeated all over the West. But
in the first decade of the new century, logging in all national forests
was in steep decline, for reasons both economic and idealistic.

No change in government could alter that. Timber for home-
building came from tree farms in Canada, because it was much
cheaper to ship that wood to market than to yank it from an isolated
place like the Bitterroots. Communities valued their public forests for recreation and the biological mix. Yew trees were a source
for a cancer treatment. Even Wallace, with a population barely a
third of what it was in 1910, reinvented itself as an outdoor destination — a base for skiers, bikers, and wilderness seekers. What Elers
Koch and another forest ranger, the writer Aldo Leopold, had envisioned long ago had come to pass: by 2005, about thirty-five million
acres of Forest Service land were designated as official wilderness
areas, land set aside by law as places where "man himself is a visitor
who does not remain," never to be logged, roaded, or sold off. One
of those areas was in the High Lonesome where Koch and his wife
spent so much of their time, just over the divide along the Lochsa
and Clearwater rivers. Another, farther south, the River of No Return Wilderness, is the largest in the continental United States. The
land itself, to the eye of a beholder, can tell a story of the 1910 fire,
though the marks grow harder to see with every passing day.

When the Rockefellers and the Weyerhaeusers had pushed
through these woods, it appeared that a new order was at hand. But
it had not lasted. The trains are gone. Avery is a barely inhabited
hamlet along a lonely road, and most of those inhabitants work for
the Forest Service. It might as well be called Pinchot again. The
railroad, the most costly of the transcontinental tracks, is no more,
its steel lines pried from the ground and sold for scrap. That job of
ten thousand workers had been dismantled, just as the ranger cabin
had once been torn apart to make way for the Milwaukee Road.
The tunnels remain, those big holes bored into the mountain where

trains took refuge during the fire. In the summer months, the tunnels and the ground leveled for the tracks of the Milwaukee Road are open to mountain bikers who want to experience the Bitterroots on two wheels, at their leisure.

There is nothing left of Grand Forks, not even a foundation footing from one of the saloons, nothing but grass and third-growth timber in the flat of a meadow, a little creek flowing past, bullfrogs in the shallows. Same with Taft, that roaring burg, burned to the ground, not a wisp left behind. Nature has reclaimed that ground. Up in the far reaches of the St. Joe River, where Joe Halm went for shelter from the firestorm, an angler with a few days of idle time can find some of the finest cutthroat water in the world. Up higher are bull trout in the cold, deep pools of the headwaters. There is no way to get into that country except by horse or human hoof. It has never been logged. The most remote pocket of the Coeur d'Alenes is just as Pulaski had experienced it on those Sunday picnics with Emma, just as Roosevelt envisioned it, just as Pinchot remembered seeing it for the first time, taking his breath away—there for fresh eyes, for people yet to be born, there to be discovered anew.

NOTES ON SOURCES

Prologue

Details of how the fire started and how it spread, from Records of the Forest Service, Region One office, Missoula, Montana; Records of the Forest Service, National Archives, Pacific Alaska Region, Seattle, Washington; and Records of the Forest Service, National Archives, College Park, Maryland.

Carl Getz quoted on panics, from *Seattle Times,* August 26, 1910.

Fire Chief Kelly, "Let the bastards go," quoted in *Northwest Disaster: Avalanche and Fire,* by Ruby El Hult, Binfords & Mort, 1960.

Edward Pulaski, family reaction, and quotes, from "Memories of a Forest Service Wife," personal notes by Emma Pulaski, on file, Forest Service Region One headquarters, Missoula.

Additional Pulaski information, from Forest Service personnel files, Missoula, and from *Early Days of the Forest Service,* vols. 1–3, on file at the Forest Service Region One office, Missoula.

Greatest force yet assembled to fight a wildfire, from *Burning an Empire: The Study of American Forest Fires,* by Stewart Holbrook, Macmillan, 1945.

Theodore Roosevelt quoted on rich men, from *Theodore Roosevelt: An Autobiography,* Macmillan, 1913.

Roosevelt quote on losing species, from his letter of February 2, 1889, *Theodore Roosevelt—Letters and Speeches,* Library of America, 1951.

The Forest Service staff and budget around Wallace, Idaho, and the Coeur d'Alene National Forest, from files at the Museum of North Idaho, Coeur d'Alene, Idaho.

William Howard Taft, his feelings on being president, from *William Howard Taft: An Intimate History,* by Judith Icke Anderson, W. W. Norton, 1981.

Deployment of the 25th Infantry, from National Archives, Seattle, the Museum of North Idaho, and various newspaper accounts.

How the fire spread, from Records of the Forest Service, National Archives, Seattle, and files at the Museum of North Idaho.

Details on how Wallace, Idaho, looked, from *Mining Town: A Photographic Record of T. N. Barnard and Nellie Stockbridge from the Coeur d'Alenes,* by Patricia Hart and Ivar Nelson, University of Washington Press, 1984.

President Roosevelt in Wallace, from Hart and Nelson, *Mining Town.*

Anti—Forest Service sentiment, various editorials from *Butte Miner.*

Death of Boyd and the parrot, from Hult, *Northwest Disaster,* and various newspaper accounts, *Idaho Press* and *Spokane Spokesman-Review,* August 21–22, 1910.

Evacuation and the trains, from *Wallace Press Times,* August 21, 1912, story on anniversary of fire.

Hysterical people, reaction during the evacuation, from *Spokane Spokesman-Review* and *The Missoulian,* August 21, 1910.

Forest Service message on town burning, from National Archives, Seattle.

1. *"A Peculiar Intimacy"*

Wrestling, Roosevelt and Pinchot at governor's mansion, from *Breaking New Ground,* by Gifford Pinchot, commemorative edition, Island Press, 1998.

Owen Wister remark on Pinchot, quoted in *Theodore Rex,* by Edmund Morris, Random House, 2001.

Made an ass remark, from Gifford Pinchot's diaries, multiple dates, from the Papers of Gifford Pinchot: Letters, Books, and Diaries, Library of Congress.

Roosevelt on corruption in Albany, from his autobiography.

Roosevelt on climbing the Matterhorn, from *Theodore Roosevelt—Letters and Speeches.*

Roosevelt hunting grizzly bear with a knife, from *The United States Forest Service: A History,* by Harold K. Steen, University of Washington Press, 1976.

Roosevelt's appreciation of wilderness, Roosevelt on acting unafraid, Roosevelt on Harvard, Roosevelt sparring mate wanted for burglary, and Roosevelt on saving bison: from his autobiography.

Roosevelt, the death of his wife and his mother, and his diary entry, from the Theodore Roosevelt Association, www.theodoreroosevelt.org/life/timeline.htm.

Roosevelt, unable to say wife's name after her death, cited in *New York Times Book Review,* January 11, 2009.

Roosevelt on his ignorance of poverty early on, from his autobiography.

Roosevelt on the western roundup, from *Selections from the Correspondence of Theodore Roosevelt and Henry Cabot Lodge, 1884–1918*, Scribner's, 1925.

Roosevelt quote on what he owes to the West, from his autobiography.

Pinchot on craving action, on being alone, from Pinchot, *Breaking New Ground*.

Pinchot early life, and gilded idlers, from Pinchot, *Breaking New Ground*, and from Pinchot papers.

Pinchot in France, from his diaries, November 3, 1890.

Pinchot on being footless and useless, from his diaries, July 8, 1891, and from Pinchot, *Breaking New Ground*.

Pinchot's grandfather the logger, other family connections, from *Gifford Pinchot and the Making of Modern Environmentalism*, by Char Miller, Island Press, 2001.

Pinchot on meeting John Muir, from Pinchot, *Breaking New Ground*.

Muir's early life and philosophy, from *The Life of John Muir*, by Donald Worster, Oxford University Press, 2008.

Muir and Pinchot relationship, from *The Battle Over Hetch Hetchy*, by Robert W. Righter, Oxford University Press, 2005.

More on Muir and Pinchot, from *Shapers of the Great Debate on Conservation*, by Rachel White Scheuering, Greenwood Press, 2004.

All slept in tent except Pinchot, from Steen, *The United States Forest Service*.

Pinchot comment, rotten as usual, from Pinchot diaries, July 8, 1891.

Pinchot and Muir at the Grand Canyon, and the tarantula, from Pinchot, *Breaking New Ground*.

Pinchot boxing again and wrestling with Roosevelt, from Pinchot diaries, November 11, 1899.

Cleveland action put forestry on the map, from Pinchot, *Breaking New Ground*.

Pinchot, of all the foes, fire is the worst, from *A Primer of Forestry*, by Gifford Pinchot, National Archives, Seattle, 1900.

Timber owners' abuse, from Pinchot, *Breaking New Ground*.

Roosevelt comment after death of McKinley, September 23, 1901, from *Selections from the Correspondence of Theodore Roosevelt and Henry Cabot Lodge*.

Roosevelt on wanting a radical Republican Party, from his autobiography.

Roosevelt quote, peculiar intimacy, from letter to Gifford Pinchot, February 24, 1909, *Theodore Roosevelt—Letters and Speeches*, also cited in *The Forest Service*, by Michael Frome, Westview Press, 1984.

2. Roost of the Robber Barons

William Clark background, from *Montana: A History of Two Centuries,* by Michael P. Malone, Richard B. Roeder, and William L. Lang, University of Washington Press, 1976.

More on Clark, from *The Montana Heritage,* edited by Robert Swartout Jr. and Harry W. Fritz, Montana Historical Society, 1992.

Mark Twain quote on Clark, from *Biographical Directory of the United States Congress,* www.bioguide.congress.gov.

Clark's worth, reported in *New York Times,* May 27, 1906.

Roosevelt on being a westerner, from Morris, *Theodore Rex.*

Roosevelt on Clark's face, quoted in *The Selected Letters of Theodore Roosevelt,* edited by H. W. Brands, Cooper Square Press, 2001.

Roosevelt money-getting quote, cited in *Theodore Roosevelt Cyclopedia,* edited by Albert Bushnell Hart and Herbert R. Ferleger, Roosevelt Memorial Association, 1941.

Roosevelt and Pinchot on the fights ahead, from *Theodore Roosevelt and His Time,* by Harold Howland, Yale University Press, 1925.

Roosevelt quote, skins the land, conservation talk of May 6, 1903, from Hart and Ferleger, eds., *Theodore Roosevelt Cyclopedia.*

Background on John Muir, from *The American Conservation Movement: John Muir and His Legacy,* by Stephen Fox, Little, Brown, 1981.

Muir on wilderness as a tonic, from John Muir, *Our National Parks,* Houghton Mifflin, 1901.

Muir on stuffing Roosevelt, from Morris, *Theodore Rex.*

Roosevelt quote on whether there is a law that prevents him from creating wildlife refuge, from *The Presidency of Theodore Roosevelt,* by Lewis L. Gould, University of Kansas Press, 1991.

J. J. Hill quote, give me enough Swedes, from *The Pacific Northwest: An Interpretive History,* by Carlos A. Schwantes, University of Nebraska Press, 1993.

Hill's background, from *James J. Hill and the Opening of the Northwest,* by Albro Martin, Minnesota Historical Society, 1991.

Six dollars an acre, from www.historylink.org.

Roosevelt and early dealings in his administration with men of wealth, from *Theodore Roosevelt and the Politics of Power,* by G. Wallace Chessman, Little, Brown, 1969.

J. P. Morgan quote, he can give it back, from *The American Century,* by Harold Evans, Knopf, 2000.

Worth of Rockefeller, Weyerhaeuser, and Morgan, compared to Bill Gates, from "The Wealthy 100," by Michael Klepper and Robert Gunther, as updated in *New York Times,* July 15, 2007.

Roosevelt on titans buying the judiciary, letter of October 8, 1906, from *Theodore Roosevelt — Letters and Speeches.*

Roosevelt, tires me to talk to rich men, from Morris, *Theodore Rex.*

Butte mayor's quote, bring on the feed, from *Collier's,* July 1907.

Origin of the Square Deal in Butte, from Morris, *Theodore Rex.*

Astor parties on Fifth Avenue, from *New York Times,* May 27, 1906.

Elitists and google-eyed quote, from *A Fierce Discontent: The Rise and Fall of the Progressive Movement in America,* by Michael McGerr, Oxford University Press, 2005.

Rangers in Colorado, from McGerr, *A Fierce Discontent.*

Roosevelt landslide, Alice's reaction, from Morris, *Theodore Rex.*

Roosevelt skipping through the White House, from Gould, *The Presidency of Theodore Roosevelt.*

Roosevelt letter to Kermit on the greatest majority, November 10, 1904, from *Theodore Roosevelt — Letters and Speeches.*

Transfer of the Forest Service details, from Steen, *The United States Forest Service.*

Roosevelt quote, forests belong to the people, letter of November 27, 1905, from *Theodore Roosevelt — Letters and Speeches.*

Pinchot quote, fight, fight, fight, from Pinchot, *Breaking New Ground.*

Pinchot, understanding beneficial effects of fires, quoted in *National Geographic,* October 1899.

3. The Great Crusade

William Greeley on admiration for Pinchot, from *Forests and Men,* by William Greeley, Doubleday, 1951.

Greeley on seeing Roosevelt onstage, from Greeley, *Forests and Men.*

Greeley, additional biographical background, from Forest Service history, www.fs.fed.us.

Pinchot on the little guy, and fight, fight, fight, from Pinchot, *Breaking New Ground.*

Koch background and his admiration of Pinchot, from *Forty Years a Forester,* by Elers Koch, Mountain Press Publishing, 1998.

Koch, early assignments, from Koch, *Forty Years a Forester.*

Early ranger requirements, from Steen, *The United States Forest Service.*

The High Lonesome, from *The Big Blowup: The Northwest's Great Fire,* by Betty Goodwin Spencer, Caxton Printers, 1958.

Pinchot, Forest Service stood up for small man, from Pinchot, *Breaking New Ground.*

Pinchot reporting to Roosevelt on Heyburn from Wallace, from the Pinchot papers.

Greeley on supermen, from Greeley, *Forests and Men.*

Roosevelt on Pinchot, quoted in Gould, *The Presidency of Theodore Roosevelt.*

Ladies and Pinchot, Barrymore's comment, from *Big Trouble: A Murder in a Small Western Town Sets Off a Struggle for the Soul of America,* by J. Anthony Lukas, Simon & Schuster, 1997.

Pinchot, most eligible bachelor, from Miller, *Gifford Pinchot and the Making of Modern Environmentalism.*

Love affair with Laura, background and general information, from "The Mystery of Gifford Pinchot and Laura Houghteling," by James G. Bradley, *Pennsylvania History,* Spring 1999.

Pinchot, my soul doesn't grow, from Pinchot diaries, June 24, 1894.

Pinchot on the wealth at Vanderbilt estate, from Pinchot, *Breaking New Ground.*

Laura, all from Pinchot diaries as cited in the text; quote on things looking brighter is from January 22, 1894.

Pinchot on taking a wife, editor from London, from letter of April 2, 1910, Pinchot papers.

Pinchot and Roosevelt, how they worked, from Pinchot, *Breaking New Ground.*

Roosevelt on the power to create reserve, from Morris, *Theodore Rex.*

Background on Senator Mitchell, his scheme, dying in jail, from Oregon Historical Society, www.ohs.org.

Joe Cannon, from *Tyrant from Illinois: Uncle Joe Cannon's Experiment with Personal Power,* by Blair Bolles, W. W. Norton, 1951; and from Miller, *Gifford Pinchot and the Making of Modern Environmentalism.*

"Drenched!" from Pinchot diaries, October 11, 1905.

Fine gallop with Roosevelt, from Pinchot diaries, February 26, 1902.

Pinchot as Roosevelt's faithful bodyguard, from Steen, *The United States Forest Service.*

Too stout, from Pinchot diaries, November 11, 1905.

Roosevelt told me, from Pinchot diaries, October 13, 1903.

Pinchot, the earth I repeat, from Pinchot, *Breaking New Ground.*

Senator Heyburn, from "Senator Heyburn's War Against the Forest Service," *Idaho Yesterdays,* Winter 1970.

Heyburn, not backing the young student, from archives, University of Idaho Special Collections, Moscow, Idaho.

Heyburn, geese, from *New York Times,* September 6, 1906.

Roosevelt's view of opponents, "unscrupulous demagogues," from Hart and Ferleger, eds., *Theodore Roosevelt Cyclopedia.*

Roosevelt on Heyburn, from "Senator Heyburn's War Against the Forest Service."

Muir, how he shaped conservation, summarized from *The Eight Wilderness Discovery Books,* by John Muir, Mountaineers Edition, 1992.

Muir quote, Pinchot is ambitious, from Gould, *The Presidency of Theodore Roosevelt.*

Roosevelt on the floor of the White House, "oh this is bully," from Greeley, *Forests and Men.*

Roosevelt and Pinchot laughing as senators approached, from Pinchot, *Breaking New Ground.*

Roosevelt, closing quote on the Forest Service and fighting fires, from letter to Pinchot, August 24, 1906, *Theodore Roosevelt—Letters and Speeches.*

4. Deadwood Days

Taft, the town, from Koch, *Forty Years a Forester.*

Taft, the name of the town and Chicago reporter's description, from *Names on the Face of Montana,* by Roberta C. Cheney, Mountain Press Publishers, 1983.

Antics of people in Taft and neighboring tent towns, from *Up the Swiftwater,* by Sandra A. Crowell and David O. Asleson, Museum of North Idaho, 1980.

Pinchot's *Primer of Forestry,* United States Department of Agriculture, 1899.

Koch, from his book, *Forty Years a Forester.*

Undesirable prostitutes, from Koch, *Forty Years a Forester.*

Building the railroad, details, from *The Milwaukee Road,* by Tom Murray, MBI Publishers, 2005, and from an exhibit at the Museum of North Idaho.

Roar of laughter in tent towns, from Joe Halm's account in *Early Days of the Forest Service.*

William Weigle and attempt to evict saloonkeepers, and Halm's account, from *Early Days of the Forest Service.*

Escorting escaped convict and his escape, from Weigle in *Early Days of the Forest Service,* and Crowell and Asleson, *Up the Swiftwater.*

Timber doesn't need protection, from Frome, *The Forest Service.*

Pinkie Adair, interviewed by Sam Schrager, 1977, from unpublished oral history project, courtesy of the Latah County Historical Society, Moscow, Idaho.

One ranger with such a large tract is helpless, from *Early Days of the Forest Service.*

Background on Edward Pulaski, from his personnel file, Forest Service Region One headquarters, Missoula.

More on Pulaski, from background on file at the Wallace District Mining Museum, Wallace, Idaho.

Background on the Kelley brothers, from Crowell and Asleson, *Up the Swiftwater.*

5. Showdown

Incoming president Taft, from Anderson, *William Howard Taft.*

Pinchot's view of Taft, from Pinchot, *Breaking New Ground.*

White House meeting of Roosevelt, Pinchot, and Taft, from Pinchot, *Breaking New Ground.*

The pledge from Taft, from Pinchot, *Breaking New Ground.*

Pinchot's view of Taft, weak but not wicked, and Roosevelt saying he was a better man for having known him, from Pinchot, *Breaking New Ground.*

Cloudy days, Laura, from Pinchot diaries, various days.

Pinchot championing the cause, quoted by Taft, from Anderson, *William Howard Taft.*

Death of Mark Twain, from *Mark Twain: The Illustrated Biography,* by Geoffrey C. Ward, Dayton Duncan, and Ken Burns, Knopf, 2001.

Massive cut planned for the spring, Nancy Warren, quoted in *American Forests,* September 1928.

Huge growth spurt in the West, from U.S. Census Bureau, www.census .gov.

Senator Heyburn working against the Forest Service, from files at the Forest Service Region One headquarters, Missoula.

Pay complaints of rangers, from files at the Forest Service Region One headquarters, Missoula.

Forest rangers' need for a living wage, April 29, 1910, memo on file at the Forest Service Region One headquarters, Missoula.

Pinchot's worst fears of Taft, from *Progressive Politics and Conservation,* by James Penick Jr., University of Chicago Press, 1968.

Grey Towers background, from National Park Service, www.fs.fed.us/ na/gt.

Giving up public land, from Miller, *Gifford Pinchot and the Making of Modern Environmentalism.*

Pinchot paying rangers out of his own pocket, from *New York Times,* September 13, 1909.

Amiable man quote on Taft, from *The American Past: A History of the United States from Concordia to Hiroshima,* by Roger Butterfield, Simon & Schuster, 1947.

Muir quote, above the fray, from Scheuering, *Shapers of the Great Debate on Conservation.*

Pinchot quote on standing for Roosevelt policies, from *New York Times,* August 22, 1909.

Ballinger quote on giving land to corporations, from Scheuering, *Shapers of the Great Debate on Conservation.*

Pinchot face-off with Taft, should have been fired, from Pinchot, *Breaking New Ground.*

Guggenheims' wealth and control, from *Collier's,* November 13, 1909.

Pinchot on pushing too far, from *New York Times,* September 13, 1909.

Pinchot and landing the big fish, from *Fishing Talk,* by Gifford Pinchot, Stackpole Books, 1993.

Forester letter creates sensation, from *The Missoulian,* January 7, 1910.

Pinchot reaction on being fired, with mother, from Pinchot, *Breaking New Ground.*

Letter from forest ranger to Pinchot, thought you were a Greek god, January 24, 1910, from Pinchot papers.

Roosevelt on Taft, from Anderson, *William Howard Taft.*

Pinchot's talk to foresters after being fired, from Miller, *Gifford Pinchot and the Making of Modern Environmentalism.*

Rangers under siege, needing help, more funds, from Records of the Forest Service, National Archives, Seattle.

Editorial on Forest Service, from *Butte Miner,* August 12, 1910.

6. Summer of Smoke

Pulaski, quote and details, from Records of the Forest Service, Region One headquarters, Missoula.

Pulaski, additional biographical background, from "Pulaski: The Man, the Tool," *American Forests,* July 1984.

Pulaski's notebook and writings, from Records of the Forest Service, Region One headquarters, Missoula.

Fire conditions, dry in summer, from William Weigle's account, "The Great Idaho Fire of 1910," *The Timberman,* July 1934.

Weigle, on townsfolk refusing to work, from *Idaho Press,* July 21, 1910.

Forest rangers suspicious of set fires, from Professor J. E. Kirkwood's notes on a summer spent in the woods in 1910, Records of the Forest Service, Region One headquarters, Missoula.

No states grew faster than Washington, Idaho, from U. S. Census Bureau, www.census.gov.

The Pulaskis on the St. Joe, and Indians, from Emma Pulaski's "Memories of a Forest Service Wife."

Information and history of the Coeur d'Alene Indians, from *The Coeur d'Alene Indian Reservation,* Ye Galleon Press, 1970, and *Saving the Reservation: Joe Garry and the Battle to Be Indian,* by John Fahey, University of Washington Press, 2001.

Indians, lottery, and reservation reduction, from *History of Idaho*, by Hiram T. French, Lewis Publishing, 1914.

Greeley's memos to rangers, from Records of the Forest Service, Region One headquarters, Missoula.

Newspaper editorial on green rangers, from *Butte Intermountain*, August 15, 1910.

Newspaper editorial, abolish the Forest Service, from *Helena Independent*, August 4, 1910.

Ranger comment, just bed them down anywhere, quoted in Spencer, *The Big Blowup*.

7. Men, Men, Men!

Koch and booze, recruiting in Taft, from Koch, *Forty Years a Forester*.

Other ranger experiences around Taft just before fire, from *Early Days of the Forest Service*.

Greeley quotes to reporters, from *The Missoulian*, July 15, 1910.

Curing cancer and bald heads making people smart, from random wire-service stories in *The Missoulian*, January 10, 1910.

Koch and his bride, the Kipling verses he cited, all from Koch, *Forty Years a Forester*.

Wild days in the town, bullet in tongue, from Crowell and Asleson, *Up the Swiftwater*.

Pinchot's passion for the outdoors, description of the Grand Canyon, from Pinchot diaries, April 19, 1891.

No money to pay firefighters, from Koch, *Forty Years a Forester*.

No money to pay rangers' salary, from Albert Cole's recollections in *Early Days of the Forest Service*.

Butte Irish, from *The Butte Irish: Class and Ethnicity in an American Mining Town, 1875–1925*, by David M. Emmons, University of Illinois Press, 1990.

Story of the Irish firefighter Grogan, from his claim file at the Records of the Forest Service, National Archives, College Park, Maryland.

More background on Grogan, from Crowell and Asleson, *Up the Swiftwater*.

Comments of Wilson, the agriculture secretary, from *National Geographic*, January 1911.

Taft's massage, his routine on holiday, from *Leslie's Weekly*, July 21, 1910.

Taft's insecurities, insulting nicknames, from Anderson, *William Howard Taft*.

Pinchot on Taft, from Pinchot, *Breaking New Ground*.

Weigle happy to have troops, quoted in *Idaho Press*, August 9, 1910.

Buffalo Soldiers, their history and pay, from National Park Service, www
.nps.gov.

Number of blacks in the region, from U.S. Census Bureau, www.census
.gov.

The Brownsville incident, from *A Fierce Discontent: The Rise and Fall of
the Progressive Movement in America*, by Michael McGerr, Oxford University Press, 2003, and from the Park Service history of the Buffalo Soldiers,
www.nps.gov.

Additional background on the 25th Infantry, from *Buffalo Soldiers, 1892–
1918*, by Ron Field, Osprey Publishing, 2005.

Senator Tillman's racist comments, from *The Betrayal of the Negro: From
Rutherford B. Hayes to Woodrow Wilson*, by Rayford W. Logan, Da Capo
Press, 1997.

Taft's reaction to a request for interview, from Anderson, *William Howard Taft*.

James J. Hill on Taft, from Martin, *James J. Hill and the Opening of the
Northwest*.

Peary and Roosevelt, from *True North: Peary, Cook and the Race to the
Pole*, by Bruce Henderson, W. W. Norton, 2005.

Taft quote, from Anderson, *William Howard Taft*.

8. Spaghetti Westerners

Italians get old quickly, from *The Immigrants Speak*, by Salvatore J.
LaGumina, Center for Immigration Studies, 1979.

Background on Italian immigration experience, from the author's visit to
the Fondazione Giovanni Agnelli, Torino, Italy, October 16, 2007.

Why Italians from the north left Italy, from the author's interview with
Professor Paola Corti, University of Torino, October 17, 2007.

Lives of Bruno and Viettone, from their claim files at the Records of the
Forest Service, National Archives, College Park, Maryland, and from the author's visit to their hometown, Rivara Canavese, Italy.

Death of twelve-year-old Italian girl, from *The Survey*, January 17, 1911.

Sentiment toward immigrants, scum of creation, from *This Fabulous
Century, 1900–1910*.

Anti-Italian sentiment, from *Wop*, edited by Salvatore J. LaGumina,
Straight Arrow Books, 1973.

Plantations trying to get Italians, from *The Survey*, January 17, 1911.

Orphans and treatment of immigrants in Morenci, from *The Great Arizona Orphan Abduction*, by Linda Gordon, Harvard University Press, 1999.

Italians in Washington State, and Indians, from *La Storia: Five Centu-*

ries of the Italian-American Experience, by Jerre Mangioni and Ben Morreate, HarperCollins, 1991.

Italians seeing their first blacks, from LaGumina, *The Immigrants Speak.*

Days the Italians were hired, from claim files, Records of the Forest Service, National Archives, College Park, Maryland.

Pinchot in Italy, from Pinchot diaries, May 1910, and from his book *Breaking New Ground.*

Roosevelt in Africa and Italy, from *When Trumpets Call: Theodore Roosevelt After the White House,* by Patricia O'Toole, Simon & Schuster, 2005.

Roosevelt letter to Lodge on mistake of Taft, May 5, 1910, from *Selections from the Correspondence of Theodore Roosevelt and Henry Cabot Lodge.*

Heyburn's views on states' rights, from *The Outlook,* March 19, 1910.

More on Roosevelt and Pinchot scheming, from O'Toole, *When Trumpets Call.*

Roosevelt, Man in the Arena speech, and Africa, from www.theo doreroosevelt.org.

9. Firestorm's Eve

Prediction on the winds, *Seattle Times,* August 12, 1910.

Halm, the athlete, from *Chinook 1907,* published by the junior class of Washington State College, Pullman.

Halm, on how dry the forest was, from his recollections in *Early Days of the Forest Service.*

Behavior of black troops, from *Idaho Press,* September 8, 1910.

North Pole and Negro not named, from *The Outlook,* March 12, 1910.

Black dialect in headline, from *The Missoulian,* July 8, 1910.

Comment, six good Greeks, from *Company Town,* by Keith C. Peterson, Washington State University Press, 1987.

Weigle quote, God only knows, from Hult, *Northwest Disaster.*

Problems of Italian immigrants in the cities, from *The Survey,* January 17, 1911.

Italians, on receiving the roughest treatment in Idaho, from *Idaho Ethnic Heritage,* vol. 2.

Pulaski details, from Emma Pulaski's "Memories of a Forest Service Wife."

Italians had a saying about the streets being paved with gold, from *Coming to America: Italian Americans,* by Barry Moreno, Barron's Educational Series, 2003.

Pulaski's thoughts, doubts, and guilt, from Pulaski's response to questions on what happened, internal Forest Service correspondence, from Records of the Forest Service, National Archives, Seattle.

Pulaski's surprise at the chef's hat, from Hult, *Northwest Disaster.*

Koch on how fire is like war, from Koch, *Forty Years a Forester.*

Koch on manpower requirements, from Koch, *Forty Years a Forester.*

The town of Taft, people getting drunk before the fire, from Koch, *Forty Years a Forester,* and from Haun's report in Records of the Forest Service, National Archives, Seattle.

More on Taft, reaction of forest rangers to town, from Koch, *Forty Years a Forester,* and from memories of Roy A. Phillips in *Early Days of the Forest Service.*

10. Blowup

Fire description, from W. G. Weigle's "Report on the 1910 Fires," on file at the National Archives, Seattle; from Koch's report, "When the Mountains Roared," on file at the Forest Service Region One headquarters, Missoula; from Spencer, *The Big Blowup;* from Halm's published account, "The Great Fire of 1910," *American Forests and Forest Life,* July 1930; and from William W. Morris's account, "The Great Fires of 1910," on file at the Forest Service Region One headquarters, Missoula.

How a fire grows, feeds on itself, nature of fire, from *Fire in America: A Cultural History of Wildland and Rural Fire,* by Stephen J. Pyne, University of Washington Press, 1997.

The velocity of fire in the Rockies, from *Young Men and Fire,* by Norman Maclean, University of Chicago Press, 1992.

11. The Lost Day

Weigle's account of being in the fire, from his "Report on the 1910 Fires," and from his "The Great Idaho Fires," *The Timberman,* July 1934, reprinted in *Idaho Yesterday,* Fall 2001.

Weigle's thoughts just before the storm, from *Butte Miner,* August 14, 1910.

Description of Wallace as the fire spread, from *Seattle Times,* August 26, 1910, and from L. Worstell's account on file at the National Archives, Seattle. Additional information from Hult, *Northwest Disaster.*

No horse fast enough to outrun the fire, from personal accounts on file at the Museum of Northern Idaho, Coeur d'Alene, Idaho, and from Records of the Forest Service, National Archives, Seattle.

Carl Getz and the horror, quoted in *Seattle Times,* August 26, 1910.

William Chance quotes on following him, from Records of the Forest Service, Region One headquarters, Missoula.

Ed Pulaski quote on no use, from the account by Foltz, a witness, in "Pulaski, Two Days in August, 1910," cultural resource inventory from Records of the Forest Service, Region One headquarters, Missoula.

Pulaski's details from his own account, "Surrounded by Forest Fires," *American Forests and Forest Life*, August 1923, and from Forest Service archival report put together for the 1984 dedication of a memorial, on file at the Wallace District Mining Museum.

More Pulaski details, from "Pulaski, Two Days in August, 1910."

Death of the Italians, Ranger Bell's account, from Koch's report, "When the Mountains Roared"; from Spencer, *The Big Blowup;* and from claim files of the Italians at the National Archives, College Park, Maryland.

Weigle returns to town, what he found, his reaction, from his account, "Report on the 1910 Fires," National Archives, Seattle.

Weigle, all crews lost, from his "Report on the 1910 Fires."

12. The Lost Night

Magazine description of the fiercest forest fire ever, from *Collier's,* September 24, 1910.

Maclean quote, from Maclean, *Young Men and Fire.*

Greeley quoted on all hell breaking loose, from Greeley, *Forests and Men.*

Wallace, account of its being doomed, then surviving the fire, from two editions, published on same day, *The Missoulian,* August 21, 1910.

Accounts of flames burning homes, from *Seattle Times,* August 25, 1910.

Soldiers on the train, overseeing the evacuation, from Hult, *Northwest Disaster.*

Quote of the fire chief, from Hult, *Northwest Disaster.*

How the fire affected property owned by Senator Heyburn, from *Idaho Press,* August 25, 1910.

Wallace evacuation and the plight of the hospital, from *Idaho Press,* August 22, 1910; Spencer, *The Big Blowup;* and Hart and Nelson, *Mining Town.*

Emma Pulaski quotes, from her "Memories of a Forest Service Wife."

Boss is dead quote, from Pulaski's own account, and from Stockton's account as reported in Crowell and Asleson, *Up the Swiftwater.*

Death of the Italians, from their claim files, Records of the Forest Service, National Archives, College Park, Maryland.

Additional information on the Italians, from consulate's report, Records of the Forest Service, National Archives, College Park, Maryland.

Quote on being cooked alive, from Crowell and Asleson, *Up the Swiftwater.*

Arthur Hogue quote on what fire looked like, from Spencer, *The Big Blowup.*

Eighteen bodies burned, death of Grogan, suicide of firefighter, from Koch, "When the Mountains Roared," Forest Service Region One office, Missoula.

Cause of Weigert's death, and conclusion of suicide, from claim files, Records of the Forest Service, National Archives, College Park, Maryland.

Times of death for firefighters with Grogan, from Records of the Forest Service, National Archives, Seattle.

Common laborer, from Records of the Forest Service, National Archives, Seattle.

Two Englishmen, final letter: on Holmes, from Records of the Forest Service, National Archives, Seattle, and for the other victim, from *The Missoulian*, August 25, 1910, and Hult, *Northwest Disaster*.

13. Towns Afire

Taft burning, from Koch, *Forty Years a Forester*, and from Koch's report, "History of the 1910 Fires," on file at the Forest Service Region One headquarters, Missoula.

Quote, I've lost all my crews, from Spencer, *The Big Blowup*.

Sky turning a ghastly color, from Koch, "History of the 1910 Fires."

What town of Taft was like, from *Doctors, Dynamite and Dogs*, by Edith M. Schussler, Caxton Printers, 1956.

Wence, the Northern Pacific section man, quoted in *The Missoulian*, August 24, 1910.

Whole canyon on fire, from Koch, "The 1910 Fire Season."

Quote from man in Mullan, from *The Missoulian*, special commemorative edition, August 2000.

Death of towns, from Koch, "When the Mountains Roared," and from individual ranger reports on file at the Forest Service Region One headquarters, Missoula.

Evacuation of Grand Forks, from Hult, *Northwest Disaster*, and from Crowel and Asleson, *Up the Swiftwater*.

What it looks like, from the author's visit to the site, August 15, 2007.

Pinkie Adair story, from oral history project, Latah County Historical Society.

Additional Pinkie story, from Crowel and Asleson, *Up the Swiftwater*.

14. To Save a Town

Here lies a coon, from *Gems of Thought and History of Shoshone County*, edited by George Hobson, Kellogg Evening News Press, 1946.

Avery troops, from official report of 25th Infantry, Records of the Adjutant General's Office, National Archives; Lieutenant Lewis's report, from Forest Service Region One office, Missoula.

Kid on the train, from *Hardship and Happy Times,* edited by Bert Russell, Lacon Publishers, 1978.

Pinkie Adair, from oral history project, Latah County Historical Society.

Black troops "stuck to their posts like men," from Crowell and Asleson, *Up the Swiftwater.*

Negro soldiers' heroic service, from *Seattle Times,* August 22, 1910.

Description of blacks, from *Collier's,* September 24, 1910.

Race quote, a whiter set of men, from *Seattle Times,* August 28, 1910.

15. The Missing

Weigle, from his narrative in "Report on the 1910 Fires," on file, National Archives, Seattle.

World was black to my eyes, Pulaski, from his account,

Emma's view, from her account, "Memories of a Forest Service Wife."

Nicholson, lack of compensation, from Records of the Forest Service, National Archives, Seattle, and from Spencer, *The Big Blowup.*

Weigle, never have I seen conditions so appalling, quoted in *Seattle Times,* August 23, 1910.

Headlines, from *Spokane Spokesman-Review,* August 25, 1910.

Halm believed lost, from *Idaho Press,* August 24, 1910.

Debitt, food supply short, from Crowell and Asleson, *Up the Swiftwater.*

Halm's death reported, from *New York Times,* August 27, 1910.

Halm, from his account in *Early Days of the Forest Service.*

Haines volunteers to search, from Weigle, "The Great Idaho Fire of 1910."

Halm, from his account in *Early Days of the Forest Service.*

Patrick Sullivan, compensation, death, from the Records of the Forest Service, National Archives.

16. The Living and the Dead

Dead bodies as charcoal, from *Seattle Post-Intelligencer,* August 23, 1910.

Pinkie Adair, from oral history project, Latah County Historical Society.

Quote, fire worse than San Francisco earthquake, from *The Missoulian,* August 25, 1910.

Quote, United States just ended its latest war, from *Collier's,* September 24, 1910.

Deaths at Big Creek, from Weigle, "Report on the 1910 Fires"; Spencer, *The Big Blowup;* and Halm, in *Early Days of the Forest Service.*

Weigle throwing guy down stairs, from *Idaho Press,* August 25, 1910.

Lullaby story, several versions, this one from Koch, *Forty Years a Forester.*

Emma taking care of Ed Pulaski, from her "Memories of a Forest Service Wife."

Italians and consulate's efforts to compensate them, from Records of the Forest Service, National Archives.

17. Fallout

Pinchot placing blame for cause of fire, from *New York Times,* August 27, 1910.

Pinchot quote, more blame, from *Everybody's Magazine,* October 1910.

Blame, back and forth, from *Idaho Press,* September 8, 1910.

Revolutionary speech, from *The Autobiography of William Allen White.*

Taft reaction, from Chessman, *Theodore Roosevelt,* and from Miller, *Gifford Pinchot and the Making of Modern Environmentalism.*

New Nationalism speech and reaction, from *The Missoulian,* September 1, 1910, and Theodore Roosevelt Association, www.theodoreroosevelt.org.

Pinchot on rebuke to reactionaries, from Anderson, *William Howard Taft.*

Taft retreats to bed and weeps, from *The Autobiography of William Allen White,* and Anderson, *William Howard Taft.*

Great fun quote, from Pinchot diaries, March 13, 1911.

Opposition to the Forest Service died, from Steen, *The United States Forest Service.*

Zane Grey forester book, *The Young Forester,* Grosset and Dunlap, 1910.

Death of Senator Heyburn, from obituary in *New York Times,* October 18, 1912.

18. One for the Boys

Replanting Bitterroots, and Morris's observations on the land after the fire, from "Experiences on a National Forest," by William W. Morris, part of *Early Days of the Forest Service,* on file at the Forest Service Region One headquarters, Missoula.

Pulaski and claims, from "Pulaski, Two Days in August, 1910."

Pulaski self-description, from *American Forests,* July 1984.

Back and forth on Pulaski claims, from memos on file at the Forest Service Region One headquarters, Missoula.

Cost of a memorial, memos on file at the Forest Service Region One headquarters.

Pulaski death, from Forest Service biography, files.

Pinchot appearance and not feeling well, from photographs and Pinchot diaries, January and February 1911.

Pinchot feeling cheerful, from Pinchot diaries, March 1911.

Tree dedicated, from National Park Service website, www.nps.gov/muwo/historyculture/stories.htm.

Heyburn as intense partisan, from the Museum of North Idaho news clips on his life, collected in a single bound file at the museum.

White, mostly rich men quote, from *The Autobiography of William Allen White.*

Roosevelt at the end, from Gould, *The Presidency of Theodore Roosevelt.*

Taft quote on his presidency, from www.whitehouse.gov/about/presidents/williamhowardtaft.

Quote, life at its warmest, from Pinchot, *Breaking New Ground.*

What fire meant to Forest Service, quote, from *Scorched Earth: How the Fires of Yellowstone Changed America*, by Rocky Barker, Island Press, 2005.

Weigle's second and third acts, from Forest Service archives, Ketchikan, Alaska, www.fs.fed.us/r10.

Ranger Debitt's life after Forest Service, from Crowell and Asleson, *Up the Swiftwater.*

19. Ashes

Missoula arrival, plans, from Pinchot diaries, several pages quoted in *The Conservation Diaries of Gifford Pinchot*, edited by Harold K. Steen, Forest History Society, 2001.

Pinchot, note on *Gone with the Wind*, from Pinchot diaries, December 3, 1937.

Cornelia and politics, from Miller, *Gifford Pinchot and the Making of Modern Environmentalism.*

Landon comment, from Pinchot diaries, September 18, 1936.

Defeat of Landon, from Pinchot diaries, November 5, 1936.

Koch on lessons of fire and wilderness, from his *Forty Years a Forester.*

FDR appraisal of Pinchot "conservation road," from Barker, *Scorched Earth.*

First CCC camp, from Steen, *The United States Forest Service.*

Pinchot quote, I have been a governor, from *Gifford Pinchot: Private and Public Forester*, by Harold T. Pinkett, University of Illinois Press, 1970.

Pinchot and Henry Graves, from Forest History Society, www.foresthistory.org.

Greeley vs. Pinchot, from "A Clash of Titans," *Evergreen*, Winter 1994–1995.

Greeley on fires, from his *Forests and Men.*

Industry praising Greeley, from "A Clash of the Titans."

Greeley on stopping fires, from Spencer, *The Big Blowup.*

Mrs. Greeley quote, from Miller, *Gifford Pinchot and the Making of Modern Environmentalism.*

Maclean quote, from his *Young Men and Fire.*

"Absolute devastation," from Pinchot diaries, August 11, 1937.

Jack Ward Thomas on fire, quoted in Barker, *Scorched Earth.*

"Nobody seemed to know us," from Pinchot diaries, August 10, 1937.

Death of Koch a suicide, from his son's introduction to Koch, *Forty Years a Forester.*

Death of Ione Adair, from *Idahoan,* November 26, 1977.

Pinchot commenting on slash, from Pinchot diaries, August 11, 1937.

Pinchot, great days, from Pinchot diaries, August 24, 1937.

Pinchot, greatest sight, from Pinchot diaries, August 26, 1937.

FDR and Pinchot, conservation congress, from Cornelia Bryce Pinchot's account, first published in *Forest History Today,* Spring 1999, and from Miller, *Gifford Pinchot and the Making of Modern Environmentalism.*

Pulaski dedication details, from the author's visit to the site, and from *Spokane Spokesman-Review,* August 21, 2005.

ACKNOWLEDGMENTS

Every coming-of-age story has its keepers. For the Big Burn, most of these archivists, historians, librarians, and storytellers are in warrens and backrooms of the West. I'm grateful, first and foremost, to the U.S. Forest Service, especially at the northern regional office in Missoula. Not only have they kept an exhaustive and detailed record of the 1910 fire, but they have been eager to share it—which has only increased my admiration for this agency. In particular, I would like to thank Carlie Magill, the archive manager.

The president of the Pulaski Project, Jim See, in Wallace, Idaho, is one reason why the name Pulaski continues to find a home with new generations. He launched a conference on a snowy spring day in the Silver Valley that helped to get me started on this book. Also in Wallace, the city's fine Carnegie library and the Wallace District Mining Museum were excellent firsthand sources on the Big Burn. I owe a debt to the Museum of North Idaho in Coeur d'Alene, a great source of original homesteading documents, and the Clearwater County Museum in Orofino, which holds a trove of early Forest Service memoirs among its backroom treasures.

Thanks to Julie Monroe and Nathan Bender, in the Special Collections and Archives Division at the University of Idaho, for pictures and other help, particularly the prints from the Barnard Stockbridge Studio Collection. I was guided to those prints and other pictures from the era by Patricia Hart and Ivar Nelson, scholars and lovers of the West. And without Ann Catt, the curator at the Latah County (Idaho) Historical Society, I never would have had the words of Pinkie Adair, as told in a series of oral histories late in her life.

At the Library of Congress in Washington, I'm indebted to Jeffrey M. Flanner, the head of the reference and reader service section, for guiding me through the many letters and notes of Gifford Pinchot and Teddy Roosevelt, and to the library's crosstown colleague in recordkeeping, the National Archives.

I'm certainly not the first writer drawn to the story of the 1910 fire, and won't be the last. But among the other accounts, I would like to acknowledge Betty Goodwin Spencer for her pioneering work in *The Big Blowup* and the historian Stephen J. Pyne, who knows more about fire than anyone, for his book *Year of the Fires*.

At Stanford University, where I found an editing refuge in the Bing Wing of the Green Library, I have the Bill Lane Center for the American West to thank.

For bookbuilding, the kind that moves ideas from thoughts to printed page, I owe much to editors Anton Mueller and Andrea Schulz, and to my longtime agent Carol Mann. Thanks also to Laurence Cooper for fresh eyes and a sharp pen. And for finding an audience, a tip of the hat to Carla Gray and Lori Glazer at Houghton Mifflin Harcourt.

Finally, thanks to my brother Kelly Egan, who first took me into the St. Joe country, some of the finest cutthroat water in the land. Your secrets are safe.

INDEX